Map by Robert MacLean

MAP of

THE TERRITORY Sometime Called

The HAMPSHIRE GRANTS

LATTERLY

The STATE OF VERMONT

Showing Adjacent Sections of

NEW ENGLAND, NEW YORK AND CANADA

*

Brattleboro, Vermont MCMLXXVI

Scale ⊢———⊣ = 40 MILES

ATLANTIC

MASS.

R.I.

SPRINGFIELD

CONN.

HARTFORD

NEW HAVEN

LONG ISLAND

Housatonic River

SALISBURY

CORNWALL

Hudson River

NEW YORK

PHILADELPHIA

MAC LEAN

The Damndest Yankees

The Damndest Yankees

ETHAN ALLEN & *His Clan*

by Edwin P. Hoyt

THE STEPHEN GREENE PRESS

Brattleboro, Vermont

Acknowledgments

A GOOD DEAL of the research for this book was done in the Vermont Historical Society rooms in Montpelier, and I am indebted to any number of helpful people there. Also various librarians at Castleton State College and at Castleton Public Library were helpful. Leo Towers, former Town Clerk of Castleton and a moving force in the Castleton Historical Society, was a marvelous source of information about the doings around those parts. I also consulted records, documents and various writings at the Connecticut Historical Society offices in Hartford, and at the public libraries in Salisbury and Sharon, Connecticut, which have a good deal of material about the Allen clan.

EDWIN P. HOYT

This book has been produced in the United States of America. It is published by The Stephen Greene Press, Brattleboro, Vermont 05301

LIBRARY OF CONGRESS CATALOGING IN PUBLICATION DATA

Hoyt, Edwin Palmer.
   The damndest Yankees.

   1. Allen, Ethan, 1738–1789. 2. Allen, Ira, 1751–1814. 3. Vermont—History—To 1791. 4. Allen family. I. Title.
E207.A4H65   974.3'02'0924 [B]   74-27455
ISBN 0-8289-0259-3

76 77 78 79 80 9 8 7 6 5 4 3 2 1

Contents

CAST OF CHARACTERS *vii*

CHAPTER ONE *Cornwall Days* *1*

CHAPTER TWO *The Broader World* *7*

CHAPTER THREE *The Hampshire Grants* *13*

CHAPTER FOUR *The Education of Ira Allen* *20*

CHAPTER FIVE *Judge Livingston's Court* *24*

CHAPTER SIX *Stephen Fay's Tavern* *29*

CHAPTER SEVEN *Holding Off the Yorkers* *38*

CHAPTER EIGHT *The Onion River* *50*

CHAPTER NINE *The Land Shark* *60*

CHAPTER TEN *Lot 1* *66*

CHAPTER ELEVEN *Three Encounters and Two
                Traps* *73*

CHAPTER TWELVE *Tension* *82*

CHAPTER THIRTEEN *Ticonderoga* *90*

CHAPTER FOURTEEN *Revolution!* *99*

CHAPTER FIFTEEN *The Limitations of Guerilla
                War* *104*

CHAPTER SIXTEEN *The Captive* *112*

CHAPTER SEVENTEEN *Pirates or Patriots?* *121*

CHAPTER EIGHTEEN *The Long Voyage
                Home* *130*

CHAPTER NINETEEN *The Dilemma of the
                Grants* *137*

CHAPTER TWENTY *The Low, Low Time* *143*

CHAPTER TWENTY-ONE *The Price of
                Independence* *149*

CHAPTER TWENTY-TWO *The Struggle* *154*

CHAPTER TWENTY-THREE *The Hero's
                Return* *161*

CHAPTER TWENTY-FOUR *The Republic* *169*

CHAPTER TWENTY-FIVE *Family Rupture* *175*

CHAPTER TWENTY-SIX *The Future of the
Republic* *181*

CHAPTER TWENTY-SEVEN *How Wise the
British . . .* *188*

CHAPTER TWENTY-EIGHT *The Haldimand
Affair* *195*

CHAPTER TWENTY-NINE *The Most Dangerous
Game* *200*

CHAPTER THIRTY *The Lone Republic* *211*

CHAPTER THIRTY-ONE *The Troubled Days of the
Republic* *216*

CHAPTER THIRTY-TWO *The Happy
Warriors* *220*

CHAPTER THIRTY-THREE *The End of the
Dream* *230*

CHAPTER THIRTY-FOUR *A Man of Desperate
Fortunes* *233*

CHAPTER THIRTY-FIVE *The Long Ordeal* *245*

CHAPTER THIRTY-SIX *Envoi* *251*

AFTERWORD *The Allens in Historical Literature* *254*

INDEX *257*

Illustrations

Following page *126*

PLATE 1: *Profile portrait engraving of Ethan Allen.*

PLATE 2: *Ethan, from a historical periodical of the 1860's.*

PLATE 3: *The Mead statue of Ethan, in Montpelier, Vermont*

PLATE 4: *The lost Kinney statue of Ethan.*

PLATE 5: *Ira Allen in his forties.*

Principal Characters

ETHAN ALLEN   Hero of Ticonderoga; author, Deist, toss-pot, Colonel in the Continental Army and leader of the Green Mountain Boys.

IRA ALLEN   His youngest brother; land speculator, soldier, a founder of the Republic of Vermont.

HEMAN ALLEN
HEBER ALLEN
ZIMRI ALLEN
LYDIA ALLEN   } their brothers and sisters
LUCY ALLEN
LEVI ALLEN

MARY BROWNSON ALLEN   The mature wife of Ethan's youth.

FANNY MONTRESOR BUCHANAN ALLEN   The youthful wife of Ethan's maturity.

STEPHEN FAY
REMEMBER BAKER   } Green Mountain Boys
SETH WARNER
JUSTUS SHERWOOD

BENNING WENTWORTH   Royal Governor of New Hampshire; patron of the Hampshire Grants.

CADWALLADER COLDEN   Royal Governor of New York; rival claimant to the Hampshire Grants.

GENERAL JOHN STARK   Revolutionary General; leader of the Colonial forces at the Battle of Bennington.

GENERAL JOHN BURGOYNE   Commander of the British forces in the Champlain-Hudson Valley.

COLONEL BENEDICT ARNOLD   Ethan's rival at Ticonderoga; leader of the Colonial expedition against Quebec; later turned his coat.

THOMAS CHITTENDEN   Ally of the Allens; leader of the Vermont Republic and later Governor of the State.

ISAAC TICHENOR   "The Jersey Slick"; Adversary of the
Allen faction in Vermont politics.

GENERAL FREDERICK HALDIMAND   Governor Gen-
eral of Canada; negotiator of Vermont's restoration to the
British Empire.

GENERAL GEORGE WASHINGTON   Commander in
Chief of the Continental Army.

The Damndest Yankees

Cornwall Days

SCARCELY anyone in the twentieth century has ever heard of Joseph Allen. He lived in Cornwall, in the narrow valley of Connecticut's Housatonic River in the eighteenth century. In many ways Allen was a typical settler, but without him and his strong-minded sons—Ethan, Ira, and the rest—there would today be no state called Vermont, and New York would have swallowed up a goodly chunk of New England. They tried, those Yorkers did, but Joe's boys led all the rest in pushing them back and carving a new state out of Green Mountain rock.

The reason for Old Joe's beliefs and his actions, and for what came later, can be found in the New England of the early eighteenth century. At that time, eastern Massachusetts and parts of Connecticut were crowding up. People like the Allens were moving to newer lands to the west, where there was more room. In 1720, when Joseph Allen was twelve, his family moved to the budding community of Litchfield, where they owned a large tract of land. By this time, Joe's father had died. His mother died shortly after the family moved to Litchfield. With several of his six brothers and sisters, Joe tried for the next ten years to make a living from their farm. He married Mary Baker of Woodbury and began to raise a family of his own. But in time it was the same old story: Litchfield was growing crowded, and land prices were rising sky-high. The wilderness beckoned.

Earlier it had been simple enough to move west, as Joe's family had moved to Litchfield. By the mid-eighteenth century, however, the colonies were becoming more clearly delineated, and New York, which was very large and very strong, contested the movement of New Englanders into the area west of southern Connecticut. New York colonists had been settled there for a long time, and most of the eastern New York lands had been sold and cultivated.

To the north, though, opportunity still beckoned. In 1731 the Connecticut government at Hartford had ordered the western counties of the state laid out into townships. One of these was the township of Cornwall on the Housatonic. It was divided into fifty-three parts; some were set aside for ministers of the Gospel and a school, and the rest were sold.

Joseph Allen held a principle handed down from his father and his grandfather: Buy land and more land as long as you can get it and afford it. Joe bought some five hundred acres in Cornwall for the equivalent of twenty cents an acre, and along with fewer than a dozen other families he went into the wilderness to live. It *was* wilderness, too—virgin land sixty miles square, with a little native pasture and meadow, but mostly wooded and filled with wild turkeys, bear, deer, and all the chattering denizens of the forest.

It was a difficult land, this part of northwest Connecticut where the Allens settled. The clouds often hung in over the Housatonic, day after day, winter and summer. Even in times of drought, the sky would cloud up with promise of rain but no rain would fall; the gray clouds would just hang there, all day long.

It seemed to settlers that Cornwall had a vertical landscape. The mountains came down to the edge of the Housatonic and jutted into the river. Most of the land was covered with oak, chestnut, and hickory, and only on the narrow river plain was there much pine. But if there were many trees, there were even more rocks, so many that it seemed hardly possible for a man to be able to wring a living from the land.

Yet Joseph Allen went there willingly and settled down in a log cabin. In the fall of 1738 he and four others were chosen to lay out fifty acres of land for each of the Proprietors, or Principal landowners in the new Town. They agreed to split the bill for the survey and divide the cost of building roads. Joe was a young man then, in his early thirties, and the prospect of surveying a huge chunk of wilderness did not daunt him. The fee of ten shillings a day was not inconsiderable, since the surveyors would be spending most of their time in the wild, living off dried beef and hardtack and a little rice. Someone had to do the job, someone with an abiding interest in this rough frontier.

Guided by these stalwarts, the township of Cornwall began to

take shape. Joe Allen spent the next few months deeply immersed in the affairs of the new community. He was chosen as
tax collector, and his first duty was to collect twenty-six shillings
from each property owner to defray the costs of the survey.

Joe was also one of the far-sighted townsmen who insisted
that they lay out the town's roads then and there and allocate
six rods for each right of way—or ninety-six feet—almost twice
the breadth of a modern local roadway. Joe planned a highway
from Cornwall to Litchfield and one leading south to Kent.
The property owners appointed him to the committee that
would actually lay out the roads and clear the timber, allocating
twenty-five pounds for the job.

When Joseph Allen came to Cornwall he brought his wife and
his newborn son, Ethan, to the raw territory. Soon other children arrived: Heman, born in 1740, Lydia in 1742, Heber in
1743, Levi in 1745, Lucy in 1747, Zimri in 1748, and Ira in
1751. Despite the harsh life of the frontier, all eight young
Allens survived childhood, an unusual feat for the times.

The children—all of whom were given Biblical names except
Lucy—were baptized and brought up in the Congregational
Church. Although Joseph did not hold completely with the
tenets of his church, he was forgiven during these early years
because of his worth to the general good of the community of
Cornwall. He did not share in the soul-searching of the devout:
he was a much milder man in matters of religion, and believed
in the essential goodness of all humanity. He also believed in
the worth of property, and he taught his children that land was
everything and would be everything in the expanding continent on which they lived. All the Allen children grew up with a
belief in land, as a source of wealth and as a comfort to a family.

In 1739 Joe was chosen moderator of the town meeting in
Cornwall. There were about forty rude log cabins in the community then, and there was little difference between the richest
and poorest of the settlers. They all lived in log houses, ate off
pewter plate, and warmed themselves at wood-burning fire-
places over which their wives cooked the meals.

Joe kept cows, a pair of oxen, horses, and pigs that foraged in the woods. Each morning Joe dressed in his leather breeches, homespun shirt, and broad, round-toed shoes. In the winter he wore leggings; in the summer his legs were bare. In cold weather he wore a long tailcoat and a cocked hat to church and to all important affairs; otherwise he wore a fur cap and a rough jacket. He hewed wood, burned stumps, cleared land, plowed, planted, and harvested his winter's food. If he and Mary went over the rough roads to Litchfield to call on relatives or friends, they rode the horse, Joe riding in the saddle before and Mary sitting behind him.

Indians were not a problem to the Cornwall settlers: the closest tribe, a band of Mohawks, hunted and fished along the Housatonic down at Kent and never threatened the Cornwall settlement. Nevertheless, the early years were hard in Cornwall. Had it not been for a fine sense of sharing among the members of the community, the settlers might have been wiped out because of their very isolation. Provisions were short. An entire food supply had to be wrested from the land during the summer months, and that supply had to be carried over through the winter until the next spring. The settlers lived on grain and on venison, bear, and squirrel meat. "So great was the expense, fatigue and hardship that I endured for the first three years," wrote one of Joe Allen's neighbors, "that I would not suffer them again for the whole township."

Joe worked hard. He carved his own piece of property out of the wilderness and supported his children on it well enough. The first of them, Ethan, was educated from an early age by his mother and father, then by the preacher and the scholarly people of the community. When Ethan was in his teens, Joe made the big decision that the boy would be spared from farm duties for a time so that he might go away to school.

Up in Salisbury, to the northwest, the Reverend Jonathan Lee advertised that he was prepared to take on a certain number of boys for training in Greek, Latin, arithmetic, logic, rhetoric, and other studies they would need to enter Yale College in New Haven. Ethan was a big strapping boy, strong of tongue and strong of muscle, and he had a good sound head on his shoulders. Joe knew that Ethan would become a leader of men if given the opportunity. Nowhere was there better chance for leadership than through schooling, and training at Yale College.

So in the middle of the 1750's young Ethan rode to Salisbury and was duly brought to the Reverend Mr. Lee's house to board and undertake his studies. Since his previous education had consisted mostly of listening to his elders and reading the Bible and Plutarch's *Lives,* there was a great deal of learning to be done. The principles of grammar were not exactly foreign to the boy, but he did not know the rules, and found himself plunged suddenly into a whole new world. Ethan's mind was retentive, though, and his spirit contemplative. He did well in his new environment.

The Salisbury to which Ethan Allen was sent by his father was a remarkable place, and it exerted a lasting influence on the young man. Located by Lake Wononskopomuc, its climate was gentler than Cornwall's. Where Cornwall was rimmed with rock and its terrain was rough, Salisbury was located on a rolling plain, with good native meadow land that meant less work for the farmers. Salisbury was settled at about the same time as Cornwall, but by the year Ethan arrived, Salisbury's population had grown to eleven hundred, which made it the hub of northwest Litchfield County.

The Reverend Mr. Lee had no complaint about his scholar. The prospect was that Ethan would spend a year or two in Salisbury, depending on his progress, and then apply for admission to Yale College. But Joseph Allen died suddenly in the spring of 1755 at the age of forty-seven, leaving a widow and eight children. Ethan, as the eldest, became responsible for the farm and the family. He left school and headed home to take on his new responsibilities.

Though his schooling was cut short, Ethan had absorbed more learning than most of his neighbors had. He had memorized large segments of the Bible and remembered them well. He had sharpened his intellect even in the time he spent with the Reverend Mr. Lee, and had acquired a healthy respect for knowledge and the scholarly view of life. All these attributes were to stand him in good stead and to guide his way through a

remarkable series of adventures. For Ethan and his siblings had
the fortune, good or bad, to be born into the most exciting
period of the eighteenth century. They would come to maturity
just in time to participate in the revolutionary activity of the
age and to choose their sides in the struggle that was to come.

The Broader World

EVEN after he returned home, Ethan Allen remembered fondly the sights and sounds of Salisbury and the books and stirring conversations he had enjoyed there. He could not forget the place, although duty drove him home to take up the role of supervisor of family affairs in Cornwall.

Everybody worked to bring in the crops that would sustain the family over the long winter months. Brother Heman, only two years younger than Ethan, was the second in command, and Ethan declared then and later that Heman was the bastion of the family. Heber, Levi, Zimri, and even six-year-old Ira did chores each day. There were horses to hitch to the plow, cows and horses to feed and water, eggs to gather for the kitchen, butter to be churned, and milk to cool. The girls spun and knit and wove the homespun clothing that everyone wore. With Mother Allen plus the eight of them, there were enough hands to make light work of it, but Ethan was the organizer.

He was also an adventurer at heart. When the French and English renewed their continuing quarrel in the New World in 1755, the Connecticut government raised several regiments to fight the French in the Champlain Valley. Samuel Bellows of Salisbury raised a company that year, and in it were several men Ethan knew. The next year, while Ethan toiled in the family fields, Captain Jeffrey of Cornwall led the local regimental contingent against the French. Still Ethan was too occupied with family affairs to go.

The following year, 1757, France's Marquis de Montcalm was reported to be moving down to attack Fort William Henry, which controlled Lake George and the entrance to the Hudson River valley. Ethan could no longer be contained. No one would have blamed this twenty-year-old who had so heavy a family responsibility if he had stayed home. But Ethan shouldered a musket, strapped on a powder horn, and joined the settlers who were assembling at Salisbury to relieve Fort William Henry. Big, ruddy Ethan Allen was not the least impressive of them.

The company marched through Berkshire County in Massachusetts and toward the wild lands to the north, intending to turn west to the fort. But before they reached Lake George a messenger arrived with the mournful news that the fort had already fallen to the French. The American and British forces were not strong enough to rout them. The relief force turned about and headed home. Ethan's war was over for the moment.

The taste of adventure had sharpened Ethan Allen's appetite, and the sight of the wild lands to the north of Massachusetts had set his imagination working. Every month it was harder for him to remain in the narrow confines of Cornwall. Still, Ethan remained for five years, buying and selling land and working the farm to support the large Allen family. He was often out in the woods, trapping, hunting, and fishing.

Ethan was twenty-five, and still chafing under the restrictions of life on the farm in Cornwall, when he finally took the opportunity to get away. His brothers were grown—even baby Ira was nearly twelve years old. Heman, Heber, and Levi could take responsibility for the farm now. So Ethan headed for Salisbury and a business of his own.

The hills of northwest Connecticut had deposits of low-grade iron ore that could be used to make pots and other utensils. A number of small foundries or furnaces had grown up. In Salisbury someone had discovered a hill that contained more than the usual amount of ore. Ethan traded and bought until he had a piece of that mountain and the right to cut timber to support an iron mine. He went to work to create the biggest furnace operation in the region.

That same year, 1762, Ethan married. He was certainly not too young for the match, but his bride was scarcely an ideal mate for him. Mary Brownson was half a dozen years older than Ethan, and completely opposite to his adventurous, extroverted personality. Ethan had some scholastic pretensions and considered himself to be philosophically inclined, but Mary, the daughter of a well-to-do miller in Woodbury, could not write

her name. She was dowdy and over-religious by Ethan's standards, and she had absolutely no sense of humor. Nothing about
her could have been expected to attract a man like Ethan. Yet
they were married in Roxbury by the Reverend Daniel Brins-
made and came home to the Cornwall farm to live while Ethan
got his business affairs in order. Their first child, Loraine, was
born there.

In 1763 Ethan brought Mary and their daughter to Salisbury.
The huge demand for iron kettles, which were used by farmers
in making potash, kept Ethan's foundry busy. He bought more
timber lands to supply fuel. He arranged for the damming of
waterways to supply power and for roads to give access to raw
materials. Soon he was building a new furnace, twenty-four feet
high, capable of making two tons of iron at a time. The business
employed fifty men, which made it the largest manufactory in
the area.

The drain on Ethan's time and resources, and the need for a
good manager and a partner, persuaded him in 1764 to bring
his brother Heman into the business. Heman was unmarried,
two years younger than Ethan, and a stolid, sturdy type of man
who could be relied upon. Ethan's dull marriage and business
responsibilities seemed to weigh heavily on him. He was a lively
fellow who liked to spend his evenings in the taverns, talking
politics and philosophy over many more than a single glass. He
saw, as his father had taught him, that there was money and
power to be had in land speculation, but it took time and
energy. Unless he had help with the foundry he could not in-
dulge in speculation. So Heman came to Salisbury and became a
partner in the foundry. They all lived in the fine house Ethan
had bought from Eliphalet Buell.

Although the Allen brothers were among the most successful
men in Salisbury, they were still rough frontiersmen. They did
not get on very well in the town. Soon they clashed with their
neighbor, Samuel Tousley, whose pigs wandered onto the Allen
land and rooted about, eating the Allen produce and raising
hob with the Allen scheme of life. The Allen boys seized the
Tousley porkers. They put them in a neighbor's sty and would
not return them to Tousley.

A furious Tousley went to court, and the judge issued a writ enabling Tousley to repossess his pigs. Tousley was so angry that he brought another suit against the Allen brothers for pig theft and trespass on his property.

Ethan went to court and offered their defense. Tousley had committed a nuisance, he said, and the Allens had merely taken the pigs into custody. The court held, however, that the Allen brothers had taken the law into their own hands, and they were fined ten shillings. The court also held that Tousley had been damaged in the amount of five shillings, which the Allens had to pay. The Allens left court in a high fury. The feud continued a few days later. Samuel Tousley met Heman Allen and they got into an argument about pigs, money, and other matters of finance and morality. The result was that Heman punched Samuel Tousley in the face. Heman was hauled into court, where he was fined sixteen shillings for assaulting his neighbor, and warned to behave himself.

The Allens were free spirits, not inclined to conform with their neighbors' wishes, or with laws they found oppressive. Ethan, in particular, was always ready to ignore the law when he felt he was being wronged. One day he got into a quarrel with George Caldwell, another Salisbury man with whom Ethan had had unpleasant business dealings. Ethan stopped Caldwell on the road and dressed him down verbally. When Caldwell retorted, Ethan set upon him and beat him. The court fined Ethan ten shillings for this breach of the peace.

Yet Ethan was not just a street brawler. Many of his quarrels with authority came over matters of principle. For one thing, there was the matter of smallpox inoculation.

Years back the Indians and others had learned that an effective method of preventing the ravages of smallpox was to inoculate oneself with serum from the sores of a smallpox victim. That way one was likely to catch a minor case of the disease, recover, and then forever after be immune. Many New Englanders tended to believe that smallpox inoculation was the work of the devil. It was neither clean nor godly to take festering pus from one man's wounds and force it into a healthy body. In Salisbury it was against the law to inoculate except with the express consent of the selectmen—and that consent was given, apparently, by whim and usually only when it was too late to do any good.

Ethan Allen objected to a law that said the selectmen had control over his body through the superior authority of the Connecticut legislature. He advertised his intention to violate the law, and he did so, inoculating himself without the selectmens' consent. Then he repaired to a local tavern for refreshment. In the course of the jolly conversation Ethan let it be known what he thought of the legislators who would pass such a stupid law and the local selectmen who would try to enforce it. As he warmed to the wine and his subject, he went further. He challenged the local selectmen to do something about the fact that on this very day he had inoculated himself. If they did not like it, he was prepared to take them on, individually or together, and whip the lot of them to a fare-thee-well.

In 1765, when this incident occurred, the church had lost some of its power over the individual—otherwise Ethan would have felt the full wrath of society. As it was, he was again hailed into court to answer to a charge of blasphemy for the language he had used in the tavern. Nothing much came of that complaint; but, with one thing and another, Ethan was getting fed up with Salisbury.

In the fall of 1765 Ethan moved his family to Northampton, Massachusetts, where he went into business with a New York merchant named Sampson Simpson. Mr. Simpson believed a fortune could be found in the hills of the Bay Colony, and when a deposit of lead was discovered his enthusiasm grew. Ethan, never lacking in enthusiasm, took over as manager of the partnership. He dreamed of a steady stream of silver and iron coming from that mine, but as the months wore on the deposit of lead seemed in danger of petering out without providing the fortune the partners had envisioned. Northampton, too, palled on Ethan. He began to spend more time in the taverns, and when in his cups was easily persuaded to air some of his advanced social and philosophical views. He did not believe in the salvation of a pious few, or in hellfire and brimstone, he swore, nor did he hold with most of the things the church fathers professed as articles of faith. In the eyes of those same church fathers, Ethan's heretical views were likely to corrupt his fellow boozers, and perhaps even the little children of Northampton. In July, 1767, the selectmen met and handed down their decision: Ethan Allen and his family were to leave the town.

Where to go? Ethan headed back for Salisbury, where he could at least occupy half of the Allens' big house. Heman, still unmarried, did not need much space, and he was a graceful man who could put up with much, even the prickly nature of his brother. On Ethan's departure for Northampton, Heman had gone into business for himself as the operator of a general store. It was a task for which he was eminently fitted for he had the sobriety and the gentle disposition that make a good storekeeper.

When Ethan arrived in Salisbury he was met by a big family. The brothers were centering their activities around Heman and the store. Heber, the third brother, who was twenty-four, had come recently from Cornwall to help in the store and to court Sarah Owen. Levi, who was two years younger, had also come up to the bigger community—probably so Heman could keep an eye on him, for Levi was a scamp. He was always in mischief, and sometimes more than that. He had a dark side to his character, combining the irascibility of Ethan with a negative turn of mind. Ethan was willing to fight a man and then shake his hand afterwards. Levi would avoid the fight, but he would lie awake long hours considering how he might destroy his enemy. In Cornwall he had already been involved in several scrapes and was developing so bad a reputation that the townsfolk were glad to see him leave.

Sisters Lydia and Lucy would marry and go to Massachusetts and southern Connecticut; they would not be a part of the Salisbury Allen family, and their connection with events to come would be minor.

The Hampshire Grants

GIVEN Ethan Allen's temperament and his age—thirty years— it was unthinkable that he could settle down and join Heman in the store venture in Salisbury. He needed adventure and open spaces. Ethan was wise enough to know that his abilities did not flourish on cobbled streets or in the drawing room. He was a philosopher of the woods, and to the woods he must repair.

Earlier, Ethan had attempted to become housebroken, at least in his own way. During the days when he and Heman were running the iron foundry, Ethan had struck up an acquaintance with Dr. Thomas Young, who practiced medicine a few miles away in Amenia, New York. Dr. Young possessed a store of general knowledge that established him in the community as a scholar and man of vast learning. He was good for Ethan, for he stimulated the Allen imagination and provided knowledge about the world that Ethan could not gain elsewhere. Many an evening the pair sat up late, the doctor recounting what he had learned from books and papers, Ethan recounting what he had seen and learned in the woods.

Ethan felt a compulsion to write. Then and afterwards he scribbled down his thoughts whenever he had leisure time. From the long discussions and the scribblings came the joint decision of the learned doctor and the backwoods philosopher to write a book, a philosophical treatise aimed at helping to free men's minds from the fetters of established religion.

The times were ripe for such writings. The growth of interest in the physical world was working to produce new interest in science. Many men were testing the nature of matter itself. And the more they probed into the secrets of the universe, the less satisfied they were with the old religious views, which attributed to an almighty God a constant and working control over the daily affairs of men. Dr. Young introduced Ethan to the philosophers and scientists, Ethan responded with his own observa-

tions, and together they began to write their book. The theme
was Deistic: the authors accepted the existence of a great pro-
genitor, a God who had started things going in the universe.
But beyond that, they rejected the idea that a trinity of God
existed or could exist. The Church of England, the Puritans of
America, and all organized religions, were built on fraud, the
fraud of believing in the supernatural.

Unfortunately Dr. Young left the area in 1764, before the
book was finished, and he took the manuscript with him, promising to keep in touch. With him also went the warmth and
influence of their discussions, and Ethan did not continue on
his own in the literary project.

His philosophical activity temporarily suspended, Ethan's mind
turned to the lands north of Connecticut, between the Connecticut River and Lake Champlain, which he had seen on the
abortive mission to Fort William Henry seven years before. By
law these lands belonged to New York, but there was confusion
as to ownership of the property, and a good deal of dissatisfaction. The confusion had existed a long time. First the Indians
had quarreled over the region, and then the French and British.
By 1763 the British had won control. The ensuing confusion
about the British colonial policy governing the area was caused
by the failure of the Crown to understand the vastness of the
American continent.

In the seventeenth century King Charles II granted his
brother, the Duke of York, the vast tract of land we now know
as New York. But the maps of the day were totally unreliable,
and New York's eastern boundary was uncertain, for the cartog-
raphers and clerks did not know the course of the Connecticut
River. As long as the French and Indian skirmishes occurred in
the area the question of ownership was not pressing. After peace
came to the region, however, settlement increased. Owners and
claimants of the land began to clash.

Beginning in 1749, Governor Benning Wentworth of New
Hampshire had granted a number of townships west of the
Connecticut River to friends, relatives, and people who would
pay large sums of money for the land. Wentworth's grants of

land were in this vague area, which did not belong indisputably
to any colony, but to which New York had at least as good a
claim as Wentworth's colony of New Hampshire had. Had New
York complained, Wentworth most probably would have
backed away. But New Yorkers and their governor were much
more concerned with protection of the property they already
had, and Wentworth's action went largely unchallenged. During the next fifteen years, the governor issued more than 130
"Hampshire Grants," totaling some three million acres.

In the beginning Wentworth's relatives and cronies thought
they had a good thing—they would buy the Hampshire Grants
and then increase the price and resell them to make their fortunes. Seeing these same economic possibilities, the governor
and council of New York realized their colony was being deprived of revenues from lands the king had—they claimed—
granted to the Duke of York. They sent agents to London to
complain of Wentworth's action in selling off *their* territory. In
1764, while Ethan Allen was making iron in Salisbury, King
George gave New York undisputed right to the lands west of the
Connecticut, including the land Benning Wentworth had
parceled out as the Hampshire Grants.

Undisputed right? Hardly. Those who had bought their lands
from Wentworth or from Wentworth's assignees were very
ready to dispute. Most of the lands were held by speculators and
absentee owners, but in the southwest part of the territory, just
north of the Massachusetts line, some two hundred families had
actually moved onto their lands, built their cabins, cleared
meadow and pasture, and were trying to make the hard living of
the New England settler. In 1765 New York began sending in
surveyors, and without so much as a by-your-leave they marched
across the settlers' lands and laid out their posts and chains
across their farms. Furthermore, New York made it clear that it
had no intention of honoring the Hampshire Grants of Governor Wentworth. The landowners went to London to petition
the king for redress.

The Crown stalled, ordered New York to stop issuing patents
for lands equivalent to Wentworth's grants in the area, and
promised to look into the situation. This decree came in July,

1767, and the confusion that ensued allowed men to come to the area to do whatever they believed they could do to make a profit. The settlers held to their New Hampshire titles and stood fast. Speculators began selling out cheaply to settlers and adventurers; by 1769 the population of the area had tripled, and New York was concerned lest the royal delay cause it to lose all its titles to the Hampshire lands. So the New York colonial government, in defiance of royal mandate, began issuing its own patents to the lands—many of them superseding or overlapping the Hampshire Grants.

That year the battle became personal and thus very serious, for it concerned men who were actually on the land and others who came with new pieces of paper intending to drive them away.

Ethan went up to the Grants to see for himself what was happening, and he came home knowing a tremendous clash was not far off.

In the summer of 1769 a farmer named James Breakenridge planted his corn and small grains on the farm he occupied near Bennington. He held this land in accordance with a grant from Governor Wentworth. He knew that New York also laid claim to this land, but as far as he was concerned New York and her governor, Cadwallader Colden, could go to the devil. Breakenridge and his fellows had raised the money to send Samuel Robinson to London. Robinson had sought the ear of the king, and the king had promised that all would be settled amicably. Breakenridge was willing to settle peaceably, but he was not willing to pay New York for the lands he had bought once from New Hampshire.

As it turned out, the "Yorkers," as Breakenridge and his fellows called them, had no intention of asking Breakenridge to pay. They intended to come in and push him off his land. Governor Colden had turned over Breakenridge's land to a group of speculators headed by Major John Small and a minister of the Gospel, the Reverend Mr. Slaughter. These men had asked for a commission to survey and divide the tract among them so they could speculate and grow rich. They dispatched their preliminary agents, who were greeted coldly by Breakenridge. The colonial government then sent the surveying party back accompanied by a New York justice of the peace, who had a copy of the law to show any and all who might wish to see it.

In the middle of October the New York party arrived at the Breakenridge farm—the surveyors with their chains and Justice John Munro with his law book—and prepared to survey the land in behalf of the New York "owners." Farmer Breakenridge told them to get off his land. Justice Munro stepped up and said it was not his land, but the land of Major Small and the Reverend Mr. Slaughter, according to New York law.

"I hope you will not try to take advantage of us," said Farmer Breakenridge, gesturing around him, "for our people do not understand law."

Justice Munro looked around at the faces of the other farmers who had assembled to see what would happen on the Breakenridge farm during this confrontation. He noted that most of the men facing him carried long rifles. He noted that their gaze was not only unfriendly—it was distinctly uncompromising.

Justice Munro did his best. He stood on a stump and he read the law to these backwoodsmen. He called on them to disperse, go home and tend to their own affairs, and let the surveyors proceed.

Not a man moved. Breakenridge repeated his demand that the surveyors get off his land. Since the Yorkers could count some sixty settlers, each armed with a rifle (or at least it seemed so), Justice Munro counseled wisdom instead of violence, and the surveyors went away. They parted on friendly enough terms —like boxers shaking hands before they set to.

Breakenridge and his fellow farmers harvested their corn and kept steadfastly at the never-ending job of making a living from the land. But they sensed they had not seen the last of the Yorkers.

Down in Albany the furious Major Small cursed Breakenridge, and the sanctimonious Reverend Slaughter prayed for

God to guide the stubborn farmer in the ways of righteousness, which meant giving the Reverend his land. Small and Slaughter persuaded the New York colonial authorities to prepare ejection suits against Breakenridge and a number of other farmers and landholders in the Bennington area who occupied land granted by Wentworth.

Some of the people who owned Hampshire-Grant land near Bennington actually lived in and around Salisbury, Connecticut. They learned that next summer the New York Supreme Court would hear the Breakenridge case in Albany. They did not like that news at all. New York judges deciding on New Yorkers' claims to lands that New York said it owned could dispense only New York justice. They called a meeting at Sharon, over the hill from Salisbury, and they pledged money to stop the Yorkers. A second meeting was held at Canaan, off to the east of Salisbury. The proprietors of the disputed lands realized that they had to do something drastic to protect their interests. They agreed to tax themselves for the general good, fifty cents for each land right, and pay the money to Charles Burral. He was to do what had to be done to keep the court action in motion until June, when they would have another meeting.

When the landholders met again Ethan Allen came down from Sheffield, Massachusetts, a few miles north on the plain from Salisbury. Ethan had installed Mary and the children in Sheffield, and got Zimri, who was just twenty, to manage the farm for him so he could turn his hand to other matters.

Even those who were delicately pleased to have Ethan gone from Salisbury knew that he was a man to be reckoned with. His friends had little but praise for the rugged Ethan; his enemies knew his strength. When he appeared at their meeting and indicated that he would be glad to undertake the management of their case for the Hampshire Grants, the landowners were pleased. Most of them had their farms and enterprises. Ethan was at loose ends, and his woods lore was such that none could match him. He was a fierce advocate of personal freedom, a fact most of these men knew whether through personal observation or from reading and hearing of Ethan's troubles with the

law whenever someone stepped on Ethan's toes. So it was decided: Ethan would be their man. He would go to Portsmouth,
the capital of New Hampshire, and get Governor John Wentworth to straighten out the mess his uncle had created for the
settlers on the Hampshire Grants—the land that soon would be
known as Vermont.

The Education of Ira Allen

THE frontier to which Ethan Allen was committing himself was a lonely, forbidding, and sometimes dreaded place. A few years later, in assigning an officer to command the vital fort at Ticonderoga, the American general Horatio Gates would send the young and vigorous Arthur St. Clair, with the comment that only a man of such magnificent physique could survive the murderous climate of the region.

It was not so much different down in northwest Connecticut where Ethan and the other Allens lived. Ira, the youngest of the family, had an adventure about this time that showed just how miserable and frightened a man could be in the cold grasp of nature. He was living in Salisbury with Heman and Levi, while Ethan and Zimri lived a few miles up the plain in Sheffield. Heman and Levi bought 350 hogs, and Ira agreed to go into the woods with them and tend them during the fall while they fattened up on beechnuts in the forest. The Allens were engaging in a speculative venture that had great promise, for domesticated animals were always in short supply in the western part of the colonies. But the hogs had a proclivity for escape that was marvelous to behold. A swineherd was definitely needed at all times.

Ira, Heman, and Levi set out with several hired men to drive their 350 charges from Salisbury into the wilderness. In the area lived the Macintire family, with whom Ira would stay while he fattened up his hogs. While the prospect of being a swineherd was not overly enticing, a winter with the Macintires was more so, for the family had two daughters in their twenties and Ira was a vigorous eighteen-year-old.

Off they set one October morning at dawn. Before they had gone a mile, cold rain began to fall, and by sunrise it had turned to sleet.

The drovers had divided the hogs into three sections, with Ira and a hired man named Abner Owen taking the first. So cold was the drive that Owen became numb with fatigue and sat down on a log to rest. He slumped forward and nearly lost consciousness. Ira saw that Owen would soon succumb to the dreaded cold.

Faced with the stupefied Owen, Ira did the only thing he could. He picked up his drover's stick and slashed his companion across the shoulders once and then again, rousing him from the frightening torpor. They went on, but Owen became weak again, and five miles from the Macintire house they had to abandon the hogs and head for shelter.

Heman found that another hired man, Edward Akins, had collapsed and could go no further, so Akins was put up on the horse along with Heman and they moved on. Finally they came to a line of marked trees and knew they were heading toward some kind of human shelter. They moved as quickly as they could, the hogs forgotten for the moment, for dusk was falling and to remain in the woods without shelter would endanger the lives of at least two of them. All were soaked to the skin, their clothes freezing to their bodies.

The Macintires hurried the weary travelers in and warmed them by the fire. Akins was so badly off that the Allens despaired for his life, but Mrs. Macintire managed to get three little doses of warm milk down him, and he began to revive. By morning he was fit again.

Soon the hogs were rounded up and driven into a grove of beech trees not far from the Macintires, and Ira stayed on to care for the animals. Every day or so he went out with salt to find his charges and bring them back together again. Ira whiled away the days doing chores at the Macintire's, and the nights telling stories and listening to the chatter of the girls.

Outdoor life in the woods was not the only danger the settlers faced in these frontier lands. Men were not particularly friendly to strangers, and those to whom villainy came easily had good opportunity to assault the solitary traveler. Ira was a big strapping boy, and he soon learned the ways of the wilderness and of man in this forbidding land. Of the two, the wilderness treated him better.

Early in January of 1770, Heman decided to sell the fattest of his hogs, and the drovers came to pick them up at the Macintire's. The remaining animals were kept in the woods for another six weeks. A tremendous snowfall in February sent Ira scurrying. The hogs would certainly starve in this weather: when Ira went out to find them in the eerie silence after the storm, they were wallowing in three-foot drifts, and the beech-nuts were buried.

Ira set out at dawn on snowshoes for Conway, hired a horse, and rode to Deerfield to buy corn for the pigs. When the Deer-field storekeeper and the farmers learned that someone was in the village trying to buy a quantity of corn, they got together and doubled the price. Outraged, Ira drove on to Muddy Brook where the farmers again tried to cheat him, and to Sunderland, where he finally managed to get three hundred bushels at a fair price and hire a barn to use for the rest of the winter. Ira settled in at a local deacon's place for the rest of the winter. After a few weeks he needed more corn, but he discovered all the local farmers were united on cheating him on the price. It was not every day that a chance to fleece a stranger came along. Ira was not fleeceable: he scoured the countryside around the village until he found honest farmers who would sell him grain at a fair price.

Ira was also learning how to achieve goals without resorting to force or violence. On this trip, he stopped at a public house kept by a Captain Warner, knowing full well that the Warners liked to cheat and abuse strangers if they thought they could get away with it.

Beardless Ira walked into the tavern and went to the corner away from the fire, as if he were afraid and knew his place was low. Shyly, he ordered a small glass of rum. The landlady took one look at him and gave him the tiniest bit possible. Then he asked for dinner, and she found him a plate of old crusts and bones. Ira sat down at a table and ordered a pint of cider to go with the mess. He made a show of pushing the bones and crusts around with his fork, and then called loudly for his bill without having touched a bite. He put down two pieces of gold.

"I am sure it will be high, madame," he told the landlady,

"since you have obviously spent at least a week preparing this repast. I think I'll go into town and kill one of my hogs instead."

The landlady came scurrying up, all apologies. Out she dashed into the kitchen and reappeared with a steaming plate of the best food in the house. Ira sat at the table, grinning, and drank his cider. The group of men who had been clustered around the fire, tankards in hand, laughed as the landlady came back into the room all aflutter and did her best to placate the "quality" traveler she had offended. Ira began joking with the men and spent a very pleasant evening, while the Warners quivered in the background.

Ira came home from this first adventure on his own a sturdy and independent young man who had learned much about the world around him. He was as hard as nails and even more resilient. The long winter in the woods had strengthened his constitution so he could bear almost any challenge to it, as he quickly showed on another occasion, when he came down with fever. He was put in bed, but this did not agree with him, and he decided to undertake more drastic treatment. He got out of bed, dressed in his underclothes and wrapped a blanket around himself, and went to the mill pond near the house, where the water was so cold, winter and summer, that it seemed near freezing. Ira stripped off his blanket and clothes, dived into the water, and swam out. He was shaking with cold, but he dived in again and swam out—and then stood shivering on the log he had chosen as a diving board. He had vowed to dive in three times, but he was so cold that he could not feel the log with his feet, so he wrapped the blanket around his body and ran briskly back to the house. He sat down by the fire, began to sweat, and went to bed. He then had another attack, but ended up sweating out the fever and breaking it.

Judge Livingston's Court

IN the summer of 1770, the children of old Joseph Allen had their first tragedy.

When Ira had recovered from his bout with fever and was up and around again, he learned that sister Lydia was not well. He rode the forty miles southeast to Goshen to brother-in-law John Finche's house to visit and comfort Lydia.

He arrived to find her on her deathbed. Ira refused to accept the verdict, and sat up with his sick sister for three days and three nights, trying to rally her. The doctor came, shook his head, and said that Lydia's only possible chance lay in certain very strong medicines. The trouble was that no one in this frontier country had them; the nearest source of supply was Esopus, New York, which was sixty miles away—a journey through woods even thicker than those in which Ira had spent the winter. If Lydia needed the medicine, though, distance and difficulty meant nothing. Ira saddled his horse and set out. On the road, as he arrived at a tavern at full gallop, he would stop, explain his mission, and pick up a new horse. Thus riding "express," he made the sixty-mile journey in a day, got the medicines, and headed back.

Having been up for three nights running, Ira was understandably sleepy. He fell asleep on the back of his horse, but was awakened rudely when the animal stopped at an obstruction. It was a close brush with danger, but the Allen luck had held. Ira shook the sleep from his eyes and continued back to Goshen, where he arrived at dawn. The medicines were given to Lydia, but she was too ill for them to help. A few days later she died.

Ethan, during this time, had been deeply involved in the affairs of the settlers on the Hampshire Grants. He had left Sheffield in May to go to Portsmouth, New Hampshire, to see Governor John Wentworth. There was no doubt in the minds of the settlers around Bennington and the landowners from Connecti-

cut that their grants were valid. From time to time the New
Hampshire legislature took action in matters that concerned the
Hampshire Grants, which added to the feeling that New Hampshire land rights were established, no matter what London and
New York might say. But when Ethan Allen reached Portsmouth, he discovered that matters had changed considerably in
the past few months. Governor Wentworth, prompted by a
sense of family responsibility, had earlier advised the settlers on
the Hampshire Grants to tell New York to go to the devil. New
York had promptly complained to London and the king had
rebuked Wentworth for defying the Crown. So the governor
was in no mood or position to espouse the cause of the settlers
around Bennington, even if he felt like it. He did offer Ethan
every courtesy, supplied all the papers that purported to show
the legality of the grants, and did all he could except the one
thing that would have counted: the governor did not undertake
to fight for the rights of the settlers his uncle had established on
the land. The best he could do was to advise Ethan to find the
most competent lawyer in New England, and to the governor's
mind this was Jared Ingersoll of New Haven, Connecticut.

Ethan tarried long enough in Portsmouth to buy three
Hampshire Grants parcels for himself from their original
owners. As long as he was involved in the Grants, he figured, it
was probably a good idea for him to be financially interested as
well.

Ethan rode to New Haven, two hundred miles from Portsmouth, and found Jared Ingersoll. Armed with Governor John
Wentworth's letter of blessing, Ethan persuaded Ingersoll to
undertake the defense of the settlers on the Hampshire Grants
against the New Yorkers who would oust them. The trial was
set for that summer in Albany, and Ingersoll agreed to be there.
Ethan headed home to Sheffield, where he stayed until the
summer.

The trial, which opened at the end of June, became a series
of hearings to determine the rights of the colonists and colonies.
As might have been expected, the wealthy New Yorkers appeared as fine figures. The farmers from the Hampshire Grants
arrived at court in their homespun; the owners of the New York

patents appeared "in great state and magnificence," as Ethan put it; "the defendants appearing but in ordinary fashion, having been greatly fatigued by hard labor wrought on the disputed premises, and their cash much exhausted, made a very disproportionate figure at court."

The settlers could hardly expect very much from a New York court. Among the owners of the New York patents were the attorney general and the lieutenant general of the state. The most prominent speculator involved was the lawyer James Duane, who would take upon himself the leadership of the New York cause. Duane was a shifty fellow, known for his speculations and his sharp dealing, and he was not very popular even in his own colony. Needless to say, he became the prime enemy of the simple settlers on the Grants, for he epitomized all they hated in their opponents: a man foppishly dressed, shrewd, and ungenerous. Duane was what in those times was called a "land jobber," or land speculator: he neither lived nor intended to live in the Grants—he was buying up land to be sold for profit. That was not unusual. Some of the Connecticut owners with whom Ethan was associated were just as speculative in their dealings. However, many of the people who appeared at the Albany court were not speculators, but the actual settlers of the lands in question.

Presiding over the New York Supreme Court was Judge Robert Livingston. Ethan and his friends did not know it, but even the judge was a holder of Hampshire Grants lands under the New York patents. The scales of justice were definitely out of balance in this case: Livingston, a wealthy and powerful figure, was not likely to favor the poor farmers of the lands east of the Hudson.

Almost from the opening, it was apparent how the trials would go. The first of them was the case of *Small v. Carpenter*, and it told the story.

Isaiah Carpenter lived on a farm in Shaftsbury, which was a few miles north of Bennington. He had bought and settled on lands granted by Governor Benning Wentworth in 1765. Four years after his purchase, Governor Cadwallader Colden of New York had deeded the same land to Major John Small.

Attorney Ingersoll arose to present the papers Ethan had secured from the governor's office in Portsmouth, proving that Isaiah Carpenter had good title to his land. Attorney James Duane, representing himself and others, rose to object to the introduction of the New Hampshire titles. They were worthless, he said. The Crown had granted the land to the Duke of York, and New York and its officials had the right of disposition of that land.

Judge Livingston sustained the objection, thus destroying the entire case of the settlers at the outset. All the rest was ceremony. Jared Ingersoll got up from his table, picked up his papers, and left the courtroom, declaring that the case was already prejudiced by the judge's ruling and that there could be but one outcome. So New York justice held that Major Small owned the land on which Isaiah Carpenter lived. The remaining eight suits went uncontested.

Ethan followed Jared Ingersoll out of the court, muttering that it was "judgment without mercy," and that it was quite to be expected, for the power and money of the Yorkers was too great for the defendants to overcome.

No one was very much surprised at this outcome. Ethan went back to his tavern to pick up his saddlebags and ride home, but before he could leave, he had a pair of callers. They were James Duane and John Tabor Kempe, attorney general of the colony of New York and a landholder in the disputed area. With them was an unidentified man who remained silent.

Duane and Kempe had a suggestion for Ethan. They had seen how much influence he had with his fellows and they knew he was the agent of the Hampshire Grant-holders. If he would go back and persuade the Grant-holders to accept the decisions without any trouble, the New Yorkers would make it worth his while. For openers, they offered him money and a horse.

All right, said Ethan, he would take them. And he did, it seems, at least by Duane's later account, although in later years Ethan denied it. To take the money was sensible in Ethan's view: if the fool Yorkers wanted to give him money and a horse, he might as well take them. He knew what he was going to do when he got back to New England.

"We have might on our side," Attorney General Kempe reminded Ethan during their interview, "and you know that might often prevails against right."

These were truthful but unfortunate words for a colonial judicial officer to utter—the men were speaking frankly.

Ethan replied in kind.

"The gods of the hills are not the gods of the valley," he said.

This cryptic remark puzzled the New Yorkers. They asked Ethan what he meant.

"If you will accompany me to the hills of Bennington, the sense will be made clear," he replied.

In their way, they would accompany Ethan Allen to those hills, and they would find their answer. They were not going to like it.

CHAPTER SIX

Stephen Fay's Tavern

OF all the animals that ranged the woods of the Hampshire Grants, the cougar, or catamount, as he was called, was the most respected by the settlers. He was brave and deft. He killed when he needed food, and then he slashed, ate, and was gone. He lived to himself, and was seldom seen. When Stephen Fay and his two sons opened a tavern on top of one of the Bennington hills, it was quite properly called the Catamount, and a big tawny cougar was killed and stuffed and mounted outside the square, unpainted building. It was significant that the cat was positioned to face westward, as if it was watchfully guarding the Grants from any threat from the Yorker domains.

In the summer of 1770 a group of settlers and landowners in the Hampshire Grants met at the Catamount to decide what course they would take in view of the New York court action. They could expect the Yorkers at any time to come storming in with writs and papers and surveying chains. What were they going to do about it?

Ethan reported to the settlers assembled at Fay's Tavern about the trials, and how Judge Livingston had flatly rejected the claims of the New Hampshire Grants. Since the Crown and the colony of New York both pretended that they owned the lands, the settlers could only maintain their rights by force of arms. The decision to fight was made by men in buckskin and homespun, standing around a rough room in the big tavern. They established, then and there, a militia of their own and a defense system whereby they would be warned when the Yorkers came.

Ethan was elected commander of the militia force, and they began calling him Colonel Ethan Allen. Two of his trusted lieutenants were Remember Baker, a first cousin, and Seth Warner, who was also Baker's first cousin.

Baker was a sturdy, freckle-faced young man with sandy hair and an irrepressible grin. He was a real soldier already, having gained experience in fighting the French and Indians. In the course of actions such as the assault against Fort Ticonderoga, Baker had tramped through the Hampshire Grants and had liked the country. In 1763 he had brought his wife, Desire, and his son to settle in Arlington, not far north of Bennington. He had a personal stake in the welfare of the cause.

Seth Warner was also a settler on the Grants. He, too, had come to Bennington in 1763, when he was twenty years old. He was a big man, six feet two in his moccasins, who by the time of the meeting knew every hill and stream in the countryside around.

But Ethan was their leader, combining the characteristics of general, politician, and philosopher. Ethan seemed to know from the beginning that the Hampshire Grants could be protected by using guerilla warfare to repel the Yorkers. His already fearsome reputation as a fighter from Salisbury days was enhanced in the time to come on the Grants. It was said that Ethan could pick up two strong men and butt their heads together with ease, that he could hold at bay a half-dozen sturdy fighters, that he could bite the heads off nails (and often did so for amusement). He certainly was a strong man, all deponents of history agree, and quick-tempered. He led the militiamen through his own strength of presence, and they never forgot it.

Sometime during the fall, Ethan went back to Albany and returned James Duane's horse, although there is no indication that he returned the money given him. He also told Duane that everything had been fixed up—which possibly meant to Duane that the settlers were being persuaded to give up their squatter's rights and accept the decision of the New York court. But if that was Duane's real belief, then it was not going to be long before he would be shaken by the naked truth: the men of the Hampshire Grants had no intention of giving up so much as a foot of land to the Yorkers.

Not all the people living in the Hampshire Grants were of one mind, of course. Some believed they ought to accept the New York claim. These people had been given titles to their claims by New York's government in areas where New Hampshire's grants did not interfere with holdings of influential New York. There was religious dissension, too. Besides the established denominations—the Congregational church and the Anglican or Episcopal church—there were men like Ethan, who was now a professed Deist. As a Deist, Ethan believed in a supreme being, but refused to accept the trappings of any organized religion. Such men have always infuriated the church at least as much as outright atheists. Ethan was heartily detested by many religious leaders on the Grants. He was, then, both a uniting and divisive factor.

New York had already learned it had friends in the Grants, and it used them to extend its authority and influence. Ethan was determined that they should not extend either one very far, or for very long.

Soon the militia that had formed under Ethan Allen gained two names. The Yorkers hardly waited until Ethan appointed Remember Baker, Seth Warner, and a handful of others as officers in the militia before they ran to New York to inform Governor Cadwallader Colden that Ethan Allen had assembled a vicious gang called the "Bennington Mobb" that threatened anyone who favored New York. Colden rose in his wrath and vowed to use the full power of the strongest colony in the north to drive this gang of upstarts off of New York's lands and back into the Green Mountains. And Ethan, ever the alert publicist, knew that his boys now had a name: thus was born the Green Mountain Boys.

The Green Mountain Boys numbered about three hundred, but as planned and trained by Ethan, they never were a real army. He took young men who already knew how to shoot and trap and walk silently in the woods, and he assembled them to protect the people of the Grants from the incursions of New Yorkers. His militia seldom drilled. They had no uniforms; a sprig of evergreen worn in the cap was as much insignia as a Green Mountain Boy needed. They met at Stephen Fay's Catamount Tavern to talk a little business and drink a lot of rum. They were fighters, and they knew that they were fighting for their freedom, but they were guerillas at best. They possessed no cannon, nor would most of them have known how to fire one. They were a handful of irregulars, held together in a common cause and, later, even more by pride. There were no terms of enlistment, and pay came when there was money. If a man's wife was sick or the plowing had to be done, he naturally begged off the current assignment; there were more than enough Boys for the job at hand. No one ever hesitated to speak his mind, and if they did not argue with Ethan, Seth Warner, or Remember Baker, it was because they respected these leaders as the best woodsmen in the Grants.

As the year 1770 came to a close, Ethan and his men began to enlist public sympathy for their cause throughout New England. This meant publicizing their position by broadsides and articles for the newspapers, which in turn meant sending men and materials down to Hartford, the nearest place where printing could be done. Ethan sent broadsides and articles signed "A Lover of Reason and Truth" to the Connecticut *Courant*. These were copied by newspapers in Connecticut and other colonies, including New York, and it was not long before the word spread that strong men were on the Hampshire Grants and intended to stay there. The word went home to England, where both New Hampshire and New York sent representatives to try to clear the titles once and for all through the king. But King George and his counselors did not take the strong steps that might have settled the matter.

The action centered in the area west of the Green Mountains and east of the Hudson. The world was warned that this was a struggle between Poor, Honest Men of the Land and Princes of Privilege. Such argument was bound to arouse sympathy in the Colonies at large, for at this time wealthy landlords and the agents of faraway England were in increasingly bad favor among the people. Ethan Allen was as good a propagandist as he was a woodsman, and soon he had hundreds talking with conviction of the mistreatment of the poor souls in the Hampshire Grants.

The broadsides were widely distributed in the Grants. There was good reason for this: settlers must be persuaded against yielding to any soothing Yorkers who would entice them into applying for New York patents to their lands. The cause could be lost if enough men admitted any right in Yorker claims. The faint-hearted must be cajoled, even intimidated, against the land thieves of New York.

Ethan and his Green Mountain Boys were very lucky when Cadwallader Colden was replaced as royal governor of New York by the Earl of Dunmore in 1771. Colden was familiar with the Hampshire Grants, and in the winter of 1769–70 he had been considering courses of action to enforce New York law. He might have put an end to the whole affair, and to the pretensions of the landowners in Connecticut, by validating the Grants of the settlers but not those of the speculators. But in the change of administration this matter was laid aside. The new governor who came to Albany knew absolutely nothing about America. He settled down in a mansion on New York City's Battery to enjoy his post and wait for a better job. Instead of calming the troubled waters, as Colden might have done, Dunmore proceeded to enrich himself remarkably by the best-known device of governors: he granted patents to hundreds of thousands of acres of Crown lands. Many thousands of these acres were in the disputed territory of the Grants. In the short year that he held office, the Earl changed the situation from serious to desperate.

In the spring of 1771, Lord Dunmore was replaced by Governor William Tryon, who had been serving in North Carolina. Tryon had just gone through a chastening experience in quarreling with backwoods settlers, and he was not eager to leap again into a military adventure.

Meanwhile, all the Allens were becoming personally interested in the Hampshire Grants. Ira, the youngest of the lot, sold his share of the Cornwall estate of old Joseph Allen in 1771, and used the money to buy several land rights in the Grants town of Poultney. Then he came north to visit Ethan and see what he had bought. He moved up the valley from Poultney to Castleton and the lake country, and then went up to Hubbardton, where the high meadows and rolling mountain lands intrigued him. He made a point of learning whose lands these were, and discovered that a good share was owned by a Captain Isaac Searles. Ira went to seek Captain Searles but learned he was in

Boston, so he returned to Salisbury to go into business with Heman and Levi as manufacturers of leather from deer hides. They set up a tannery and prepared the hides, then made leather breeches to sell to the more well-to-do colonists.

All this was Levi's idea, for he had seen it done successfully by traders in the West. Levi had left Salisbury the year before for an excursion to Maumetown, which was a long way on the other side of Detroit. He came home full of the tannery idea, and sold it to his merchant brother Heman. But typically, having had the idea, Levi was soon off in another direction, and other members of the family were left to carry out the hard work.

Ira, once again, was chosen to do the labor. Heman sent him up to Ensign's mill on the Housatonic, not far from Salisbury, to learn the trade. Ira went up with a hired man named Michael Flin, who was supposed to know what he was doing. They got through the first day's work all right and bedded down in the mill for the night. Next day, when they started the operation, the mill broke down. Flin shut the watergate and watched as Ira jumped down into the water inside to see what was amiss. Ira stood on the waterwheel, between the arms, his head at a level with the floor alongside, and then ducked down and found the trouble and corrected it. Just as he leaped out of the water onto the floor and pulled himself up, Flin started the waterwheel. Had Ira not moved when he did he would have been a goner—there was no clearance between the waterwheel and the rocky streambed; and Ira would have been swept over the wheel and down seventy feet of falls. From that moment on he watched the careless Flin like a hawk.

Ira stayed at the mill for several months learning the whole process of dressing deer hides. By the time he was finished he knew a good deal about treatment of hides and could make cloaks or ladies' muffs from furs. The Allens had another business enterprise.

But Ira had no desire to be a merchant like brother Heman, for he shared the same love of adventure that drove Ethan. In the winter of 1771 Ira finally found Captain Searles and persuaded him to sell the Hubbardton lands he coveted. In all he bought up thirty-two rights, encompassing some ten thousand acres. He paid the captain sixty-four pounds for the lands, which represented all Ira had saved in the fur business and in the tanning operation.

If the Hubbardton land was to be of any value, either for resale or for farming, it had to be surveyed. One of the decisions made by the settlers of the Hampshire Grants was that no New York surveyors were to be permitted to run lines across any of their lands. So Ira determined to learn the art himself. He procured the materials available and began to study.

While Ira was getting ready to come north, Ethan was busy with his defiance of New York. In the spring of 1771, the New York proprietors of Hampshire Grant land sent surveyor William Cockburn to Pittsford, about fifty miles northeast of Bennington. When Ethan learned that Cockburn was running lines up north, he wasted no time in assembling a band of Green Mountain Boys and going on ahead of them to investigate. Ethan soon found surveyor Cockburn. He sent him a message: the Green Mountain Boys were on the move, and if Cockburn wished to return to Albany with a whole skin, he had best be off before they arrived.

Cockburn recognized the reality of the threat, and he and his chainmen made off to the west to report to James Duane. Cockburn told Duane of his frightening adventures and how he had nearly been set upon by Ethan (he called him Nathan Allen) and his Boys, all dressed like Indians, with their faces blackened by soot. They were a horrid and murderous-looking mob, and Cockburn had no intention of returning to survey Pittsford until he had adequate protection.

Scarcely was this first skirmish won than Ethan and the Boys learned of the coming of another group of New York men to lands near Poultney. Ethan sent Robert Cochran, one of his more vigorous young lieutenants, who took a gang of the Boys down to find out what was happening. Sure enough, there were the Yorkers, trying to run their surveying lines. Cochran and his Boys laid into the outlanders, beat them up, and then sent them back to Albany. The war against New York authority was growing warm.

That summer Henry Ten Eyck, the high sheriff of Albany

County, set out on his own to enforce the laws as laid down by Judge Livingston. Early in July Sheriff Ten Eyck took a force of 150 deputies and headed for Bennington and the property of James Breakenridge, on whose farm the first confrontation had occurred two years earlier. A scout was sent ahead. When the party neared the place, the scout returned to announce that there must be three hundred men around the Breakenridge property, all armed and making noises as though they intended to fight if matters came to that.

The sheriff moved to the edge of the clearing that surrounded the house. Before him lay a big field, and he could see at least forty men spotted around it, all of them with long-barreled guns at the ready. The Yorkers stood there, not quite sure what to do next. A party of men came out of the house and met the posse to parley. Sheriff Ten Eyck looked at the Breakenridge place. It had been turned into a blockhouse. From loopholes cut in the walls the sun glinted on the steel of rifles and muskets. If it came to a fight, the defenders would not be easy to dislodge.

Farmer Breakenridge came out of the house and joined the discussion. His farm was under the protection of the people of Bennington, he said, and they would protect it. The Yorkers looked around at the resolute band of men and were persuaded that Breakenridge spoke the truth.

Sheriff Ten Eyck now had to make his decision. He read the writ of ejectment, which was his legal duty, and demanded that Breakenridge leave the place. No one moved. He ordered his men to advance and take the house. They looked around them, mumbled, and then the vast majority of them moved—backward. Soon Sheriff Ten Eyck could count only forty men ready to do his bidding. If that force threw itself against the "Bennington Mobb" it would be cut to pieces. So the sheriff turned and marched back to Albany to report another failure in force against the squatters.

Ethan Allen was not on hand the day of the Breakenridge confrontation when his organization performed so well for him. He was in Poultney on other business, but when word reached him about trouble at Breakenridge's he hurried back to Ben-

nington. Passing beneath the big cougar on its platform twenty
feet above the dooryard of the Catamount Tavern, Ethan went
inside, and over a bottle of Fay's New England rum he and
Remember Baker and Seth Warner went over the events of the
past few days. Ethan was very pleased at the restraint with
which his Green Mountain Boys had handled themselves. They
had accomplished at Breakenridge's all that anyone could have
expected of them.

Holding Off the Yorkers

AT any time, Governor Tryon could have resolved the problem of the Hamsphire Grants with a show of force. He had the power of the Crown behind him, and he had the soldiery to send in to drive the squatters off their land. Ethan Allen's band would have fought, but they would have lost. The game that Ethan had to play was complex: he must defend the Grants without provoking a real military action. Ethan kept a constant barrage of propaganda going against the "land thieves," making a big show of force as long as there was no need for it. His policy was to sow as much dissension as he could in the enemy camp by his pamphlets and newspaper articles.

Ethan was busy: he made trips north to Poultney and Castleton, where he was buying as much land as he could afford, and trips south to visit Mary on the Sheffield farm. He encouraged brother Zimri's farm work, met at the tavern with the Boys, and wrote his pamphlets against the enemy. He explored all over the north country. He skirted long Lake Champlain on the west, and when he could he bought land, or sold it if the price was right. After the Breakenridge affair, land values in the Grants suddenly shot up, and Ethan unloaded one piece of his property for four times what he had paid for it a few months earlier.

Ethan's tales and successes encouraged the other brothers to speculate in Hampshire Grants land. Heman, Heber, Ira, and a first cousin, Ebenezer Allen, all began buying property in large pieces. Levi was not so much involved. He was busy with the tanning and fur business down in Salisbury. Heman did not come up to the north country often or even consider moving there from Salisbury, where he was entrenched with his store and other business interests. Furthermore, his health was not strong enough to permit him to work in the woods. So Heman left the adventuring to his other brothers, though he provided some of the capital.

Ethan and Ira in particular were committed to adventure. Although they were regarded as outlaws by the New Yorkers, the Green Mountain Boys argued that they were obeying the mandate of a convention of the settlers who had agreed that only by force could they oppose the unjust demands of the New York landowners. The Green Mountain Boys made it plain that they intended to stay. Surveyors from New York were frequently troubled, and if they were caught in the territory they were warned first that they must not come back. If they did come back, they were caught and whipped and sent on their way with another warning. Hugh Monroe, a very determined surveyor, was caught several times. Finally Ethan's Boys lost patience with the determined fellow and decided to make an example of him. He was tried by a military court convened on the spot where he was captured, found guilty, and sentenced to flogging. He was stripped to the waist, tied to a tree, flogged until he fainted, cut down and revived, and then tied up and flogged again until he fainted a second time. On awakening, poor Monroe was flogged still a third time, until once again he fainted. This was the end. His wounds were dressed, and he was escorted back into New York territory. They warned him never again to appear in the Grants, on pain of more severe punishment.

Such incidents raised a furor in Albany, but not every man's hand was against the Green Mountain Boys. Law enforcement officers came into the Grants on several errands. One was to collect debts, and when they came for this purpose they were not disturbed. The settlers explained that they were not lawless: they accepted the law—what they did not accept was the right of the colony of New York to throw them off land they had bought and paid for.

As time went on others joined the cause, usually for reasons of their own. Colonel John Reid, a British army officer, had been given a patent by New York for lands in New Haven, Ferrisburg, and Panton. He settled them, which meant he went in and took over the lands by force and then settled people of his own choosing on them. Thus force begot force, and the issue festered like a boil. The settlers forbade anyone in the Grants to pay any attention to the property claims of New York. Governor Tryon responded by putting a price of £150 on Ethan Allen's head and prices of £50 each on the heads of Remember Baker, Seth Warner, and three other lieutenants. Ethan replied jeeringly by putting a bounty of £5 out for the capture of Attorney General John Tabor Kempe of New York, sending the advertisement to various New England newspapers. Soon people throughout the colonies were chuckling over the witty defiance of authority being displayed by the Green Mountain Boys against the strongest colony north of Virginia.

It may seem that the Green Mountain Boys spent all their time patrolling the north woods or squabbling with New Yorkers, but this was not the case. These people were primarily concerned with the land and settlement, and they worked hard at both. In the fall of 1771, for example, Ira Allen joined forces with Remember Baker to survey the town lines of Hubbardton, where they had bought property. When the pair reached Castleton, they found the settlers crabby and disinclined to help them, for the people on the land resented the newcomers. They were right, as it turned out, for the survey made by Ira and Remember played hob with what the Castleton people thought they held. In the end, Allen and Baker cut off fifteen hundred acres claimed by Castletonians and added the land to their Hubbardton properties.

It was hard work in rugged country. Ira decided to lay out some lots for sale and sent out alone into the woods with five days' provisions. He carried a gun with him, more to use the powder for making fires than anything else. Baker and his twelve-year-old son stayed behind where the party had been camping.

Ira encountered a big buck deer and took a shot at him, but his powder was wet and the gun misfired. The old buck continued to hang around the area. This was in the rutting season; the animal was furious at the intruder and was ready to fight. After five frantic minutes spent in fixing his gun, Ira took a shot. Although he had only about an eight-inch patch to aim at,

he hit the buck in the spine and broke his back. The buck could
not use his hind feet, but he had his head up and was defiantly
shaking it in his fury. Ira drew his hunting knife and prepared
to cut the buck's throat. The big animal shook him off with
such fury that he was thrown fifteen feet, lost his knife, and
wrenched his left arm. Finally Ira had to shoot the deer's brains
out. Just after, he saw another buck and gave him chase. Before
the afternoon was over, Ira had two big deer skinned and hung
up in the trees and was on his way back to find Remember
Baker and bring the venison into camp. He discovered that
Baker's adventures that day had been even more stirring than
his own. Baker had set out to blaze some trees, and he had run
into a bear. He went at her with a hatchet and finally killed her,
skinned her out, and hung up the meat. For three days the men
lived on bear meat.

His experiences in running lines in Hubbardton taught Ira
Allen one important lesson: he needed more education if he
was going to survey these wild lands. So he headed back down to
Salisbury for the winter, bound to find a teacher and learn all
that could be taught about surveying. In the midst of his studies
he caught the measles, anything but a joke in those days, and
was nearly blinded for a month.

Meanwhile that winter, Ethan was poking about in the woods
finding new lands to conquer. He also was converting every
asset that he could spare from Salisbury and Sheffield into
Hampshire Grant land. He was buying literally thousands of
acres in his own right and for his brothers. By the spring of 1772
Ethan Allen was one of the largest landholders in the Grants,
and the Allen family was certainly the largest of all. Thus the
Allens had a tremendous stake in the future of the Hampshire
Grants. If the New York laws were upheld, they would lose
every inch of their property.

For a time in the fall of 1771 Ethan and his men felt sure that
Governor Tryon was going to send a strong force of royal troops
against the Green Mountain Boys, and they made preparations
to fight. One man who was not known to the New York authorities was sent to Albany to discover what was going on—to spy,

no less. His task was to take a look at the governor and the leading military officers so he would know them if they came into the field. He would join a band of six sharpshooters who would station themselves on the road. When the troops marched up, they would pick off the governor and his aides.

There was no joking in this. Ethan was dead serious—he was ready to shed the governor's blood or his own to prevent the Yorkers from coming in and taking possession of the Grants, and his lieutenants and men were right behind him.

That autumn Ethan went out to settle the score that the Green Mountain Boys had with Colonel John Reid. He took along Remember Baker, Robert Cochran, and half a dozen other Boys. Farmer Pangborn, who had settled near Rupert, had been dispossessed by Reid and his Scottish settlers, who came in under the New York laws. It was time that Reid was straightened out.

Ethan and the Boys slipped into the settlement without arousing a whisper. They began by routing the settlers that Reid had brought in, explaining to them that they were on Mr. Pangborn's land illegally and had to get off. But two offenders merited special treatment. One was Charles Hutcheson, a former corporal in the British army. The other was Reid himself. The Boys burned Hutcheson's house to the ground while he stood by miserably, watching the destruction of his handiwork.

"A burnt sacrifice to the Gods of the world," said Ethan with satisfaction as the flames roared up.

"Now go your way," he added to Hutcheson, "and complain to that damned scoundrel, your governor. God damn your governor, laws, king, council, and assembly."

Hutcheson and Reid stood dumbly in the face of such blasphemy and treason.

"Colonel Allen" complained Hutcheson, "you curse most horrible."

"God damn your soul!" shouted Ethan in anger. "Are you trying to preach to us?"

Then he told Hutcheson and Reid in words of one and two

syllables what was going to happen to them if they dared return to the Hampshire Grants. Not only would they have a taste of the twigs of the wilderness—the beech switches that the Boys used on minor offenders to make them remember what they had done—they would also be flogged and, yes, killed if need be. And if the governor sent troops, those troops would be shot down. For, as Ethan was at some pains to inform Colonel Reid and his settler, the Green Mountain Boys numbered in the hundreds, and they were committed to the battle to the end.

The Reid-Hutcheson incident brought matters closer to a head, for the pair went to Albany to convince the governor that he must act before the Green Mountain Boys took over the whole area. Among other charges, they complained bitterly that Allen was a blasphemer and creature of the devil who denied both God and the existence of any infernal spirit. Obviously he was a witch or worse.

This defiant devil and his entourage soon returned to the Catamount Tavern of Stephen Fay in Bennington and there celebrated the coming of the New Year 1772, which they hoped would bring an end to the Yorker invasion. But in their hearts they could not but know that it would not be so, that the struggle was real and would be long.

The Green Mountain Boys were totally open in their defiance of New York, and an outsider might even consider them objectionable about it. One settler with New York leanings complained that it had gotten so that no one dared speak a word in favor of the New York government without being in danger of at least a flogging. On this New Year's Day, Benjamin Buck, a traveler from New York, happened to be in the Catamount Tavern when Ethan and his Boys were whooping it up. The wayfarer sensed where he was and offered to take his meal in another room than the big common room, but Ethan would have none of it. He wanted an audience. At this meeting the new proclamation of Governor Tryon was read aloud amid hisses, boos, and groans. The proclamation reaffirmed the rulings of the courts and the ascendancy of New York law.

"What do you think of that?" Ethan demanded of Buck.

"I suppose it will hold up," said Buck, definitely uneasy lest he say more.

Ethan rushed over to Buck, struck him three times with his fists, and pushed him away.

"You are a damned bastard of old Munro [the New York justice of the peace assigned to the Bennington area]. We shall make a hell out of his house and burn him in it, and every son of a bitch that will take his part."

Buck picked himself up and tried to placate the furious Ethan. "It doesn't make any difference who is right," he said. "All I meant was that New York has the power to have its own way."

The veins stood dark on Ethan's forehead.

"How can you be such a damned fool?" he shouted. "Have we not always overcome them?"

There was more of this, more taunts at Governor Tryon.

"And as for that lying bastard Tryon, let him *try on* and be damned."

If traveler Buck had not been totally converted to the New York cause before he came to the tavern, he was converted by this outburst, and lost no time rushing to Shaftsbury where Justice Munro lived in a perennial stage of siege, to report the new wickedness of the Green Mountain Boys. Munro duly informed Albany, and the pot continued to boil.

One of the hot spots of pro–New York sentiment in the Grants was the area around Clarendon, south of what is now Rutland, known to the Yorkers as Socialborough. A handful of settlers had come here under an early title granted by Governor Pownal of Massachusetts at a time when the Bay Colony had briefly laid claim to this land. Finally the people offered the Green Mountain Boys a real insult: they began calling the area by the name Durham, which had been given it by Governor Tryon.

Ethan decided that the citizens of Clarendon needed a good, horrible example to bring them back into the fold. So, one winter day, he set out with a hundred of the Boys for the wayward village. His example was to be Benjamin Spencer, a justice of the peace under the New York government. Spencer was to be frightened half to death and forced to flee the area.

The woods were full of spies, and before Ethan and the Boys could surround the Spencer place, the justice had word of their coming and had hightailed it into the woods. Ethan drew a pistol and went into the house, but no one was there.

It was late afternoon. Ethan spent an hour scouting around the place without finding much. Then, good commander that he was, he prepared against any countermeasure by marching off to a point three miles away, where the Boys made camp and set up guards for the night. That night, Ethan took ten men and went back to Spencer's, hoping to surprise the gentleman in his bed. But Spencer was a wily fellow and he had not dared return home, suspecting just such a visit. Instead of Spencer, all Ethan found was a small dog that Spencer called Tryon.

Tryon, was it? Ethan spat and set to work. He and his men slashed the dog to bits, and Ethan held up a hunk of the poor little creature and declaimed.

"Thus we will do unto Tryon."

As miserable a performance as it was to take out his ill temper on a hapless animal, Ethan's action again created precisely the effect he wished. When Spencer came back next day, learned from sympathizers what had happened, and saw the pieces of his little pet, he was truly alarmed. He fled the area and stayed deep in the heart of New York country for the next few months. Ethan thus accomplished what he set out to do, and turned onward to the next task.

Justice of the Peace Munro of Shaftsbury was perhaps Ethan's most unflagging opponent. A brave man, Munro continued to live in the heart of the Hampshire Grants, knowing that the Green Mountain Boys would attack him on the slightest provocation. One day in the early spring of 1772, Munro decided to carry the fight to the Green Mountain Boys. In the dark of night, he led a posse against Remember Baker. They attacked the Baker house in Arlington as the family was sleeping and set about capturing them. Baker's wife was pushed aside by the Munro men, and they seized his gun from beside the fireplace before he could get to it. But Remember got hold of his axe and began flailing that around his head, driving the Yorkers back. He leaped for the loft and climbed up into the top of the house. There he chopped a hole through the roof and pulled himself out before the Yorkers could get him. He slid down into a snowdrift beside the house and prepared to escape, certain that even Yorkers would not harm his wife and young son.

But the Yorkers were too many for him. He was spotted and encircled. In the struggle Baker's thumb was cut off by a Yorker sword slash, and he was beaten half into insensibility.

Baker then was tied up and bundled off in the sub-zero weather wearing only his winter underwear. The Yorkers put him in a sleigh under heavy guard and set off toward Albany, where Munro hoped to exhibit his captive and secure the plaudits of the community, a reward from Governor Tryon, and the bounty on Remember Baker's head as one of Ethan Allen's captains.

But the Yorkers made a big mistake in not taking Mrs. Baker along, for Remember's wife was a true daughter of the woods and a tough citizen of the Grants. No sooner had they left the farm than she was off running to a neighbor's house to tell the tale. Within an hour, a dozen men from Arlington and Bennington were on horses, speeding along the Albany road in pursuit of the kidnappers.

One of these men was Justus Sherwood, a bright young fellow who had recently settled on the Grants. In a few years, Sherwood was to play a curious rôle in the Allen's history. Tonight, however, he raced along on his horse, shouting and encouraging the others. They had come up fast, this crew of Ethan's young men, knowing there was no time to be lost if Remember Baker was to be saved from the Yorkers.

The pursuers clanged along the hard road through the snow, their horses heaving and blowing steam. The sleigh slid through the crunch, Justice Munro gazing often behind him. Then, in the small hours of the morning, when the sleigh was deep in Yorker country halfway to Albany, the pursuers overtook Munro. Seeing these whooping Green Mountain Boys coming down like a black cloud, all but two of the posse members fled, leaving Munro and one other to defend themselves. Such was the power of the propaganda Ethan had been manufacturing for two years that most Yorkers believed the Green Mountain Boys were bloodthirsty supermen.

The Boys put a sword to Munro's throat and unbound Remember Baker, then wrapped him in cloaks and robes taken from his captors. He was weak from loss of blood, and they hurried him back to the Catamount Tavern, where he was put to bed and treated by Dr. Jonas Fay.

Justice Munro was flung into a room in the bowels of the tavern along with his man, and left to consider his fate. If he had had only ten men who would have stood with him, he grumbled, he would have had Baker good.

While the Boys considered what they would do with the notorious Munro for his perfidious action, something happened in Albany that changed the atmosphere. Governor Tryon sent a letter to a Bennington minister, the Reverend Mr. Dewey, suggesting that it might be possible to settle the affairs of the region without further bloodshed. Why did not the people of the Grants send some representatives to Albany? The governor would be glad to see anyone except Ethan Allen, Remember Baker, Seth Warner, or Robert Cochran. Governor Tryon held out against those four, the leaders of the Green Mountain Boys, because all of them had offered violence to his people.

By that time Ethan Allen was back in Sheffield, visiting his wife. He was also calling at Heman's store in Salisbury to talk over affairs with his brother and arrange for money to purchase more land in the Grants.

Down there, away from the hurly-burly of Bennington, Ethan got the news of Remember's capture, and he wrote a stirring pamphlet, several broadsides, and newspaper articles about it, not failing to castigate the New York governor and his minions at every turn. Ethan's writings were pure hyperbole— he invented situations and even characters. Evil Yorkers always tortured good men and laughed. A tremendous dog was set on poor Remember, in this fabricated tale, and that captain's blood gushed forth red and true as the Yorkers half killed him.

In Ethan's absence, Stephen Fay, who was also a captain of the Green Mountain Boys, and his son, Dr. Jonas Fay, were selected to go to Albany. As a gesture of good will, Justice Munro and his accomplice were released, although the charges against them were most serious, and they made their way safely back to Yorker domain.

Nothing much came of the attempt to settle the claims peaceably. How could it? James Duane and the other land speculators were determined to have their land under New York law, and the settlers were determined to keep it under the Hampshire Grants. While the Fays went to Albany and were courteously received, long discussion produced nothing but verbiage, and they came home to continue a correspondence that did not change affairs a bit.

Meanwhile, many of the Green Mountain Boys were still sore as boils over the kidnapping of Remember Baker and the easy treatment given Munro. Seth Warner, in particular, was furious, and one day he rode down to Shaftsbury, to demand that Munro return the gun his men had "stolen" from Remember Baker on the night of the kidnapping. Justice Munro felt secure in his own bailiwick, and when Warner came up on his horse and stated his business, the justice grabbed the bridle of the Green Mountain Boys captain's horse and declared that Warner was under arrest for giving assistance to an outlaw.

This was a grievous error, even though Munro was in his own front yard. Seth Warner drew his sword, smacked Munro a good hard blow on the head with the flat of it, and got down to view the senseless body, not much caring if it was alive or dead. Then he went to the house, picked up a rifle, and rode off. Munro recovered, much to the disgust of many a Hampshire Grantsman. In Poultney, where Remember Baker, Ethan, and Ira owned large chunks of land, the town voted to give Warner a hundred acres for his public service in wounding Munro. In Albany, the governor added Seth Warner's name to the list of most wanted men, along with Ethan's and Baker's.

At about this time, Ira Allen was back in the Grants, having mastered the art of surveying, and he learned that Yorker surveyor Cockburn was up near Bolton in complete defiance of the orders he had received a few months earlier to keep his nose out of the area. Ethan, who had meanwhile returned from the trip south, sent Warner and Baker north with a force of Green Mountain Boys to get Cockburn out of there. They found the Yorker, threatened him, and would have flogged him good and hard except for the peace talks that were still going on with Governor Tryon.

By midsummer it was apparent that the talks would come to nothing, so the state of siege was strengthened. It has been suggested that Ethan wrecked the talks because he was sure that Governor Tryon would not accept his claims to land, since he had not settled it. As a matter of fact, though, many of the men in the Green Mountain militia owned land they had not settled. The only settlers that Tryon would have been willing to accept were that handful of original families who had been on the Grants when the trouble started. Now, by the summer of 1772 all the Allens and many another had cast their lots with the forces of rebellion. They could not and would not settle for any Yorker-dictated peace that would bring the area west of the Green Mountains under New York control. They were bound to forge on and fight if necessary.

The Onion River

AT the tender age of twenty-one, Ira Allen was a full-fledged lieutenant in the Green Mountain Boys, a position he held more despite his brother's eminence than because of it. Young Ira was perhaps the finest woodsman of the lot. He spent most of his time in the north country surveying lands for himself and his family and friends. When the Green Mountain Boys wanted someone to spy on the Yorkers, likely as not Ira would be chosen, for he could walk through the woods with the quiet of an Indian. Since he was not so well known to the enemy, he could also mingle in the cities without much fear of recognition.

As a bachelor, Ira needed little money, nor did he have use for a farm or house. So his savings grew as he worked and surveyed. It was not unusual in the perennially cash-short frontier for him to take a chunk of land as a fee for surveying a lot. And when opportunity came he converted far-flung pieces of land either to cash or to land where he wanted to consolidate his holdings.

During these survey trips Ira covered even more ground than Ethan. He went north in the summer of 1772 and visited the country along Lake Champlain. He was particularly taken with the land along the Onion River (in modern times known as the Winooski), which emptied into Lake Champlain. This was the region where Burlington would be located, in time to become Vermont's largest city. Somehow Ira sensed that the big timber and gently sloping land of the broad valley were the best in the whole region, and he came back from his survey trip full of talk about the Onion River country and the future.

Ethan was skeptical about moving so far afield. He was satisfied to speculate in lands in Poultney and Castleton, which were near enough to Bennington for him to continue to manage the affairs of the Hampshire Grants settlers and the Green Mountain Boys.

Ira was stubborn, convinced that the Onion River territory was the best. He went down to Salisbury and had a long talk with brother Heman, the capitalist of the family. Heman listened; then he pointed out a few facts of life to his youngest brother. Land speculation was a difficult undertaking, and it required a lot of capital, he said. From what he knew, Ira did not have the capital or the income to manage such a program.

But Ira argued. He would survey the land and take a piece of it in payment for his work. He could convert all his assets into land on the Onion River.

Heman was no fool. He saw the determination of his youngest brother. Over the years he had watched Ira grow into a strong and resilient character, more agreeable, more forthright by far than Ethan or the others. If Ira was that determined, reasoned Heman, he would go along with him. So he gave Ira a letter of credit for £200, and Ira bought fifty-two rights of land and tied up another six. He also went to the proprietors of the town of Mansfield, not far from his own interests, and arranged to survey the town, lay it out in fifty-acre lots, and build six houses so the settlement might begin. For this, the proprietors agreed to pay Ira ninety pounds when he returned with the papers of survey in the autumn.

Heman was pleased to see such a sign of good sense and aggressiveness in his young brother, and his enthusiasm for the Onion River increased. Heman asked how Ira intended to support this venture now that he had spent all his money. Ira shrugged; he would find some way. Live off the land if he had to. He was unconcerned.

On the morning that Ira got ready to leave for the north country, Heman stopped him as he was going out of the house and handed him thirty-two dollars. That ought to take care of his expenses, the elder brother said, and he could pay it back whenever he got around to it.

Ira had been more than a little worried about how he was going to finance the venture. He had expected to go to Bennington and persuade some of the Boys to enter it with him, but he knew well that they were always short of cash. Now he had no more worries.

In Bennington, Ira talked again to Ethan, but Ethan was obdurate. He was too busy to fool around with Onion River property. So Ira sought out cousin Remember Baker and offered to take him into partnership on the deal, if Remember would furnish all the supplies and hire all the men necessary for the trip and the cabin-building. Remember would get his share when the proprietors paid.

Baker agreed. He went to Skenesboro, at the head of Lake Champlain, to buy supplies, and Ira went to Crown Point, by way of Hubbardton, to take care of some surveys before they left. On the way to Crown Point, Ira was afflicted by boils, a problem that bothered him a great deal at this time, sometimes almost immobilizing him. But he stumbled on, found a boat, and made his way by water down to Skenesboro just as Baker was arriving.

There were seven men in the party that set out in a big bateau to go down the lake (north) to the mouth of the Onion River. Remember Baker had a hunch there might be a New York surveyor somewhere around these parts, and he and Ira decided to look for him while most of the party went on with the big boat to bring it to the falls of the Onion River. Ira and Remember set off and soon found a cache of food. They concluded it must belong to the surveying party of Benjamin Stevens, who had taken Cockburn's place. Remember helped himself to some food; then he and Ira returned to the falls. A day or so later they brought the Boys back to Stevens's camp, where they captured two men Stevens had posted.

Hoping that Stevens and his other men would return, Ira and his party waited. By dark that day, the Yorkers had not returned, so the Green Mountain Boys went to their own camp, where they assigned a lookout for the rest of the night. At dawn their guard awakened them quietly. Stevens was coming up the river. Ira's party took him as soon as he landed. A year or so earlier, the prisoners would have been flogged and sent to Albany with just enough sustenance to get them to the places of their Yorker friends. But times had changed. Ethan had indicated a go-slow policy on physical punishment on the bare chance that something might be salvaged through negotiation with Governor Tryon. So Stevens and his men were released, along with their boat and stores, with no more than threats and an admonition to keep away from the Hampshire Grants on pain of death if they were caught there again. Stevens left, but soon reported to James Duane, his boss, who made a formal complaint that Remember Baker and Ira had led in the violence against the surveyors. For the first time, Ira's name began to be known to the Yorkers, and the story Stevens told about his capture made Ira overnight a fearsome character and labeled him one of the most dangerous of the Green Mountain Boys. The Yorkers asked a price of one hundred pounds for his capture!

Ira set about exploring the mouth of the Onion River, and all his previous dreams came true. He set up camp next to a big pine tree on the bank opposite an island. Traveling the river below the falls, he was delighted to find wide natural meadows on both sides of the river. Here was green land that could be farmed without clearing, land that should be worth three or four times the usual. While the others sat on the bank and drank Jamaica rum captured from the Yorkers, Ira went tramping in the fields.

"I went up the open meadow," he said, "where the blue grass was thick, until I came to the sight of a lonely elm."

He computed the field to have about fifty acres of rolling meadow, and he promised himself that one day he would own that field and live near it. He called this area Lot 1 and Lot 2. Ira never did own it in later life, for he and his associates gave Isaac Vanornam, a member of Ira's surveying party, one of the lots for his services, and sold Vanornam the other a bit later.

Ira's survey of the Onion River lands was done under the most difficult of circumstances, and the party was dogged by misfortune. John Whiston, one of the party, was blazing a corner of the first lot when his ax slipped and he laid bare his shin so that the bone stuck out for two inches. The others stopped working and started to take him back to civilization. By the time they reached the river's mouth, Whiston's leg was red, swollen, and in danger of gangrene. Remember Baker made poultices of basswood bark, male elm, spikenar, and beech leaves, then bandaged the wound in balsam fir. They kept treating Whiston for six days, until he was able to walk. He did not have to go back down the lake, but stayed on the job.

Ira's bateau was too heavy to take upstream, so they built a bark canoe. Portaging and paddling, they slowly made their way up the Onion. They reached Mount Mansfield and found the site of the town they were to survey. Ira and Baker set out to explore. They saw a huge old black spruce tree atop the mountain, and they climbed it up to the small branches. With a sense of dismay, Ira looked about him at the panorama.

He had bartered, begged, and traded all he owned for the rights to a third of this town—and now he saw an expanse before him of solid timbered land, and not one good farm site.

Well, said Baker, that would teach him to invest his money sight unseen.

But Ira said he would make the best of it, and the survey continued. They had found it so hard to get up river that they packed only light provisions. The remainder of their party, which was more heavily laden, was delayed by the rough terrain, and the advance group ran short of food. But Isaac Vanornam and one other man went back to the river to fish, and in a day the pair caught all the trout they could carry, dressed them out, and brought them back to the party.

Day after day, Ira and Baker ran lines, set posts, and chopped blazes, for they were the surveyors. Then Baker cracked his compass, which put him out of action. He took over the building of the six houses that Ira had promised, and Ira continued the survey alone.

As October grew late, the blue-green of the mountains became hazy, and then the rains fell and brought the chill. One morning they awoke to see a light blanket of snow on the tops of the mountains around them. Winter was coming soon. The weather changed. Instead of sun, it rained, snowed, or sleeted, and soon there was not a dry stitch of clothing in the camp.

The houses were built; the survey was finished. It was time to go home. Baker had to get back to his wife and son and his farm. But Ira had lust for the land in him, and he insisted that he wanted to see the territory to the east, where he had heard of great marvels. So they agreed to part. Remember Baker and Peter Hurlburt went down the river to reach the lake and take the bateau back to Crown Point. Ira asked for volunteers to go east with him, and Vanornam decided he wanted to see the country. So did the now-recovered Whiston and two others. These adventurers set out through the virgin wilderness.

Ira and his party headed east and south. Ira was afflicted with painful boils again—four of them on one knee. Almost immediately they ran out of provisions. Captain Peleg Sunderland was to have brought a supply of food up the river to them before they left the site, but he never showed up. Now they had to press on under difficult circumstances.

It began to snow. They set a course for the Water family's house in Pittsford to the south, but the men disagreed on the direction they should take. All right, said Ira, each man would cut a stick and lay it down with the point toward the Water house. They did. The sticks faced in a semicircle—so varied were the views as to their course. Ira solved the problem in a businesslike fashion, using his surveying knowledge to set up a triangle between Lake Champlain, their present position, and Pittsford. In the end they all agreed that his course was the one to follow.

Next morning they set out, Vanornam leading because Ira was lame from his boils. It had snowed during the night and the white fluff kicked up around their ankles, but they went on.

The rigors of this trip were to be repeated endlessly in the tales of the Green Mountain Boys and other Pioneers of America. Ira tells it very well in his own account:

I found my boils more troublesome. Indeed my knee was quite stiff. The question was to get across the river. Vanornam proposed to make two rafts, which all instantly agreed to, leaving me to rest till one was completed, when Vanornam was to pass with me, the rest to follow as soon as might be.

One raft being completed, Vanornam and I embarked, putting a large firebrand on the raft. We pushed off with our setting poles, and found a strong current on the river, which drove us down as we passed; and to our great misfortune, we were twice wrecked on piles of gravelstones, (collected by fish, as the Indians in-

formed, to secure their spawn, or young.) After passing the last
when two thirds across the river, we were so wrecked that our
raft would not bear the weight of more than one.

Vanornam leaped into the river to return, that I might gain the
opposite shore; which I attempted, but I found that the raft was so
wrecked and that the current was carrying me down stream, so that
the raft would sink in deep water before I could gain the other
shore.

I therefore found it necessary to quit the raft and gain the other
shore from which I came. The water was almost to my armpits.
The cold affected my boils exceedingly . . .

Ira, limping, marched on past the men and boldly stepped
into the river, forgetting the rafts, and forded it easily. The
others followed, amazed, not questioning his leadership.

But on the second day, Ira had to face a small rebellion. The
men were uneasy. They had no food and their gun was bent so
that Vanornam missed a shot at a moose. They thought Ira was
taking them too far south, and that they would miss Pittsford.

It took an hour of argument to persuade them to go on, and
thereafter they stopped many times to check their progress. So
they went. They moved east and south, searching for game. But
the game did not appear, and soon they were out of provisions,
far from the lake waterway, and faced with a march through
unknown country to reach that first point of civilization, Pittsford, some seventy miles away.

It was a hungry, exhausting, and sometimes frightening time.
Up the side of the Green Mountains they went and along one
part of the range. Where they could find deer trails that led in
the right general direction, they skirted the brush, but sometimes they had to break straight through in order to keep on
their way south.

They searched vainly for deer. They shot three partridges,
and that was all the five men had to eat during the last three
days of their journey. When they reached the Water home at
Pittsford, almost overcome with hunger and weakness, the
people clustered around and fed them. First a crust of bread and
a little water; then, as they revived, the women brought out
pudding, and gave them that. After they had downed the pud-

ding, and waited a bit, they had mutton and turnips. One man stuffed himself, and fell into a coma. They could not awaken him, and they walked him and carried him for an hour before he revived from the effects of the food. Ira learned then and there that no man should eat much when he has grown so hungry as to become faint. The lesson was to serve him very well in the years to come in his long treks through the wilderness.

As Ira came home from Pittsford, now recovered from exhaustion and hunger, he passed by the Reid place in Rupert and stopped to check. Colonel Reid's tenants were still trying to keep the settlement alive. When Ira appeared, the only person he saw was a miller, who had managed to repair the water mill that ground the corn for the area. If that mill could be kept running, Colonel Reid would have more than a foothold again. So Ira forced the miller to break up his millstones with a sledgehammer and threw them into the river.

That was that, said Ira. Speaking as a lieutenant in the militia he warned the miller not to try to repair the mill again. Otherwise, he said gravely, the miller would suffer the displeasure of the Green Mountain Boys, and he knew what that meant.

Those Yorker landholders were wily. By this time, three years after the dispute had become open warfare, it was hard to persuade any sensible American colonial to settle in the York shadow of the Grants. The Green Mountain Boys became displeased too easily. So the big New York landholders went abroad to Scotland with brochures and promises of land for settlers. A number of Scottish emigrants arrived and made their way to the New Haven area, about fifteen miles inland from Lake Champlain. Learning that they were coming, Ethan Allen rushed a bunch of the Green Mountain Boys to New Haven to build a stockade, and when the advance party of Scottish settlers arrived to view the land and split up the patent into family plots, they were met cordially enough by Ethan, who explained the problem in the shadow of his fort.

The Scotsmen were aghast. They had been told that they might come and settle these good lands under the best of conditions, their spokesman said. They had not been told they were stepping into the middle of a land dispute.

Well, said Ethan, that was the way it was. And it was a pretty grim matter.

The Scotsmen looked up to the loopholes in the stockade and agreed. They had come to farm, not fight. Their spokesmen stepped forward and told Ethan they were quitting the area. They wanted no part of the dispute. Ethan uncorked all the Allen charm, and the men left in peace and goodwill to go and settle along the Mohawk River.

Back in Bennington, Ira began talking about the Onion River country in the north, and so bedeviled an only mildly interested oldest brother that finally Ethan agreed to go on up there and see what Ira's enthusiasm was all about. They went up north, Ira working with his compass, Ethan shooting deer.

Ethan led Ira a fast pace through the mountains, and Ira had difficulty in keeping up. ("The real facts were that for a few days he could out travel me in the wilderness," Ira wrote later.) But Ira was able to do things Ethan could not, such as subsist on raw salt pork and very little food for days. In the end each came out of the adventure knowing the other was a fine woodsman with superior qualities of his own. Out of this trip came a bond of friendship that passed beyond the disparity of their ages. Ethan was in his middle thirties, Ira in his early twenties. Ethan began to yield in his opposition to investing money or time in the Onion River area.

Ira went back to Connecticut that autumn to confer with his other brothers and to deliver the survey of Mansfield that had been made that fall. He was troubled by one matter: if he told the exact truth about the nature of the land, he would have difficulty in collecting his money. The owners would not like the prospect of settling in pure forest. And the survey told too much, for the corners of the lots were almost all described as "running from a blaze" on a spruce or fir tree, and that would raise questions. So Ira invented a tree—the gum tree.

What was a gum tree? asked the proprietors. Why, it was a tall tree with gum, like the gum of a cherry tree. This was true enough, but not very accurate, for the tree was the spruce. The ploy gave the proprietors of the land an image of open fields and cherry trees, while Ira knew that dense forest stood sentinel above the land.

If there was anything in the world Ira wanted to do it was to sell that Mansfield land, and he now devised a strategy. The brother of one of the major proprietors owned two lots. This brother was a stupid fellow, and Ira collared him one day and made a great pretense of trying to buy up the brother's two lots for himself, indicating that no one had ever seen such land (which was certainly true). When the stupid young brother told his elder sibling that Ira wanted to get hold of all the land he could in Mansfield, the proprietors got hungry, held onto what they already had like death was after them, and tried to get more.

In the end, they came to Ira Allen and suggested that he sell them back the twenty lots he had bought earlier. Well, he said, he might be persuaded, for a price. They paid his price, and they paid him ninety pounds for the survey ("which I considered of more consequence than the whole town," wrote Ira). He went home to Salisbury to tell the tale of the gum trees to Zimri and Heman. They sat at the dinner table in the big white clapboard house on Heman's farm and laughed until they could hardly stay in their chairs. Ira had indeed come of age.

CHAPTER NINE

The Land Shark

IRA now owned thirty rights of land in the Grants, but he wanted to dispose of all but Onion River property and concentrate his holdings there. The deciding factor in the family councils that ensued was the situation of the Hampshire Grants. Ira said, and Ethan quite agreed, that if the people of New England did not settle the Hampshire Grants, then the Yorkers would infiltrate and win by sheer population pressure what they had failed to achieve so far.

Remember Baker came down from Bennington to converse with the others on the problem. They finally agreed to a vast undertaking on the Onion River in which Ethan, Heman, Zimri, Ira, and Remember Baker were the partners. Levi was off on business of his own; Heber had staked his whole future in Poultney and could not be dissuaded from his course. Heber was close to their cousin Ebenezer Allen, who had already established himself in Poultney in 1771. By this winter of 1773, Heber was deeply involved in the actual settlement, worrying over such practical problems as the amount of land it would take to attract a midwife to settle there to aid the women of the town. He was coming to settle in the area, to raise his corn and take it thirty miles to Manchester for milling. While Ethan was an important proprietor in Poultney, he had no intention of settling there, at least not now that he had turned to the Onion River country.

Ira busied himself in these winter months trying to improve his position in the Onion River properties he had visited on behalf of other owners.

Those thirty rights of land he owned in the Onion River territory towns of Bolton, Duxbury, Moretown, and Middlesex were mortgaged to Samuel Averill in Rawmag, not far from Ira's cousins' house at Judeah in Connecticut. Ira owed Averill one hundred and fifty pounds, fifty to be paid the following May, the rest in two other payments six months apart. Ira also held a bond that entitled him to buy six more lots as he paid off the old ones. The rub was that having been there, Ira did not want any of these lands; he preferred some choice lands in the town of Middlesex. But it would never do to come out openly and express his desire. Not having visited the Onion River lands that he owned, Mr. Averill could be expected to be very suspicious of anyone who had been there who made any proposals about them.

Ira wanted to see Mr. Averill and work out a trade, but he did not want it to look as if that was his motive. Fortunately, not one but two sets of Allen uncles and aunts lived near the Averills. Nothing was more natural than that a dutiful nephew should visit his uncles, so Ira went there, and in celebration a ball was arranged by his female cousins. It was easy enough to be sure that the sons of Mr. Averill were invited, and they all met and talked about the affairs of youth at Ira's uncle's house. Not one word did Ira utter about his adventures in the Onion River country.

Mr. Averill soon learned of Ira's presence in the area. He was curious about the Onion River trip, since he was a primary landholder there. He sent word to have Ira call on him, and Ira replied that he would certainly do so on his journey home, which would start in a few days.

Ira went by the Averill place and was invited to stay an extra day and then to join Mr. Averill on a journey to Salisbury. Averill had to go up to Bennington on land business, and this was to be the first leg of the trip. So there were several days in which the canny landholder cross-questioned Ira, trying to get out of him every bit of information possible about his large holdings. When they reached Salisbury and put up at Heman's house, Averill finally came to the point. He would tear up Ira's mortgages on the original land, he said, if Ira would give up the claim he had on the additional lots.

Ira pretended to consider this for some time, and then said that he did not think so. These were all beautiful lands, he explained, and he had gone to a lot of trouble to explore them, so they were worth much more now than they had been earlier. Averill left, disappointed, but said he would come by on his way back from Bennington if he had a chance.

Heman had heard this last conversation. He raised his eyebrows as Ira let the landholder go, and suggested that Ira was being a fool to turn down so ample an opportunity. Averill might have forgotten all about it when he came back, it was so inconsequential a matter to so large a holder. Ira had best write him a letter up at Bennington.

But Ira was playing his own game, and he refused.

Averill came back and sure enough, he rode right by the Allen place without stopping. Heman saw him, and at supper he and Zimri never let up talking to poor Ira about the chance he had lost to make some money.

Ira listened, face set, and said nothing, except that he was going to get something out of all this.

Before he did, though, he, Ethan, and Remember Baker set out on a very dangerous journey.

In conversations in Salisbury, the two Allens and Baker had learned that some holders of Onion River lands named Burling lived down in White Plains, near New York City. The Burlings were eager to sell, and the Allens and Baker were eager to buy these valuable lands. The three of them, armed to the teeth, set out for White Plains, deep in the land of their enemies. Each of them had a price on his head, set by the New York governor. They pretended to be British army officers on their way from Quebec to New York City to take ship for London. That would account for the arms and for their travel together.

At the same time Heman took a different route to White Plains. He was also involved in the land deal, but he was so well known as a merchant because of his frequent travels to New York City that it would endanger their whole disguise if they associated with him. So Heman went alone by carriage and coach. When they all reached White Plains they carefully put up at different taverns and had nothing to do with one another.

Heman carried out most of the negotiations, the others only signing papers prepared for them. They finished, and next morning Heman was scheduled to go down to New York City with Zimri to buy some other land. Since Ira, Ethan, and Remember would all leave next day, they saw nothing amiss in getting together for one night of celebration.

That evening, Heman came to their tavern to lodge, and asked about the three British officers. The landlord advised that those three much preferred their own company. He would not admit Heman to their presence until the merchant ordered up a huge bowl of punch, which the landlord delivered to the Britishers himself. The brothers were united, finding it hard to play their roles until the man had left the room. Then they broke down into laughter and congratulations on the success of their business mission.

Next morning, they called for their bill all together, and the landlord was shocked to see the familiarity among the four of them. He was shocked even more when they announced their names. Ethan Allen and Remember Baker were well known desperadoes, and Ira was not far behind on the lists. The men made sure that a peddler who was en route to New York that day learned their names, for they might as well have a little fun with Governor Tryon now that they had done their business.

What a commotion the peddler stirred in New York! He went immediately to the Battery and was given admission to the governor and council. They proposed to send a party of light horse to capture the brigands. James Duane was wiser. He calmed the governor. These were the Green Mountain Boys, and they would never be caught in such a trap, he said. It was obvious that they had sent the peddler to warn the governor, hoping for just such an action. They were undoubtedly heading back into Connecticut and to the Grants.

And he was almost right, except that the party stopped off that night in New York colony again to stay with a Quaker preacher, Benjamin Ferry, who owned lands up in the Grants. Ira made arrangements with Ferry to take seven rights in Shelburne, on Lake Champlain. He would lay out other lands for Ferry and his family and would be paid for his surveying.

So here was another bit of business and a further incentive for Ira to return to the Onion River country. He thought about it all on the way home to Salisbury, where he turned right and went off to visit those uncles again. The others headed straight for Heman's house.

Ira went first to the Baker's. He made much of hiring cousin

Jesse to go up to the Onion River with him that summer to help with surveying, certain that Jesse would get the word around the territory and it would soon reach the Averills. It did. Ira then made it a point to arrive at Averill's house at nightfall, apparently on his way back to Salisbury. It was only good manners for Mrs. Averill to invite him to put his horse in the barn and spend the night, even if her husband was out— which he happened to be. Besides, Mr. Averill was expected to arrive late that night and would be able to see Ira in the morning.

Ira knew that the house was anything but soundproof. He figured that if he pretended to be asleep when Mr. Averill came home, he could hear what the Averills said to each other in the privacy of their bedroom. So he played at being sleepy after dinner, and finally Mrs. Averill suggested that he go to bed.

Ira had some difficulty staying awake until two o'clock, when Mr. Averill got home, but his plan worked. Mr. and Mrs. Averill did talk over the Onion River country and Mr. Averill's ideas. Ira had planted with the wife the thought that he and other landholders in the area were agreed to building roads and other expensive improvements, and that Mr. Averill would be expected to bear his share of the expense. Since Averill was the biggest landholder of all, this did not make him very happy, and he confided that night to his wife that he intended to do something to put an end to that foolishness.

Next morning, Ira came down to a big breakfast, and immediately afterward, Averill took him aside for a business talk. Ira went through all his plans again, innocently, talking about cutting a road, running town lines, and laying out lots for preachers, midwives, and other useful persons.

Mr. Averill tried one tack and then another to change the course of events. He was a speculator. He had no intention of ever going to the Onion River—he wanted to sell off his lands at high profit after holding them a while longer. Any expense he incurred was undesirable.

Ira, on the other hand, was desperately eager to get rid of his holdings in Bolton and Duxbury. What he really wanted was the lands in Middlesex held by Mr. Averill. As they talked,

Averill suggested that it would be good for both of them if Ira would give back his deed for all those lands in different towns. Ira said that might be true.

All right, said Mr. Averill, he would be glad to give Ira a deed to ten lots in one town or maybe two towns, if Ira would cancel out the other agreement.

Fine, said Ira. He would take all his lands in Bolton.

Bolton? Why, those were the best lands of all, said Mr. Averill. (Obviously they were best, otherwise why would Ira want them?) Ira, visions of forest-covered mountains in his head, assured the old man that the lands in Bolton were far from the best, but Averill would not be swindled. No, he would give half the land in Moretown and half in Middlesex, he said.

Ira looked very doleful. Neither were very good, he said, and there was not ha'penny's choice between them. But since some friends of his were settling in the area, perhaps it would be best to take all the lands in one place. All right, said Mr. Averill triumphantly. Then Ira could take them in Middlesex, which was the place Ira had spoken about least. Ira agreed reluctantly, and Averill executed the deeds before Ira could change his mind. Thus Ira Allen acquired ten rights of land free and clear in the one town that he wanted, without a penny of cost, exchanging all those old pieces of paper for them.

Happily Ira returned to Heman's house to find his brother back from New York City with many tales. In the course of the evening, Heman and Zimri asked Ira how he had come out in his negotiations with Mr. Averill.

Ira was nonchalant, but his eyes danced. Yes, he said, he had settled his affairs with Mr. Averill. What did they guess he got for all the old promises and pieces of paper scattered over the Grants?

"One right of land clear?" asked Heman. That would be fair enough.

"Two rights of land?" asked Zimri, with the optimism of youth.

Not so, said Ira. He showed them the deed for ten rights of prime meadow land in Middlesex town.

Even Heman, the family horse-trader, was impressed.

Lot 1

BY the spring of 1773 the Allens had committed themselves to settlement of the Onion River country, a commitment that was to have far-reaching consequences for the history of the land. Ira set out from Salisbury for Arlington, where cousin Remember Baker lived. Together they went over the plans and agreed that Ira would mark a road from Castleton to the new territory. Ira set out, taking Isaac Vanornam with him. He moved up to Poultney and then to Castleton and along the road laid out to Hubbardton. He and Vanornam each had a compass, a pair of pistols, a hatchet, and a blanket.

Ira headed from Hubbardton to Otter Creek, then followed the creek down to the Middlebury falls. It was May, with cold rain driving through the forest. In the end, after supperless nights and hard work, Ira and Vanornam marked out a road seventy miles long from Castleton to the Onion River land, over which people could travel with provisions and livestock.

They also established a settlement at Colchester. Remember Baker had not been idle while the younger men were cutting the road. Baker had come up by water in a party of bateaux, bringing stores and workmen. They met, and Ira set off about his surveying while Baker planned out the village and the farms for the community.

That summer Ethan showed real interest in the new lands. From the Burlings and others the Allens had acquired large tracts in the area for about ten cents an acre. Ultimately they held more than forty thousand acres. All the Allens but Heber and Levi were involved. Ethan, the publicist of the family, wrote an advertisement for the Connecticut *Courant,* and the Onion River Company began the business of selling land, guaranteeing the titles it conveyed under the New Hampshire Grants. Any land speculator would have known how precarious that authority must be, but any settler would also know that

Ethan himself was moving up to the Onion River country in the spring with a hundred Green Mountain Boys, and that guarantee was more persuasive than Governor Wentworth's ever could be.

Heman, down in Salisbury, was the principal land salesman for the group. He sold twelve hundred acres to people who promised to help clear the land and settle the country. Thomas Chittenden and Jonathan Spafford were two of these grantees.

Up in the Onion River country that summer, Ethan and Ira supervised the building of a store, which was also used as a blockhouse. It was a building twenty feet wide by thirty-two feet long, built of timbers eight inches thick. On the second story they cut thirty-two portholes for small arms. The second story hung out over the first so the defenders could throw boiling water and could shoot down on attackers below. The roof was built so it could be thrown off the building in case it caught fire from burning arrows. The whole was built over a spring so there would never be a water shortage, and all the doors and windows were double. The building was nearly invasion-proof.

In the Onion River country no man stirred without a pair of pistols in his belt. They were living in a state of siege, and they knew it. Their settlement of the Onion River land was the most important development in the defiance of New York since the sheriff came to the Breakenridge farm and tried to throw James Breakenridge off his land. Everyone concerned knew that the Yorkers would not stand by idly and see the Allens cement the Hampshire titles.

Ethan also went to New Haven that summer to discourage the irrepressible Colonel Reid, who had settled his Scotsmen there again. When Ethan and the Green Mountain Boys arrived there, joined by Ira, Remember Baker, and the gang that was working over the roadway Ira had laid out, they attacked the settlement. They let their horses into the fields to eat the corn, burned the houses of the dozen settlers, destroyed everything of value, smashed the mill and its stones, and burned the haystacks.

Ethan stood by to see that no person was hurt by his enthusiastic troops. He gave the Scotsmen a lecture and sent them back toward Albany with the message that if Reid or any one else tried to come back here, they would get the same treatment.

"I have run these woods in the same manner these seven years," he warned, "and never was catched yet."

Ethan then offered these burned-out settlers a chance to start life anew on some of the Onion River Company's lands to the north, but so scared were the Scots, and so upset by the destruction of the fruits of their labor, that only one man took him up on the offer. The others decided to leave the Hampshire Grants.

In the smoke from the burning cabins, the Green Mountain Boys disbanded and the men made their way home to finish up their farm work for the year, having struck the hardest blow yet against the Yorkers.

The quiet war between the Yorkers and the Green Mountain Boys continued. The pressure never let up. The Yorkers sent surveyors when they dared, but the Allens and others usually found them, chased them out, or captured them.

The Company's work was done by Ira and Remember Baker for the most part. Ethan was the organizer and promoter, with a thousand things on his mind. Heman and Zimri were both slender and frail and not at all built for long hard treks through the woods, living on salt pork and water, and enduring cold and misery for nights on end. They became the managers, the salesmen, the storekeepers. The younger, Zimri, Ira's personal agent, bought and sold the lands the woodsman had acquired in Castleton, Poultney, and Hubbardton, with an eye to investing everything in the Onion River Company.

Heman had another thought in mind. When the Onion River Company was established, his mind ran to thoughts of mercantile business as the place became settled. Chittenden and the others had promised that they would actually settle the land by 1774, and that did not leave much time to get established. Heman believed that Skenesboro, at the south end of Lake Champlain, was the most logical point for a trading establishment, but not having been up north into the woods, he trusted

Ira's judgment. Ira looked around the lake and came back to report to Heman against Skenesboro. It was full of swamp fever, he said, and a most unhealthy place for a person of Heman's delicate constitution. Further, although it was the head of navigation for the south of the lake, it was too close to the Hudson River and its many trading places to be profitable. No, said Ira, he much preferred Burlington Bay, right up there in the Onion River country. That site, Ira predicted with confidence, would develop into the most populous place on Lake Champlain. Ira was so sure of his judgment that the next time he traveled to the Onion River country, he surveyed a number of lots of a hundred acres each around the shores of Burlington Bay.

Remember Baker and the others wondered if Ira had gone out of his head. Baker saw the land—a poor pine plain that promised little to the farmer. He knew that there was plenty of fine fertile farmland all around the place that could be surveyed instead. What in the devil was Ira up to?

Ira simply did not discuss it. He knew that no one could foretell for certain the direction in which population would grow. Holding an opposite opinion from his cousin, Ira kept it to himself, acted upon it, and forbore argument. Perhaps that is why he and Remember Baker got on so well together.

That they did. The explorers and adventurers of the Allen party always got on well, and they seldom lost a chance for a joke or a little foolery. This season they tried to make Ira the butt of it all for his apparent poor judgment in laying out lots on the barren pine plains.

One day the party assembled in the fort, where Remember was keeping store and doing a brisk business in rum and punch. Stephen Lawrence was there, and Joshua Stanton. They had been out fishing, but had been driven in by the hard rain, and since there was nothing else to do that afternoon, they and the others gathered around the fire and ordered up a bowl of Remember's best. They started to taunt Ira about the value he foresaw in those pine plains. One chaffing remark led to another, yet it was clear that the others really wanted to know what Ira was doing. Young as he was, and short and slender, he

had already proved many times that he was the best outdoors-
man of them all, and no one called him a fool except in jest.

"I won't tell," he said, eyes twinkling, "unless you'll stand to
a double bowl of punch."

So the punch was ordered up and handed around, and when
every man had had his taste the question was pressed again.

Ira assumed his most serious mien and addressed them all as
though he were a parson on Sunday morning.

"You know that life of man by sacred writ is estimated at
three-score years and ten," he said.

They all nodded sagely, wondering what was to come.

"And yet, although some survive so long, many fall short, and
none can tell the time of his dissolution . . . ."

His hearers began to grow a little restive, as when the minister ploughed through an acre of big words.

"You also know that dry pine plain is easy digging?"

They stirred. Here now he was coming to the point.

"Well, it is also easy to move through. And if, as some say, the
spirits of the dead talk together, think of how easy it will be for
them to pass from tomb to tomb through that light dry earth,
and see from the high sand bank the busy multitude carrying on
business in Burlington Bay. . . ."

He stopped right there.

They looked up hesitantly. That was all?

Yes, that was all. That was Ira's reason, and no more promises
of rum punch would persuade him to say another thing about
it.

Of course his reason was right there, although the others
thought he had led them on very badly; it was there in that last
phrase about business in Burlington Bay. Ira always did get
pleasure out of doing things the roundabout way.

But sometimes that secretive, roundabout nature of his got
him into trouble. The summer of 1774 was one of the times.
Heman came up by boat, bringing a party of investors and
potential buyers from Salisbury. Ira was up-country surveying
when the news came that Heman was about to arrive. Ira hurried back to greet his brother, for he had the tale to tell about
the trading post, and he had the lots all laid out on the plain for

Heman's approval. He knew that this second brother, the commercial genius of the family, would appreciate his methods and motives.

Ira no sooner returned than he learned that Heman's first move when he got to the Bay was to confer with Baker and sell off Lot 1, the trading-post site, to a Captain Fry for fifteen pounds. What a good bargain they had made of it, said Heman and Baker over punch with their young relative, to get so much for that dreadful land.

Ira was so heated in his reply, so outraged that the pair of them would sell off his treasure without his consent, that he had to leave their presence. But before he left he vowed that he would buy that lot back no matter what it cost. And the next winter he made a special trip of 150 miles and paid five pounds more for it than Heman and Baker had gotten, just to prove his point.

Hot as the Allen and Baker tempers might grow at times, none of the brothers and cousins could long hold a grudge. They were not that kind of people. So two or three days later, Ira and Heman were together in a canoe on the lake, journeying up north so that Heman might have a good look at the country. They traveled all around. One night they slept on Shelburne Bay where some Yorkers had built a little cabin. In the night Ira dreamed they were being attacked by Yorkers. He awoke and cocked his pistols, which awakened Heman, who was so frightened by the prospect that he slept not another wink all night long. But that was Heman's closest call with the kind of adventure the more ebullient Allen boys encountered frequently enough.

That summer of 1774 saw the perfection and use of Ira's seventy-mile road from Castleton to the Onion River settlements, and it was not long before many a family began to move north to settle in. By the spring of 1775 some fifty families had made their homes in this new land, and the price of an acre had risen from ten cents, which the Allens had paid, to five dollars and more. But while the Allens sold to the settlers, they also bought. The summer of 1774, after Heman went back down to Salisbury, Ira was out in the woods again, looking over lands.

He no longer did the surveys himself—he was far too busy, and he had hirelings for that kind of work. He traveled throughout the country, found the lands he wanted, and took the information to Remember Baker and Ethan. Then Heman was consulted and an attempt was made to buy the lands, which were then surveyed and prepared for sale. Thus by the winter of 1774–5 Ira had been moving about Essex, and points north and east of the Onion River country. In March that fateful year, the principals of the Onion River Company held their first annual business meeting since the country had been surveyed and lots sold. They assembled at Ethan's house in Sheffield, and as senior member of the family, Ethan had the chair. They were all there, Heman up from Salisbury a few miles to the south, Zimri with him, Ira down from his surveying, and Remember Baker absent from the fort and storehouse where he now met the needs of the growing community. They added up their holdings: sixty thousand acres of land at a value of about $300,000. They had good substantial profits for their work, and Ira had even recovered Lot 1. All was well with the Allen world.

Three Encounters and Two Traps

ETHAN'S time in 1773, 1774, and 1775 was spent largely in the task of preserving the Hampshire Grants from the encroachments of the New York colonists. Without valid Hampshire titles, not one foot of the land sold by Heman, Zimri, and the rest would have been worth a penny to the Allens. The validity of the titles rested on Ethan and the Green Mountain Boys and their ability to keep the Yorkers out.

New York was involved in so many land quarrels that the Hampshire Grants did not achieve as much attention as they might have. Governor Tryon and his speculators were also fighting with Massachusetts over Berkshire County. It lay outside the twenty-mile line extending east of the Hudson River that had been established as the eastern boundary of New York. The line was not readily accepted by the New York authorities, however, and there was almost constant quarreling over jurisdiction, in which New York tried to enforce its law in the territory claimed by Massachusetts.

Thus Ethan Allen and the Green Mountain Boys had the sympathy of most of New England in their struggle against the imperious New Yorkers. There were many brushes; although the Green Mountain Boys never attempted to cross Champlain and lay any claims on the western bank, the Yorkers were overt enough in their movements the other way.

One day when Ethan was traveling along the lake, he stopped off at the public house kept by Mr. Richardson at Bridport, north of Shoreham. For some reason, Ethan was not on his guard that day and failed to see the signs of other travelers. He and Eli Roberts, his companion of the journey, were inside the public room before they noticed that two British army sergeants and ten men from the Crown Point garrison were in the saloon. It was too late to do anything but make the best of a bad situation. Ethan and Roberts hitched up their belts, displaying the pair of pistols each of them wore, and called loudly for rum. Ethan, in his boisterous, jolly way, began joking with the sergeants about their lives and jobs, in a way that left some doubt whether he knew he was in danger.

The sergeants and men were armed with guns, pistols, and swords, and the men were between Ethan and the door. There was nothing to be done but relax for the moment and see how events moved along.

Ethan and Roberts drank for a while, then they called for supper and Mr. Richardson saw that it was brought to them. As the evening grew late, Ethan yawned openly and spoke of the rigors of the day's journey. They needed a bed, he said. Mr. Richardson had to tell them that all the beds had been engaged by the sergeants and the soldiers.

That was all right, said one of the sergeants quickly.

Too quickly, thought Ethan, for it was apparent that the sergeant hoped to give up a bed or a room to the pair, then surround them in the night and pack them off to Albany to claim the price on Ethan's head.

No, said Ethan, they would not discommode the soldiers, but would sleep in the barn. It was a warm night and that would not be inconvenient. The sergeant offered again. Ethan demurred. The sergeant could not insist further without tipping his hand. Ethan generously helped allay all suspicion by ostentatiously leaving his gun in the house. He told Roberts to leave his gun, too. They had their pistols—that was common enough. But no man would leave a long gun in a public house unless he intended to pick it up in the morning.

So Ethan and Roberts went off to the barn, yawning and stretching like exhausted men, and in the spirit of conviviality, the sergeants and the soldiers came out to help them settle down (and also find out where they were).

Little by little the house began to darken. The lights in the public room were snuffed out, and candles flared against the windows of the sleeping rooms, then were extinguished. Soon a creeping sound alerted Ethan, and his hands went to his pistols. It was landlord Richardson, carrying their two guns. A moment for thanks, the muffling of the horses' hooves in the barnyard and leading them into the soft ground beyond—then Ethan and Roberts were astride and moving rapidly southward toward Bennington.

The sergeant kept silent for half an hour, then roused the men and quietly slipped out of the house, weapons at the ready, to surround the barn. Bravely, one sergeant led the way inside to take the captives—only to discover that the birds had flown.

Ethan had other worries aside from his concern over capture. The problem was Governor Tryon, who was behaving much too much like a potentate to suit the Green Mountain Boys. The governor issued a number of new patents to land-seekers, many of them covering lands held by the Allens and others. The Crown in London had forbidden such action, but Tryon was playing a political game—by appearing all-powerful, he hoped to push the holders of Hampshire Grants into seeking legalization of their holdings under New York law. The tactic had some success: a number of towns on the east side of Lake Champlain played it both ways, seeking the authority of New York, yet pretending to adhere to the Hampshire Grants.

As colonel of the Green Mountain Boys, Ethan could not abide this double-dealing, and it was essential that some unforgettable example be raised to keep the tottering in line. One of the most important totterers was Benjamin Spencer of Clarendon, that hotspot of Yorkerism.

Ethan and Spencer had had their run-ins earlier, but after the incident of the "dog murder," Spencer had seemed to be subdued. Then it came to Ethan's ears that Spencer and his neighbors had again decided to change the name of their town from Clarendon to Durham, thus emphasizing the New York title rather than the Hampshire Grant in the name of Clarendon.

This could not be allowed. One November night Ethan and a hundred of his men rode to Clarendon. They arrived at Spencer's house in the dead of night and broke down his door. Ethan and Remember Baker rushed into the house, found the justice's bedroom, and hauled him from his bed.

"You are a damned old offender!" shouted Ethan, and he ordered Spencer to get dressed.

When it seemed that Spencer was taking overlong, Ethan struck him a blow across the head with his gun butt. The whole town needed that kind of treatment, he said. Clarendon was a hornet's nest of disloyalty.

Having routed Spencer, Ethan and Remember then sent him a few miles away to the house of a loyal friend of the Green Mountain Boys. Meanwhile, they cleaned up the Yorker nest. They burned two houses, chased out other families and threatened them with violence, and manhandled a few more people. Then they rode out of Clarendon, Ethan thundering that unless the people changed their ways he would see to it that the Green Mountain Boys came back "to reduce every house to ashes and leave every inhabitant a corpse."

That was all for the night, but it was not the end of the punishment of Clarendon. Ethan ordered Spencer brought back to the village, and on his own land, in front of his own house, he was brought to judgment. For two days, while Spencer fretted in confinement, men had been erecting a grandstand and podium, and when it was ready the Green Mountain Boys brought their prisoner and assembled the townspeople on the lawn. Ethan, Remember Baker, Seth Warner, and Robert Cochran sat as judges, and all the charges against Spencer were read out in this open-air court. They said he had represented the New York government in the heart of the Hampshire Grants, and had followed New York law.

"Have I been unfair to any man?" asked Spencer, who was brave enough to stand firm against his accusers.

"No," said Ethan bluntly, "I give you that."

But that did not make any difference. Spencer's crimes were political, and thus much more deadly than any other. He was found guilty on all counts, and he was sentenced to watch the burning of his own house.

Remember Baker wanted to horsewhip Spencer too, but Ethan had gained some respect for the justice—although he called him "the old rat"—and he refused. The Green Mountain Boys set torches to the roof and it began to blaze. Then Ethan had one of those quixotic changes of heart that came over him from time to time and saved him from being either a proper hero or a proper villain, depending on one's point of view. He told the Boys to knock off the roof and save the house, for Spencer had suffered enough.

Though the house was saved, Spencer was warned either to

get out of the Grants or to resign his New York commission as justice of the peace and abide by the local laws. He did resign, and there was no more trouble from him.

There was, however, other trouble to come in Clarendon. It was brought about by the Reverend Mr. Benjamin Hough, the Baptist minister. Mr. Hough was a Bible-quoting, God-fearing man to whom Ethan's use of Scripture was no less than blasphemy. He was convinced by the Spencer episode that the Green Mountain Boys were evil unalloyed and must be dealt with summarily by the highest authority. To him that meant the governor of New York, so after the Green Mountain punishment brigade had left Clarendon, Mr. Hough mounted his horse and went to New York City, where he asked an audience before Governor Tryon and the council. These officials saw and heard him as he described the kangaroo-court proceedings in Clarendon of the Green Mountain Boys—"The Bennington Mobb." He urged that the governor send troops into the Grants to take them for New York once and for all and preserve order. If he did not, then the accursed Ethan Allen and his gang would keep the land in a constant state of terror.

Mr. Hough was a persuasive arguer, and he left New York with the feeling that he had accomplished his purpose and that Governor Tryon would soon send troops. Governor and council suggested that so sturdy a citizen as he ought to take over the justice of the peace post vacated by Mr. Spencer, who had seen the light the Green Mountain Boys offered. So the Reverend Mr. Hough accepted the commission and headed home. He almost made it.

The Green Mountain Boys had their agents in New York, and they reported that Hough had taken the Yorker post and had attempted to foment an uprising of the people against Ethan's authority. Hough was in sight of his house when he was seized by a pair of Green Mountain Boys and hurried thirty miles to Sunderland, in the heart of the land of the Grantsmen. He was held there for several days until Ethan could extricate himself from current affairs to attend to the malefactor.

Ethan came with Seth Warner and others, and they sat as a people's court in judgment of the Reverend Mr. Hough. First they accused him of his crimes and then they judged him for them. Since Hough was a man of so much influence, Ethan decided to make a truly horrible example of him. He ordered Hough stripped to the waist and given two hundred lashes. The verdict was given in front of all the people Ethan and the Boys could muster, and the basic reason for his punishment was announced: no one was to hold any office under the colony of New York within the New Hampshire Grants. Let it be remembered.

The Boys ripped off Hough's coat and shirt and hung him by his arms from a tree limb in the common. Then one began laying on the lash.

Two hundred lashes was no mean sentence. Men had died under less. But Hough was a wiry character. When it was finished he was cut down, his bleeding back was treated by a nearby doctor, and he was put to bed for the night.

Next morning, when Hough was brought before Ethan, the colonel of the Green Mountain Boys ordered the offender out of the Grants forever. Hough asked to go home and visit his family first. Ethan denied the request. Hough asked for a copy of his sentence. Ethan was glad to grant him that, knowing full well that Hough would give it wide publicity. He also gave Hough a free passage out of the territory—with a warning that if he ever returned he would get four hundred lashes and maybe worse. Hough went off to secure what help he could find to get to New York in the dead of winter.

The Hough treatment was a part of a stepped-up campaign on both sides. From New York, Governor Tryon increased the head-price on Ethan and on some of the others. The New York Assembly tried to frighten the people on the Grants into abandoning the Green Mountain Boys by passing a law the governor had urged on them, which forbade assemblies of three or more persons for "unlawful intent" and promised to punish violators with a year in prison. Officials were given permission to injure or kill offenders in the course of apprehension, without blame. Anyone who interfered with a New York magistrate in any way was subject to the death penalty. Even the burning of an outhouse was put down as a crime against New York.

The Assembly also ordered Ethan and other leaders of the

Green Mountain Boys to surrender within the next seventy days or be shot on sight. All in all, it was quite a document. The governor might have sent troops into the Grants, but he knew very well that the maintenance of martial law, which thereafter would have to be a way of life east of the Hudson, would strain the resources even of New York, and he forbore so drastic a move.

Yet the Assembly's action was a dreadful mistake from the point of view of the other colonists in New England. Ethan saw directly what it could mean to his cause, and lost no time in stirring his friends and acquaintances to action. Public meetings were called in Manchester and Arlington, and the Green Mountain Boys' leaders stood before the people and spoke of the "bloody law" of New York. Were the Yorkers ever to take over, they warned, no man's life or property would be safe.

There was a horrible example of this, too. In 1767 a farmer named Andrew Graham had built a log house on land he bought under the Wentworth Grants in what is now Windham County. He worked hard and prospered in his way, although the country was so rough he never accumulated very much. One day in 1774, a group of Yorkers came in, armed with a writ from the New York authorities, and dispossessed Graham. All this dreadful action had taken place in the eastern part of the territory, on the far side of the Green Mountains where Ethan had never attempted to hold jurisdiction, but where New York claimed all the land up to the Connecticut River, the western boundary of New Hampshire.

If the Yorkers could do it to Graham they could do it to anyone—that much was clear. And now, the ferocity of the ill-timed and ill-considered legislative action indicated that no man in the Hampshire Grants need expect mercy if the Yorkers came.

That was the burden of Ethan's argument, and he made it very strong. First he wrote a letter to Governor Tryon, signed by himself and the seven other Green Mountain Boys whose names were mentioned in the New York act. He quoted Scripture; and he quoted Draco, the harsh Athenian lawgiver; he tore Governor Tryon and the Yorkers up one side and down the other, accusing them of "insatiable, avaricious, overbearing, inhuman, barbarous, and blood-guilty" conduct. He defied New York and all its officials, and condemned them as money grubbers and land thieves, as he had so many times before.

Ethan circulated this letter widely in New York and the Grants. He wrote several letters to the Connecticut *Courant,* which had no love for New York. He composed a pamphlet bringing the whole case up to date, calling it *A Brief Narrative of the Proceedings of the Government of New York.* So important did Ethan regard this bit of publicity that he set out for Hartford himself and supervised the printing of the document. It would take a bit of time. The "brief narrative" was two hundred pages long. It detailed the struggle from the Grantsmen's point of view and called upon the forces of justice throughout the Colonies to come to the assistance of the people in the Grants. It put into print what Ethan had put into practice four years earlier: it denied the colony of New York the right to any jurisdiction over the Hampshire Grants "until His Majesty's final pleasure be known."

At this same time, James Breakenridge and Jehiel Hawley were in London, trying to press the worth of their case with the Court and the Privy Council. There was considerable sentiment in favor of their case in London, stirred constantly by copies of Ethan's pamphlets and letters to the *Courant* and the broadsides that he was so careful to have sent over.

Ethan went to Hartford late in the fall of 1774 and stayed until January, 1775, when the printing of the *Brief Narrative* was finished. He then headed northwest again with a plentiful supply of the new definitive work. Ira was with him. They stopped at inns and public places along the way and sold copies for four shillings, then worked their way homeward toward Salisbury and stopped off there for a visit with Heman and Zimri. Their coming was known, and a band of Yorkers decided they would take this chance to rid the territory of the terrible outlaw Ethan Allen and collect the price on his head.

The headquarters of the plot was over in New York, just a few miles from Salisbury. The traitor was Robert McCormick, who had learned of the coming of Ethan because he worked for Heman. McCormick had the run of the Allen house, so he was to be the decoy duck. He was assigned to discover what room Ethan was sleeping in after he arrived at his brother's house. The gang, headquartered in Amenia, had prepared a pair of sleighs and armed themselves with swords and pistols. They planned to drive up in the middle of the night, seize Ethan and anyone with him, and take them to Poughkeepsie, where they would be lodged in the stout jail, far from the Green Mountain Boys up north.

McCormick was the key. Just after Ethan arrived in Salisbury, McCormick showed up at the Allen house, and as he had done many times before, because he lived over in Amenia, he asked for lodging for the night. It was a customary occurrence; no one gave the matter any thought.

But they all knew McCormick and his ways, and Heman began to have a suspicion that something was up, because the man seemed very much ill at ease this night. Usually he was unreserved in his drinking and a jolly companion. Tonight he drank next to nothing and was very quiet.

McCormick had expected Ethan and Ira to be in the house, but they had gone out on an errand when he arrived. Heman talked to McCormick for a while, and then the tenor of the man's interest made itself known. He began asking questions about Ethan and Ira—when would they return, how long would they stay, and other little bits that excited Heman's suspicion.

So, when Heman heard the brothers' steps in the hall, he excused himself and warned them that he felt some plot was afoot. Ethan was never one to dilly-dally in any matter: he burst into the room, taxed McCormick with his suspicions, and demanded to know all about it. McCormick blanched. Yes, he had heard of a plot against the Allen brothers, he said, but he did not know much about it. Ethan turned a beady eye on him, and McCormick suddenly remembered that he had vital business in Amenia that could not wait the morrow. So he moved off into the snowy night, and when he came to the meeting place with his conspirators, he told them the jig was up—the Allens were warned. So the decoy duck got off with his neck intact, and the Allen boys did not have to bare their steel that night.

CHAPTER TWELVE

Tension

CONTINUING their journey north from Salisbury, Ira and Ethan made their way along the Berkshires to Bennington and the Catamount Tavern. The place was tense, for even this bastion was not immune from the fears of the day. Not long before, the blandishments of the Yorkers had caused Dr. Samuel Adams, a neighbor of Remember Baker's in Arlington, to take the side of the Yorkers. The doctor was a respected man and a useful one, but he had been complaining everywhere about the harsh measures Ethan was using to quell dissent from his views. Ethan and the Green Mountain Boys could not countenance this. So one day good Dr. Adams was hied before the Green Mountain Boys' "court" in the common room of the tavern. He had been up to most unseemly behavior, carrying a pair of pistols about and threatening to shoot anyone who interfered with him. Yet any doctor was a useful man, they noted, so the Boys dealt gently with him. They tied him into an arm chair and hoisted him up twenty-five feet on a sling outside the tavern so he could contemplate at close range the cougar snarling its defiance against the Yorkers. They left him there for two hours in the sight of all the people around.

It was not a harsh punishment. People were relieved that it was no worse, and the sight of the bound doctor sitting there under the jaws of the cougar caused a good deal of laughter in Bennington. When he was brought down later in the day, there was no further interference with him. He had his choice—either take the matter as a mortal insult and probably meet his death as a consequence, or consider it as a gentle reminder that if he wished to live here he must not offend the majority. There was no more trouble with Dr. Adams.

In February, when Ethan was back at the tavern worrying over the problems of the Grants and assessing the political situation, he sensed a serious change in the temper of the people. In spite of his pamphlet and the harsh New York law, the Yorkers were giving less real trouble than they had in years. Ethan was concerned. His people were growing smug and self-satisfied, and no rebellion ever succeeded thus. He even heard some remarks that the Yorkers might not be so bad as they had been painted.

A worried Ethan made it a point to attend every public meeting in the area. On February 1 at a convention in Manchester, his worst fears were confirmed: the people of the region were losing sight of the immediacy of their problem. One reason for this was the return of Governor Tryon to England, which removed from the area the man who had taken the most inflexible line against the Grantsmen. There were no current rumblings from New York.

Although Ethan was in the forefront of the convention, he ran into opposition when he wanted to adopt a fiery anti-Yorker stance. The people were settled and their farms were prospering. They did not want to come out and belabor New York's government, since no one in that colony seemed any longer to be bothering them. Ethan thought they ought to declare their independence—which would give him material for a grand pamphlet—but no such thing occurred.

Two years earlier Governor Tryon had offered a kind of accommodation to the people of the Grants, and many of them now felt that Ethan Allen had sabotaged the accord with his violence and threats. After all, a settler who was making a good living could afford to pay off a few pounds to settle an old land right, and if the Yorkers would do that, as some believed, then what was all the shouting about?

Ethan knew. The Onion River Company would be a dead duck if any accommodation were reached with New York. Any landholder who was not in possession of his land and living on it was likely to lose out—and of course this meant the Allen family and their friends who had invested so heavily during the uncertain years. These were matters for concern at the Onion River Company's meeting at Ethan's house in Sheffield in March, 1775. The restlessness of the past was dying out in such settled areas as Manchester and Bennington.

But larger events in the American Colonies were beginning to color the situation in the Grants in this spring of 1775, and

Ethan's mind opened to new ideas and new approaches. He engaged in conversation with John Brown of Pittsfield, Massachusetts, through whose territory Ethan had to pass on his way up to the Grants. Brown was an ardent revolutionist who spoke loftily of the rights of men and the oppressions of the London government. He was on his way to Canada, sent by the Boston Committee of Correspondence to discover how the Canadians felt about revolution against England. At their meeting, John Brown asked Ethan to give him safe passage and guides to take him to Montreal. Ethan assigned Peleg Sunderland and Winthrop Hoyt, a pair of his Green Mountain guides. During the discussions the question of war came up, and they talked of defenses. Brown mentioned Ticonderoga, the fort, held successively by the French and English, that dominated passage along Lake Champlain.

When Brown returned from Canada he wrote to Boston. He had not been very successful in his primary mission of getting the Canadians roused up against England, but he had acquired a good deal of information on his trip. He had learned that Fort Ticonderoga was of vital importance to the western country and must be taken in any action against the British. The people of the New Hampshire Grants had promised to do it, he said. Of course this meant Ethan and the Green Mountain Boys, for there was no other organized militia in the Grants. In agreeing to capture the fort, Ethan may well also have been thinking that the capture of Ticonderoga by Green Mountain Boys would preclude its being taken by Yorkers, and thus strike a blow, not only for the American Revolution, but against his dreaded enemies as well.

Up to this time Ethan's talk of revolution had been revolution against New York, not against the government of King George III. But the new idea brewing in Boston was for absolute independence. This idea was appealing to the Grantsmen, for it would naturally put the property of America in the hands of Americans. The New England colonies were not going to stand by and see New York hog the show, either—that much was already certain in Ethan's mind.

As all this was stirring, other pots were simmering. Although

New York laid claim to all the land west of the Connecticut River, its basic success in maintaining control had always been east of the Green Mountains in the Connecticut Valley, which was effectively cut off from Ethan's influence by the mountains that rose to his east. At the town of Westminster, on the Connecticut, men had been reading a good deal of the material emanating from Boston in recent months. They knew of the unpleasantness of taxation and repression, the quartering of British troops, the scandal of the tea tax, the Stamp Act, and all the other annoyances. In the winter of 1774–5 the people of Westminster formed their own Committee of Correspondence and kept in touch with Boston. The committee members were itching to do something in defiance. They were not, in fact, so very far from the position of Ethan Allen.

At this time, too, certain other events foretold an eventual union of the people east and west of the Green Mountains. Most important of these omens of change was the action of Colonel Philip Skene, a retired British army officer who had secured a grant to a large piece of land lying athwart the end of Lake Champlain in New York colony. Colonel Skene had settled the area, built a few wharves and a sawmill, sold lots, and set himself up as the squire of Skenesboro (later Whitehall, New York).

The colonel was vain and ambitious. He wanted to be more powerful than he was, and in the grumbling and outright defiance of the Green Mountain Boys he saw an opportunity for himself. Ethan Allen put Skene's ambition to work. Ethan, Amos Bird, and several others met a number of times with Colonel Skene and encouraged him to go to London to seek the establishment of a new royal colony that would encompass the Hampshire Grants. It would be bounded on the east by the Connecticut River, on the west by the Iroquois River and Lake Ontario, on the north by the forty-fifth parallel, and on the south by the Mohawk River. This territory would have included a great slice of New York, but in fact it was a piece mostly inhabited by Indians and trappers, and much of the land was still Crown land.

Colonel Skene was persuaded to go to London at his own

expense to seek the honors he wished. Skenesboro would be the capital of the new colony, and Colonel Skene would be Governor Skene. Ethan was content. No matter what came of it for Skene, it could do no harm for the cause of the Green Mountain Boys to have so prominent an agitator working in their behalf.

Skene's first move when he got to London was to get himself appointed governor of the garrisons of Ticonderoga and Crown Point. The next step was to get the Privy Council to make him governor of the whole disputed territory.

Although Colonel Skene's maneuvers would have served to unite the peoples on the two sides of the Green Mountains, nearly everything else that was occurring in these days was causing people to be torn asunder. Beginning in 1773 and 1774, the tea riots, the stamp troubles, and the convening of the Continental Congress in Philadelphia all showed how unsettled life was in the Colonies. Some men held for the King and New York, some held for the king and Colonel Skene, others held for the Hampshire Grants, and to hell with the king.

In this atmosphere the juggernaut of royal justice rolled into the troubled town of Westminster. The day was March 14, 1775. For some weeks there had been complaints that times were hard and that something must be done to stop the normal processes of the local courts, which were the chief instruments of New York's authority in the region. Creditors who applied to the courts could be authorized to seize their debtors' property. When a group of Connecticut Valley citizens went to Judge Thomas Chandler to protest, he promised them that the civil trials would all be delayed until a different session, thus giving indebted settlers some respite.

But the local sheriff, William Paterson, secured his income from court-ordered seizures of property, and the judge's decision did not please him at all. To make matters worse, there were many settlers who trusted neither judge nor sheriff, and they decided to seize the court and make sure that no sessions were held during that docket period.

Sheriff Paterson got wind of the plan in Brattleboro where he lived. He raised a posse of about twenty-five men, armed them as best he could, and set out for Westminster on March 13.

That evening, Sheriff Paterson and his men reached the courthouse in Westminster to find that a hundred men of the area had occupied it and turned it into a fortress.

To Sheriff Paterson this defiance was a serious matter. He marched to the front of the building and spoke loudly.

"I'll give you just fifteen minutes to get the hell out of there," he said, "and if you are not out, then by God, I'll blow a lane through you."

Inside, the men of the anti-court party, as they called themselves, were not disturbed. They had expected just such a display, which was why they had seized the court. All that was happening was confirming their distrust of British justice.

One of the leaders of the group was Charles Davenport, by trade a carpenter, by inclination an antagonist.

"It will take us just fifteen minutes," he shouted back to the sheriff, "to send you and your party to hell."

So the preliminaries were out of the way. Footsore, more than a little annoyed, and sure that the men inside had guns and God knew what other instruments of destruction, Sheriff Paterson and his posse leaders retired to a tavern, where they drank punch, warmed themselves at the fire, and decided what they would do next.

Judge Chandler heard of the commotion and went to the courthouse to see if he could prevent a deadly confrontation. Davenport and his supporters complained that the sheriff had come there with guns and other weapons; he was the one creating the trouble. The judge calmed them. The sheriff had no right to come marching in there with guns, he said, and he agreed that it was a violation of the court's decision of a few days earlier. He would go to the tavern and make sure the sheriff disarmed his men. The settlers could stay in the courthouse until morning without being bothered. He would take care of Sheriff Paterson.

He tried. The settlers believed the judge, and most left the courthouse and went home. They did leave a small armed party inside, just in case of trouble, but they did not expect a confrontation.

Whatever Sheriff Paterson told the judge, his minions and John Barleycorn contradicted. Late in the evening, four hours after they had entered the tavern, the deputies came out and approached the courthouse from all sides. They were planning a surprise attack, but the punch they had consumed made them less quiet, though more convinced of their own rectitude and potency. Sheriff Paterson stumbled up the steps. The light of the moon gleamed on the guns and knives carried by the attackers, and someone inside saw them.

Inside the courthouse, there were no guns. The men had armed themselves only with clubs. As Sheriff Paterson stumbled up the steps, one of the young men inside pushed him away. He stumbled back, and this time he was pushed and clubbed. He stepped back.

"God damn you, fire!" he shouted at his men.

They fired a ragged volley into the door of the courthouse. William French of Brattleboro, twenty-two, fell with a bullet in his head and four more in his body. Daniel Houghton was mortally wounded. Ten other men were also wounded. In five minutes Sheriff Paterson gained the courthouse, but the sound of gunfire had been sobering enough to give him some idea of what he had done.

That night men rode out in all directions to carry the black news that minions of the king had murdered innocent boys at Westminster. Men seized their muskets and their powder horns and began to move. In the morning Robert Cochran, captain of the Green Mountain Boys, was on the road, and before nightfall a hundred Green Mountain Boys marched into Westminster to settle with the Yorker sheriff if he dared show his face there again.

The people called a meeting, guarded by the Green Mountain Boys and a hundred others who had shown up to indicate their displeasure. They called the coroner, who was a reasonable man, and held an inquest. They concluded—the people and the coroner—that William French was willfully murdered by the officials of New York colony. They rounded up some members of the sheriff's posse, tied them up, and sent them down to Northampton, Massachusetts, jail to await trial for murder. But the New York authorities quickly got a writ from their own courts, and the Massachusetts judges let the men go. The people of Westminster were furious. They ordered a convention for that place in April, and at the convention declared their refusal to accept any longer the laws of the colony of New York.

Thus the people of the east side of the Hampshire Grants, after all these years, were united with those of the west side, and the concern that Ethan Allen and his men had shown over dwindling enthusiasm for their cause was allayed. Yet by the time this happened, Ethan was no longer concerned about the matter. True, he attended at the Westminster convention. True, he was one of three men who were chosen to carry on the struggle of Westminster and all the people of the Grants against the government of New York. But before he could get back to Bennington and organize his thoughts for a new pamphlet, important news reached him: guns had been fired in anger in the Massachusetts town of Lexington.

CHAPTER THIRTEEN

Ticonderoga

IRA was up in the Onion River country surveying when the muskets sounded the shots heard 'round the world. Heman Allen was down in Salisbury, taking care of the mundane details of the Onion River Company. Two years earlier Heman had married Abigail Beebe of Salisbury; everyone hoped for him a long life and many children. But Heman's health was not good these days—he had a weak chest. Still, the tragedy that befell the family this year was not his, but Zimri's: this brother died in 1775 at Heman's home.

There was no time for lamentation. The noise from Lexington and Concord meant but one thing to the Allens: *Arise.* Up in Bennington, Ethan made sure that his Green Mountain Boys were assembling and readying for whatever task they might be enlisted to perform. Down in Connecticut, Heman brought out his musket and sword and sent the word to Ethan that he was prepared to keep his long-time promise and join the Green Mountain Boys when they needed him. Ethan promptly commissioned him a captain. Up in Poultney where he was serving as town clerk, Heber sent word to his eldest brother that he, too, was ready to fight and would come when called. Down from the Onion River came Lieutenant Ira Allen and Captain Remember Baker, and soon the clan was assembled in Bennington. Lucy, their sister, was not expected to carry guns. She was living in Sheffield with her husband, Dr. Lewis Beebe, and would stay there, a happy farm wife, until she died. Lydia was dead—but better to be dead like Lydia than to suffer the fate of the last brother, Levi.

Levi Allen was thirty years old this spring of 1775. He had enjoyed a certain prosperity, much of it attributable in the beginning to family associations and help from his brothers. He was a stubborn fellow who refused to take advice or direction; thus he was not in the Onion River Company at all. He had quarreled with Heman and Zimri so much that finally he had gone out on his own. For the last two years not much had been heard about him by the others in the family. He had somehow managed to buy the whole town of Swanton, Vermont, having learned from Ethan and Ira that the Hampshire Grants lands were valuable beyond price. But suddenly he sold Swanton and moved south into Connecticut once again. For the truth was that Levi somehow had drifted away from all the others. Perhaps it was personal inclination, perhaps it was his associations outside the family. Whatever the reason, Levi Allen now professed his adherence to the cause of King George III, and instead of joining the Green Mountain Boys with his brothers, he sped away from them to the safety of the lands held by the king's men.

Ethan and the others were outraged, but at the moment they had no time to consider their wayward brother and his sins, for they were totally occupied with a new undertaking.

As soon as the cannon began to roar over Boston, the name of Ticonderoga seemed to come to everyone's lips. The British had captured the fortress from the French, who had built it in the first place to control traffic on Lake Champlain. It could accommodate a force of hundreds of men, but it had been badly neglected in recent years, and now held only fifty British regulars. The British Colonial Secretary of State, Lord Dartmouth, had been intending to strengthen the garrison for months, and in the fall of 1774 had finally so ordered in a letter that did not reach America until Christmas. By then, of course, the northern winter had set in. Now it was spring and nothing had been done. The fifty redcoats stood ready, but only two dozen of their cannon were in working order. In April, as everyone began thinking about the fort's position, the British sent a handful of men up-lake and promised to send more men and matériel.

At about this same time, Captain Benedict Arnold of the Connecticut militia raised a company of soldiers and rode with them toward Boston to see if he could get into the struggle against the British. He ran into Samuel Parsons, a merchant who was active in Hartford's Committee of Correspondence. In talking, Parsons mentioned the Colonies' grave need for artillery, and Arnold brought up Ticonderoga, where there were cannon that might be captured. Parsons went back to Hartford, raised three hundred pounds to pay soldiers, and sent a handful of men to gather recruits and move on Ticonderoga. They were led by Major Halsey, Edward Mott, and Noah Phelps—a group of ardent revolutionaries—and they bore instructions from the governor and council of Connecticut.

Meanwhile Captain Benedict Arnold had gone to Boston. When he reached American headquarters at Cambridge and talked about Ticonderoga, he found that question already under discussion. The promise secured earlier by John Brown from Ethan to take the fort had become a matter of some concern among the committees of correspondence, and the name of Ticonderoga was familiar to everyone.

The patriots could not dispatch an army to Ticonderoga because they did not have one. They could dispatch Arnold, however, with a little money and a commission that would allow him to raise a force in the name of the revolutionaries, and that is what they did. They gave him a commission as a colonel, signed by the Massachusetts Committee of Safety, and the right to win as much glory as he could. This arrangement suited Arnold very well. He liked the idea of soldiering and had read everything in the world about it, which he had leisure to do in his trade as bookseller and apothecary. But it was not easy for a captain of militia to become a colonel. Now he had the chance. All he had to do was raise a force and train it, get to Ticonderoga, carry out a pitched battle, win, and bring the fort's cannon back to Boston. Then he would be a hero. He took the hundred pounds the committee gave him and set out for Bennington, where he proposed to enlist the Green Mountain Boys under his banner. There Arnold discovered that he was late. The Connecticut men had arrived and had joined forces with the Green Mountain Boys, and Ethan Allen was already leading the whole force toward Ticonderoga.

Arnold saw his hope for glory vanishing up the Castleton road, and he leaped on his horse and gave chase. He stormed along the road until he reached Castleton and Zadock Remington's tavern, which was the headquarters of the force. There he descended, commission in hand, and sought to assert his authority. He had no soldiers, no guns, no ammunition; but he did have that commission as a colonel, a fine new uniform, and his valet on a horse behind him.

When Arnold demanded to see the person in charge, the soldiers lounging outside the tavern directed him to Edward Mott. Mott was one of the Connecticut group who had come to Bennington to enlist Ethan's aid in taking Ticonderoga, and after all the discussions and plans were made, Mott had been elected chairman of the committee of war, which was really a job as staff secretary and chief organizer. Ethan, of course, had taken the job as colonel and leader of the assault, and his Green Mountain Boys were to be the shock troops, backed by other forces enlisted in Connecticut and Massachusetts for the dangerous task.

Arnold bustled into the room where Mott was sitting. He was a splendiferous figure in his immaculate, bright blue uniform, his valet standing outside to brush him at the slightest need. Mott looked over the commission.

Arnold told him that he, Colonel Arnold, was now in charge.

Mott looked stolidly at the trim figure and said that Colonel Ethan Allen and the advance troops had already left. But he was in charge, said Arnold. Massachusetts had given the command to him.

Mott unbent enough to acquaint this bluebird of the Connecticut militia with a few of the facts of life. First of all, these men were not about to deliver up their army to Colonel Arnold, commission or no commission. Second of all, Colonel Allen was on his way, the rest of the troops were to leave in an hour to join him, and it was very doubtful if any of them would go into fight under an unknown colonel from Connecticut who might not know his mustache from his musket.

Everything Edward Mott said was quite true. Ethan and the Green Mountain Boys were so well known in all New England that when Ticonderoga was mentioned, everyone but Benedict Arnold had thought of Ethan as the logical man to lead the attack. When the Connecticut contingent had come to Bennington to meet with Ethan, Heber, Heman, Seth Warner, Robert Cochran, Winthrop Hoyt, and the rest of them, there had been no doubt as to the leadership of the expedition. The Connecticut men were bright and understanding, and they knew what they were about.

Their first move, while Arnold was rushing to Boston to get authority, had been to send Noah Phelps up to Ticonderoga to spy out the situation. Phelps was a logical choice. He was young enough and tough enough, and since he came from Hartford, it was most unlikely that anyone in the British garrison would know his face, whereas they might recognize any one of the Green Mountain Boys.

Early in May Phelps was at the fort. He went in, telling the guard he was badly in need of a shave after days in the woods, and he learned from the garrison's garrulous barber just about all he needed to know about the fort. He also learned that no one at Ticonderoga knew about the trouble in Boston that had broken into warfare. This was surprising to Phelps; he did not understand that the main line of communications from Ticonderoga led north to Montreal, rather than southeast to the embattled colonies.

On Phelps's return, Ethan marched. On May 7 he reached Castleton with 130 of his Boys and joined up with some of the Connecticut–Massachusetts men. He planned to launch the attack from Hand's Cove, across the lake from the fort. Before Ethan left, he detached thirty men under Sam Herrick and sent them to Skenesboro to seize the boats at Colonel Skene's place, just to be sure the British did not send any reinforcements from the south. He also sent Asa Douglas to get the handful of boats his family kept at Crown Point for the Boys to use at dawn on May 10 to attack Ticonderoga.

Having done all this, Ethan set out on horseback on Monday morning, May 8, for Shoreham, about twenty miles to the northwest of Castleton, even as Benedict Arnold was hurrying up from Bennington, his valet behind him, his commission in his saddlebags. The next day, Arnold and his valet arrived at

Shoreham before the Mott party, which was to join forces with Ethan that night. Colonel Arnold strode into the place where Ethan was laying out his plan, produced his commission, and announced that he had come to take command.

Ethan looked at Arnold and the paper. It was a fine commission, written in an ornate hand on long paper. Ethan had no such commission. All he had was a document from the Connecticut legislature. So Ethan nodded, and asked Colonel Arnold to come outside, so Ethan might say a few words to explain the change to the troops.

Colonel Arnold was gratified. He followed Ethan, who was dressed in his ragged Green Mountain Boys uniform (Ethan was one of the few who had any uniform at all), and they moved among the Boys, who were squatting and sitting about their campfires.

Summoning them with his loudest voice, Ethan explained that the handsome, debonair colonel had come to lead them all into battle, and he showed the commission. The plan would be the same. The pay would be the same, about two dollars per man. Only the command would be different.

The Boys in their buckskins scrutinized the cockatoo colonel in the blue uniform, and in a very leisurely way got up and began to stack their arms, the symbol of a camp at rest. It was their announcement of their intention.

Colonel Arnold watched, at first in unconcern and then in growing dismay as the import of the action grew on him. The Boys began to speak up. They were not going to serve under some pipsqueak ordered from Boston. Ethan Allen was their colonel and had been for four years. They would go into battle under him or they would not go.

Arnold still wanted that command—the glory was there to be seized. Then Ethan said no, he was not going to jeopardize the success of the expedition, and Arnold could not have command. But here is what Ethan would do: Arnold could walk with him and see what happened, though he was not to interfere.

Arnold was very unhappy, but it was the best he could do, for he could not risk being the man who *prevented* the capture of

Ticonderoga. So the spiffy colonel and his valet sat down to wait while Ethan and his dusty Boys got on with their plan.

The trouble was boats. By nightfall on May 9, a total of 230 officers and men were waiting in camp. Asa Douglas had managed to secure nothing in the way of boats. There was no time to be lost: even now the garrison across the lake might have heard them.

As darkness set in, Ethan and his men moved down the lake to a cove a mile north of the fort.

The lake was so narrow here that a man might swim across were it not for the problems of noise and wet powder. It was possible to move only with boats. Finally two were found. One was a bateau, a big French lake and river boat. The other was a small rowboat, much less useful. But there was nothing else, and by the time these were brought to Hand's Cove it was after midnight.

So the crossing began, but the boats could ferry only eighty-three men to the other side before the dawn began to show its red and gray. Seth Warner was left to bring up the others after the attack began.

On the New York shore Ethan assembled his modest band of troops and made a little speech adjuring them to success and honor, ending by telling them it was all dangerous work, and only volunteers need come forward.

Of course every man came. They turned, and in a column of three they began to move toward the fort, Ethan in front in his uniform and with a big sword at his side, and beside him the natty little Connecticut colonel, Benedict Arnold. Behind, the Boys in their buckskin and homespun shouldered their muskets and rifles, loosened their deer knives, and felt for their powder horns as they marched.

Ethan led the Boys past the old disused parts of the fort to the south side, where a wall that had been broken some years earlier had not been repaired. The garrison had no inkling of danger. There was not even a sentry on guard at the breach in the wall. With his fifty men, Captain William Delaplace could only guard the inner bastion, a sufficient precaution, he thought. But now, as the captain lay asleep in his bed, eighty-three men climbed through the break in the wall and were soon at the wicket gate that led to the inner fortress.

At the gate stood a lone sentry. He saw the Green Mountain Boys coming, leveled his gun and pulled the trigger, then beat a hasty retreat. Ethan was in the vanguard and the shot was aimed at his heart. The gun misfired. Like everything else at Ticonderoga, the sentry was not ready for a fight.

Ethan and Benedict Arnold rushed through the gate after the sentry. Ethan slashed with his sword and the soldier raised his musket to defend himself. The blow glanced off the gun and struck the soldier in the head, giving him a slight wound. The Green Mountain Boys swarmed through the place, yelling hideously. Ethan had the Boys give three mighty cheers to confuse the garrison about their strength. In the confusion Ethan ordered the sentry he had struck to take him to the commander's room, on pain of instant death if he refused. The soldier led and Ethan followed, Arnold at his side.

At the top of the stairs that led to the officers' quarters, Ethan shouted that by God someone had better come out and surrender the garrison before he killed every man in the fort. A sleepy man in uniform breeches came stumbling out of a door, and Ethan yelled at him. It was Lieutenant Jocelyn Feltham, and he could not surrender the garrison because he was a junior officer. Ethan swore at him and threatened again to lay waste the entire garrison. When Feltham demanded to know what all the noise was about at this unseemly hour, Ethan told him that this was an attack.

And by whose authority was this illegal act against the king's property being carried out, the officer wanted to know.

"In the name of the Great Jehovah and the Continental Congress!" shouted Ethan.

By this time Captain Delaplace was awake. Feltham, a bright young officer, was trying to stall for time by reasoning with these savages so his superior could rouse the guard and shoot them down. But Delaplace did no such thing. He came out himself, and demanded to know what the excitement was about. Ethan had to go through it again before he secured the surrender of the garrison at Fort Ticonderoga. Arnold produced his commission and waved it, and finally the British officers realized they were caught up in the heat of rebellion against the Crown.

Ethan and Arnold escorted their prisoners outside the block-house. The Green Mountain Boys had secured the place without firing a shot. The only man injured was the soldier smacked by Ethan's sword, and he would recover quickly enough with a bandage and a bit of rum.

So the battle was over. For the first time the Americans had taken the offensive against the British Empire in North America, and at Ticonderoga they were totally successful. They held control of the lake that dominated waterways from Canada to the Hudson River. Ethan had sealed off Yorker country forever from his own, and the Hampshire Grants could for the first time be assessed as safe.

Revolution!

WHEN the call came from Ethan Allen to all the Green Mountain Boys to join him for the Ticonderoga expedition, Remember Baker and Ira Allen were in the Onion River country tending their respective chores. It took several days for the word to reach Burlington. Ira and Baker set out for Hand's Cove, but on the morning of May 10 they were still far away. They did not arrive at Ticonderoga that day. They did, however, learn of the events, for on the lake they surprised a pair of small boats heading north for the fort at St. John's on the Sorel (now Richelieu) River to give the alarm that Ticonderoga had fallen. Captain Baker captured them both, then moved on up-lake toward the big fort.

On the morning of May 11, Ethan dispatched Seth Warner and another party of Green Mountain Boys to capture Crown Point. They had a devil of a time getting there: the wind can blow straight south along Champlain until the narrow lake seems like a wind tunnel, and row as they might, Warner's boys seemed never to make any progress in their bateau. They made their landfall just in time to meet Remember Baker and his party coming south. Together the parties assaulted the fort at Crown Point.

How self-confident and lulled the British were in North America is nowhere shown better than in the condition of Crown Point. A valuable military post, it contained fifty cannon, many of them in good shape, and an immense supply of powder and stores for an army. It was guarded this May morning by one British sergeant and eight privates, all of whom had the good sense to surrender without a shot. Captains Warner and Baker, sharing the glory, went back to Ticonderoga to report to Ethan.

It was a good day all around. Ethan learned that Sam Herrick had captured Skenesboro, the head of navigation at the opening of the lake. There Herrick had found even more food and supplies and a number of bateaux and other boats. He even captured Colonel Skene's personal schooner.

Colonel Benedict Arnold, the most "military" figure in the place, took over the management of the ordnance he had been sent out from Massachusetts to collect. He counted some two hundred cannon, howitzers, and mortars as the fruit of the week's work, most of them in usable condition. He immediately began making plans to move all this matériel to Boston for the siege of the British.

The Green Mountain Boys then did what they were expected to do after such a major victory: they got drunk. The British garrison had laid in a supply of ninety gallons of rum for medicinal and "refreshment" purposes. Ethan gave Captain Delaplace a receipt for all of it, and the Americans proceeded to hold a party. By nightfall most of the garrison was in some stage of inebriation, and visitors from the area were being welcomed as if this was an official open house.

Colonel Arnold was scandalized. What if the British tried to recapture the fortress? Obviously the Green Mountain Boys and the Connecticut men were in no condition to defend the place. He went around the camp ordering men to put down their flagons and take up their muskets, but no one paid him any attention. By Green Mountain Boy standards, the slender little colonel was a puffed-up duck, and several of them thought it a good idea to tell him so. He was poked, pushed, and had his life threatened by one big Boy with a musket. He went angrily to Ethan to complain and insist that this disgraceful conduct must be stopped and that he, Colonel Arnold, commander by grace of the Massachusetts military committee, was immediately to be elevated to command to stop it. Ethan laughed. Well, said Arnold, at least he must have joint command. That was what Ethan had promised.

Ethan Allen was a politician in his own right. He saw the dangers ahead, and he got Edward Mott and the others of the military committee to meet and issue to him a formal order of appointment as colonel and head of the garrison, acting in behalf of the colony of Connecticut. These orders would stand until changed by Connecticut's government or by the Continental Congress.

For the next four days, then, Benedict Arnold sulked in his room at Fort Ticonderoga listening to the revelry, shuddering, and worrying about what would happen when the British came. But there were no British within hundreds of miles. It was not until months later that the British high command would finally realize that Lake Champlain jutted down into the heartland of the American Colonies, and that by controlling it, the British could cut off vexatious New England from the Middle Colonies, and might then deal separately with New York and Pennsylvania rather than fight a united Colonial front.

In four days all the rum was gone, the hangovers were over, and the irregulars of the Green Mountain army were ready for action once again. Ethan was no fool. After permitting himself a brief revel as commander of the victors and saluting Congress, Connecticut, and the cougar of Bennington in His Majesty's rum, Ethan got down to work. He wrote Congress in Philadelphia to tell them the news. He wrote the Albany Committee of Correspondence, warning of the danger of a British counterattack and emphasizing the importance of the lake and its forts. If some members of that committee were old enemies from the early days of the struggle over the Hamsphire Grants, it was all forgotten now in the greater danger from the common British enemy.

How quickly attitudes changed! Ethan and his men considered themselves fighters and partisans. With Arnold, they were all falling into a mold in a moment, accepting the fact that their bits of defiance (and they were no more than that) meant a true revolution against the British government. Had Britain been the ogre she was to be painted, keeping the Colonies under strict garrison, these uprisings would have been squelched in no time and order returned. The fact was, however, that the British in America were in dreadful disarray. There were only a few hundred British troops in Canada, and they certainly could not launch an attack on Ticonderoga or on Boston. The uprising came as such a shock at home that no one in Britain was prepared for it, at least no one in power. Lieutenant Feltham and Captain Delaplace regarded Ethan and his men as villains, and villains they might be to the Yorkers and the British and to all who loved duly constituted authority. But Ethan was a hero to the people of the Hampshire Grants and New England, and he regarded himself now as a patriot, ready to follow the orders of the Continental Congress that was deliberating down in Philadelphia.

Ethan planned a second attack. Up north, where the British made far more use of the lake than the Americans did in the south, the British had garrisoned the fort at St. John's. There, in addition to soldiers, they kept an armed sloop that was able to control the entire lake, for it was the only warship on the water. Ethan felt that St. John's must be taken, and so must the sloop.

It was four days before the troops pulled themselves together. They decided to send Colonel Skene's schooner to do the job, and they put the command in the hands of Colonel Benedict Arnold. He did have that commission to wave, and it was becoming a bit embarrassing that they were not letting him do anything at all. These considerations suddenly became important when a hundred of Arnold's troops showed up on May 14. More important, Arnold had been a ship owner and sailor in Connecticut, and he was the only man among the group who had any experience on what might be called a ship. He was the logical choice to command the expedition against the warship.

On May 15 he set out with fifty men. Three days later he captured St. John's and the war sloop and five usable bateaux, all without losing a man. The British had only thirteen men in the garrison at St. John's. It was as simple a capture as Ticonderoga.

This victory gave the Americans complete control of Lake Champlain, plus a warship to prevent the British from challenging them on the lake.

Meanwhile Ethan had decided that he would bring his Green Mountain Boys north to occupy St. John's. They entered four bateaux and came down the lake only to find that Arnold had done it all and was on his way back to Ticonderoga. But Ethan did not turn back. He wanted to capture and hold St. John's as a base for an attack on Canada. On he went, against Arnold's advice.

In this case, Arnold's advice was excellent. Governor Guy Carleton in Montreal might not have heard about the attack on Ticonderoga in time to do anything about it. But St. John's was another matter—it was an integral point of his local defense. And if the eight hundred troops he had at his disposal seemed as nothing in terms of an attack on the Colonies, they were quite enough for this kind of job. Carleton dispatched two hundred regular British troops in neat marching file to St. John's. When Ethan and his ragged Green Mountain Boys reached the Sorel River, a scout told them of the coming of the troops.

The Green Mountain Boys were tired from a hard journey against bad winds down the lake. Ethan considered an ambush of the British, but was talked out of it, and the Boys moved to the east side of the river, opposite the enemy, to wait and think things over.

Next morning at dawn the British crossed over with cannon and began an attack on the Green Mountain Boys. It was the first time most of the Boys had ever heard a gun larger than a musket fired in anger. They moved out—so hastily that some said it was a rout. One man was captured and two were left to make their own way home.

Ethan rallied them and led them back up the lake to Ticonderoga. Ahead went the word. Colonel Arnold, having come back to the fort with the luxury of the British provisions he had captured, was just sitting down to supper served by his valet on the evening of May 21 when the word was brought that Ethan Allen and his Green Mountain Boys had suffered a disastrous defeat at St. John's. Colonel Arnold did anything but choke on his soup. In fact, it would be hard to find a meal that pleased him more during the whole of his adventure in the backwoods.

☆CHAPTER FIFTEEN☆

The Limitations of Guerilla War

THE Allens of 1775, and particularly Ethan, cannot honestly be assessed if they are put up against the Benedict Arnolds and the George Washingtons of their time. For there was almost no common ground between Ethan and Benedict Arnold. Ethan was a backwoodsman. Arnold was a man of affairs, a tradesman to be sure and several cuts below Washington in the social scheme, but a man who knew which fork to use and the importance of soap and servants. He regarded Ethan and the Green Mountain Boys as a wild and woolly gang who were good for very little and the performance of the troops after the victory at Ticonderoga only confirmed his view. But Arnold's opinion would not have made the slightest difference, for Edward Mott and the Connecticut committee that ran the little war around Lake Champlain had spoken clearly and succinctly earlier. He who had the troops was in charge. That's why Ethan was in charge at Ticonderoga. A few weeks after the battle, when the Green Mountain Boys dispersed to do their spring plowing and get the crops into the ground, Ethan had no more troops. He was still called commandant of the garrison, but Benedict Arnold was not long in fixing that. On May 27 Arnold announced that he was taking command. Each day had brought new recruits from the east, not dismayed at all by the fact that the fortress had been won. So Ethan had to step down, which he did with the best grace he could.

After the victories on Lake Champlain, Congress worried. Many of the people in government in the various colonies suddenly awakened to realize that they had started a war against His Majesty George III, and what had seemed such a fine idea in the northern woods did not appear so beautiful when seen from a bustling seaport. Congress was hesitant, deciding not to send the Ticonderoga cannon to Boston but to "hold them" down at Lake George for return to the British when "harmony" was restored.

Ethan, quite in character, was furious and shot off a protest to Congress about all its shilly-shallying. He regarded the British now as the enemy; it was a very simple matter, and there was no point in beating about the bush. What he wanted was to marshall a force and attack Canada before the British had time to react. Arnold might have control of the garrison at Ticonderoga, but Ethan Allen was still the most important figure in the Hampshire Grants, and what he said was heard even in the great hall in Philadelphia.

Ethan began to prepare for the invasion. He wrote numerous letters to Canadians in the north and sent emissaries to the Indian tribes to secure their support. He wrote the chief of the Caughnawagas, whose camp was near Montreal: "I want your Warriors to join with me and my Warriors like brothers and ambush the Regulars. If you will I will give you much money, blankets, tomahawks, knives, and paint. . . ."

But Ethan was not deluded by his own prose. He understood the Indians and knew that they would go with the side they believed to be most powerful and most likely to win. "They act upon political principles," he said knowingly, and if that was a cynical appraisal it was also an accurate one. The Indians were a totally pragmatic lot. The reasoning behind the quarrels of the white men meant nothing to them. They would have been quite pleased had all the whites suddenly been swallowed up by the earth gods.

Ira, in particular, was wary of Indians. That care saved him from capture and perhaps death on at least one occasion in that spring of 1775. When the garrison of Ticonderoga surrendered, the Green Mountain Boys and Arnold's troops guarded them until Colonel Benjamin Hinman's regiment of Connecticut volunteers came to relieve them by order of Congress. Colonel Hinman did not know a great deal about this country, and Ira and some of the Green Mountain Boys undertook to help him learn. At about this time Brook Watson, the former Lord Mayor of London, arrived at Ti, as the Boys called it, having been so unfortunate as to be captured in Pennsylvania. Watson had secured passports from Congress for himself and two young Canadian merchants.

Lieutenant Ira Allen volunteered to escort the party up to Canadian territory under truce. He and several of the Boys took a bateau and their three passengers and headed north. They stopped at Crown Point for a day or so. Watson made many statements about his friendship for the Americans and his sympathy for their cause, but somehow these did not sit quite right with Ira, who was a canny young man and a shrewd judge of character. They headed on and reached Canadian territory, where on the shore they saw a party of Indians.

Ira's feeling about Watson, and his suspicion of strangers in general, caused him to approach this party very warily. He ordered the Boys to prime their weapons and be ready for trouble. Brook Watson objected. There would be no trouble, he said. These were friendly Indians and they were in Crown territory.

That was just the point, Ira suggested. He reissued the order.

Watson gave a knowing look to his two young companions and the three of them reached for their pistols, as if they had made a plan to seize control of the bateau and take the Americans captive. But Green Mountain Boys were not easily surprised. Watson found himself looking down the barrel of a long rifle, and his hand eased away from his belt. He then asked, with all the dignity he could muster, to be put ashore. A disgusted and suspicious Ira Allen was ready to oblige.

The Boys rowed the boat into a swamp three miles from the house of a Frenchman, and gave their erstwhile guests instructions for reaching the place. Then they left, Ira knowing it would take the others a good two hours to make their way through the muck, and that was all the start he and the Boys would need. They returned safely.

Ethan Allen, even after the disaster at St. John's, still hoped that there would be an opportunity to attack Canada and eliminate that British stronghold by a combination of military action and political accommodation with the French Canadians in Quebec. Despite a general distrust by the French of the American colonists to the south who shared neither their religion nor most of their tradition, Ethan continued to look towards an alliance.

Consequently, Captain Remember Baker was sent on a scouting mission to Île-aux-Noix, south of St. John's. Ethan had been talking for some time to Arnold about fortifying the island. Captain Baker and his Green Mountain Boys took a bateau along the lake and approached the area in the dead of night. They landed in a bay off the island and secured their boat, then walked overland to the point where they could observe any activity on the island.

Remember Baker, who had lived and traveled among Indians for years, was not so wary of them this day as he ought to have been. An Indian hunting party traveling the territory came across their boat. Never loath to take advantage of such a chance, the Indians got into it and began rowing along the lake, past the island. Soon they passed the point where Baker and his men were stationed, observing. Baker stepped forward to announce to the Indians that they had his boat and he wanted it back. There was no trouble between the Americans and Indians, he said, and there would not be. All they had to do was to give up his boat.

The Indians were of a different mind. A boat on the lake bank, untended, was anybody's boat. Now it was their boat. They paid no attention and increased the stroke to pass the point.

Baker warned them. Unless they turned back he would fire.

One Indian brave raised his gun and took aim at the Green Mountain captain, who raised his own weapon to snap off a shot. But Remember's flint misfired, and while he was fumbling with it the Indian shot him dead.

The Green Mountain Boys began firing from behind their trees, and the Indians fled, but soon they returned in force, drove off the Green Mountain Boys, and took Baker's body to the lake bank. They cut off the head and carried it in triumph to St. John's, where they exhibited it to the British to show them what great friends to the king they had proved to be. His Majesty's officers, repelled by the Indians' lack of nicety, decently bought the head and recovered the body and buried them. But the die of the Caughnawagas was cast. They were the enemies of the Green Mountain Boys.

The death of Cousin Remember cast a gray shadow across the lives of the Allens, for Baker was a very living part of the Onion River Company and a vital force in the Green Mountain Boys' organization. But the war would not wait for grief, and neither Ethan nor any of the others had time to mourn. A few days later, Ira was off scouting St. John's and writing back to Colonel Arnold, who had established his headquarters in the comfort of the former British sloop now stationed at Crown Point.

One reason Arnold spent so much time aboard the warship was the vexing question of divided command of the forces. The Connecticut Committee of War still held that Ethan was the commander of Ticonderoga. But Ethan's troops, the Green Mountain Boys, had mostly gone home, and whatever claims Ethan could lay were given strength only by the Connecticut men. The diminutive Arnold was showing his authority more and more. Finally Ethan called a meeting of the Committee of War and suggested that it was time for a showdown.

There was only one way to achieve such a confrontation—send delegates to Philadelphia to plead the case before Congress. The committee agreed and voted to send Ethan and Seth Warner to Philadelphia to explain what had happened at Ticonderoga, and to make a case for Ethan's command and for prompt action against the British in Canada before their position was too strong.

On June 22, Ethan and Warner arrived in Philadelphia to present their case.

The first item of business was to straighten out the situation of the Green Mountain Boys. As far as New York was concerned, this organization had been nothing but the lawless "Bennington Mobb." But circumstances alter cases. Philip Schuyler, one of the great gentlemen of Albany and a prime figure in the struggle for New York suzerainty over the Hampshire Grants, was now a general in the army of the United Colonies of America, as they called themselves, and he was in charge of the northern department, which included New York and the Grants. He was eager to have fighting men, and no matter what else one might say about them, the Green Mountain Boys were good fighting men in their own territory. So Congress listened to what Ethan and Warner had to say, and recommended that New York employ the Green Mountain Boys in the New York forces.

Ethan came to his next proposal, the advocacy of an invasion of Canada. The Congress was not nearly so enthusiastic about this idea, but they referred it to General Schuyler with their tentative blessing. That was as far as the gentlemen would go.

The next step for Ethan and Warner, then, was to head for New York City to present their case, armed with the signed recommendation of Congress. Here was an odd situation: both men had prices on their heads placed by the New York authorities, whose last mention of them had been the suggestion that they could be shot on sight by lawful citizens. Yet they were now knocking on the door of the New York Assembly and offering to join forces in a common cause.

The Yorkers were not very happy about it all. Ethan and Warner were kept in an anteroom cooling their heels while the delegates to the Assembly decided whether to listen to them or put them in prison. But the common danger was real. Recognizing it, the New Yorkers swallowed their old resentments and authorized the establishment of a force of five hundred men, who would be paid from the date of the attack on Fort Ticonderoga.

In mid-July, Ethan and Warner were back in Bennington at the Catamount Tavern of Stephen Fay, organizing the military force and planning the assault that Ethan was so eager to make on Canada while there was yet time to win.

Before the beginning of the last week of July, Ethan rode on to Fort Ticonderoga, where General Schuyler had taken over command from the irritating Colonel Benedict Arnold. Ethan presented his papers and his plans, and at Schuyler's invitation took up residence at the fort to wait for the general's decision.

General Schuyler was not a man to take action swiftly. Before there could be any discussion of the final plans, the organization of the Green Mountain Boys had to be perfected.

This formality should not have been of concern to anyone. Ethan was on the New York payroll as a colonel and had already drawn an advance against his pay. But on July 26, at Dorset, the town committees of the Grants met to ratify all that had been done by Congress and the New York Assembly.

Ethan should have been there—he should have been on hand days before to rally his people. For a new element had been added to the situation in the Grants. New York was no longer the enemy. In the coming of war and a common cause, New York was an ally and the new regiment was to be enlisted under the New York military department, with General Philip Schuyler in command.

Either Ethan was blind to the dangers or he felt he had to remain at Ticonderoga for some reason. In any event, all Ethan's enemies came out of the woods. He had remarkably many of them. He had trod on the toes of the churches. He had punished several respected citizens for their adherence to Yorkerism. And now these enemies, who were original Grants settlers now growing middle-aged, saw a chance to strike back at Ethan Allen for his high and mighty ways of the past.

Ira Allen was elected a lieutenant of the Green Mountain Regiment. Heman and Heber were elected captains. Samuel Safford, a good friend of Ethan's, was elected major. But when it came to choosing the commander, Ethan was ignored and Seth Warner was chosen by an overwhelming vote.

There had been some grumbling in the ranks about Ethan's leadership. After the St. John's defeat, some men said Ethan had led them badly and had disgraced them. Later historians would claim that Ethan had left two or three men in the field—deserted them, so to speak. But this was nonsense. The Green Mountain Boys had one rule: each man took care of himself. They fought as irregulars, dispersed when told, and met again where told.

No, the men who put Ethan down were not the Green Mountain Boys, but their fathers, uncles, and cousins, members of the town committees—the politicians, as it were.

And suddenly Ethan was out in the cold.

Here was a lesson for the Allens. It was not enough to lead

the people of the Grants into action. From now on it was necessary that the opinions of the people be carefully assessed and guided. What happened to Ethan in the election at Dorset could easily happen again if they were not careful. Ethan, the leader and organizer of all that counted in the Grants, was suddenly dispossessed at a time when "authority" really began to mean something.

Yet, in retrospect, if Ethan had not been cast aside as colonel of the Green Mountain Regiment, the course of American and Vermont history might have been quite different. The Regiment, once formed, served creditably enough; but except at the coming battles of Hubbardton and Bennington, it would not really be distinguished. Off fighting under Schuyler, Gates, and Washington, as the Green Mountain Regiment did, the Allens might not have distinguished themselves any more than Seth Warner did. Warner's was an admirable record, but it was not earthshaking—and what the Allen brothers were about to do in the next few years would indeed shake the earth beneath them.

The Captive

AT Ticonderoga, where he had remained in the full belief that he would be confirmed as leader of his Green Mountain Boys, Ethan Allen took the action of the town committees much better than might have been expected. He was stunned at first. Then he saw why he had been defeated. As he wrote Governor Trumbull of Connecticut, it was the old farmers, the original settlers in the Hampshire Grants, who had defeated him. The vote had not been put to the Boys themselves, who were overwhelmingly in favor of their commander. What Ethan had not foreseen was that the cold breath he had felt in recent months would become a wind that blew him out of power. The "old farmers," as he called them, had not previously enjoyed an opportunity to show their resentment of Ethan Allen and his highhanded ways. Some of them believed it would be possible to come to an accommodation with New York, if the Allens were not working to prevent any settlement in order to protect their Onion River venture. Over the past four years, Ethan's sometimes abrasive leadership had opened wounds, and in their choice of the new officers, the Grantsmen had a chance to heal their resentment.

Benedict Arnold was pleased by Ethan's ouster. General Schuyler was surprised—but also pleased, because he had his own scores to settle with Ethan about the Grants.

By rights Ethan should have disappeared into obscurity, rejected by his own kind. But Ethan did not understand rejection. He appeared in Schuyler's room and offered cheerfully to serve under the general in any capacity. He told his friends and brothers that he quite forgave the town fathers of the Grants for their irritation with him, and that he would do anything he could to help Seth Warner.

General Schuyler at first refused to have anything to do with Ethan Allen. He had always felt Allen was a wild and undisciplined rogue. But soon came reverberations: all was not going well in the recruitment of the Green Mountain Regiment. Many of the old Boys who had served under Ethan declared they would not serve under another commander, even Seth Warner. And Warner and the others pressed Schuyler to amend the situation by employing Ethan.

Reluctantly Schuyler agreed to take Ethan as a civilian scout of the northern territory, if he would agree not to interfere in military matters. Ethan was eager to agree, and he continued to press for early action against the British in Canada. But Schuyler was not to be hurried, and now that Ethan had been rejected by the towns of his own Grants, Ethan's words were heard with something less than full respect in the New York camp.

As Ethan and the other Allens knew very well from their long treks in the forests of the northland, the season of an army in these woods was very brief. The frost could be expected early in September, and after that anything could happen. There might be snow in September. Usually there would be a long Indian summer, but it might be rain instead of warmth that greeted any army anywhere in the field. There was the certainty that December would turn cold and that January and February would be months in which no army could move at all—waters frozen, the snows deep as a man's head. To be safe, action had to begin in early summer.

Ethan knew all these things as well as any man, but this time he was trapped by the flow of events. Schuyler delayed and delayed again. July became August, and that month slipped away. Then one day very near the end of August, when men who knew the land must be putting aside any hopes of military action for the year, scouts brought word that the British at St. John's had embarked on construction of several ships. Up to this point Colonel Arnold's sloop of war was the most powerful vessel on the lake, and with Colonel Skene's schooner, the Americans maintained full control of the waterway. The British building program could change all that very quickly.

Schuyler was at home in Saratoga nursing a foot swollen with gout. In charge was General Richard Montgomery, a man of about Ethan's own age—nearly forty—who had no prejudices against the leader of the Green Mountain Boys. The force at

Ticonderoga had been augmented to more than twelve hundred men, and Montgomery decided to act. All summer long, if they had done nothing else, the Americans had been preparing for action. They had built and acquired fifty bateaux. Urged on by events and by officers eager for action to break the monotony, the general moved. By six o'clock on the night of August 28, 1775, the Colonial force was in motion. Soldiers in their bateaux were heading down the lake for St. John's.

Ethan was pleased to go along as civilian scout, although it was also his understanding that he had the right to command detachments if the situation called for it. Ira Allen, now a lieutenant in the Green Mountain Regiment, was attached directly to General Montgomery's headquarters as a scout and messenger, for he knew the northern woods better than nearly any other man now that Remember Baker was gone.

The American army moved haltingly down the lake to try to stop the British shipbuilding program and, perhaps, even to capture Montreal. That was Ethan's prodding dream.

"By doing this," he wrote later, "Canada will easily be brought into Union and confederacy with the United States of America. Such an event would put it out of the power of the western tribes of Indians to carry on a war with us, and be a solid and durable bar against any farther inhuman barbarities committed on our frontier inhabitants, by cruel and bloodthirsty savages; for it is impossible for them to carry on a war except they are supported by the trade and commerce of some civilized nation; which to them would be impractical, did Canada compose a part of the American empire."

On September 4 the American force reached and occupied Île-aux-Noix, which they found deserted. It made a fine base for the attack they expected to launch on St. John's. Ethan was with this party, and he and some of the Green Mountain Boys were sent off into the woods to pacify and recruit the Indians for the American cause. Ethan was a mountain of a man, strong and fearless, and his reputation traveled everywhere in Indian territory. He dressed in buckskins, he knew the woods as well as any brave, he could shoot better than most of them, and his feats of strength were legendary. Ethan Allen was a man among men.

He was also a visionary, who spoke with great conviction of the Yankee mission to liberate the land from the redcoats. To the Indians this meant perpetual hunting grounds and freedom of movement, and Ethan was not above promising what he could never deliver. His rhetoric was effective, and he moved swiftly and quietly through the country, talking to Indian and white settler alike about the coming of the Americans and the need to join the rebellion against the king in London.

Word of Ethan's activity soon reached Montreal, where Governor Carleton was preparing to stop the Americans. Carleton wrote home to London that these woodsmen were hurting the British cause, particularly among the Indians.

At the end of a week, Ethan rejoined General Montgomery's force, which had moved to the outskirts of St. John's. Ethan wanted to take command of a unit and lead the force against the British. But Montgomery would not have it. He had perfectly competent regular officers to lead his troops. Ethan's competence as a general was not considered very impressive, considering his previous foray against St. John's and its nearly disastrous outcome.

But on his own home ground, the green forest, Ethan had no peer save in his own family and entourage of Green Mountain Boys. Montgomery knew it. He refused Ethan's offer to lead the troops against St. John's, but he asked Ethan instead to undertake a far more dangerous mission for which the woodsman was perfectly suited. He wanted Ethan to take letters out among the Canadians and Indians once again to let them know that the American design was totally against the British garrisons and not against the people. Montgomery particularly wanted to allay the fear of the French that their Catholic religion would be banned by the Americans and that they would be otherwise molested. And he wanted intelligence. Ethan listened and reluctantly agreed to undertake this second mission.

St. John's was on the west bank of the Sorel River, only twenty-eight miles south of Montreal. From the outset, Ethan was deep in enemy territory. He went out with a party of sympathetic Canadians and only a handful of American friends.

On September 24, he was in Longueuil. He had been out for

a week preaching the American doctrine to Canadians and Indians. With a force of eighty men, he now intended to head for LaPrairie, then a picturesque French village on the St. Lawrence, just nine miles southwest of Montreal. From LaPrairie he would go on back to Montgomery's camp to report.

But that morning, Ethan and his party had gone scarcely two miles out of their camp when he encountered John Brown, the man from Pittsfield who had originally discussed with him the capture of Ticonderoga in those dim, distant days before rebellion. Brown was now a major in the American army, attached to General Montgomery's staff, and he was on the same general mission that Ethan was—recruiting Canadians and passing the word of American good will.

Ethan had recruited several hundred volunteers and sent them along to Montgomery. He had with him about 110 men at that moment. Brown had two hundred men, and he said he had an idea to offer Ethan.

They stopped at a nearby house and went inside for a private conference. Major Brown proposed that Ethan go back to Longueuil, find some canoes with which the force could cross the St. Lawrence north of Montreal, and get ready to attack the city from the north. Meanwhile Brown would attack from the south and, together, they would capture Montreal and all Ethan's dreams would be realized.

Since this plan was precisely along the lines on which Ethan had been thinking for months, and since it offered him the chance to get into action that he was denied by Schuyler and Montgomery, Ethan hastened to agree. Here is his own account of the beginning:

We were most of the night crossing the river as we had so few canoes that they had to pass and repass three times, to carry my party across. Soon after daybreak I set a guard between me and the town, with special orders to let no person whatever pass or repass them, and another guard on the other end of the road, with like directions. In the meantime I reconnoitered the best ground to make a defense, expecting Major Brown's party was landed on the other side of the town, he having the day before agreed to give three huzzas with his men early in the morning, which signal I was to return, that we might each know that both parties had landed. But the sun by this time being two hours high, and the sign failing I began to conclude myself to be in a premunire, and would have crossed the river back again but I knew the enemy would have discovered such an attempt. . . .

Ethan was in a dilemma and he knew it. He could move only a third of his troops at a time. He had no alternative but to hold, or two-thirds of his men would be captured.

Ethan sent off two messages, one to Brown and the other to a Mr. Walker in L'Assomption, a French settlement not far away, asking for help.

Meanwhile, as day progressed, people began moving about the area. Ethan had all that were seen picked up and brought to him. They protested they were on the side of the Americans, but Ethan took no chances; for the moment they were all confined. One of these men managed to escape, and hastened to L'Assomption, where he found Mr. Walker, who had raised a considerable force of men to join in the assault on Montreal. When the excited fellow brought word of Ethan's weak force and the serious danger, Walker disbanded his men and never marched.

Montreal that morning was a whirlwind of excitement and worry. Sir Guy Carleton was importuned by his staff to make his escape in the warship stationed at the city before the Americans captured him, but when a messenger appeared to reveal the weakness of the Allen force, Carleton turned to the offensive. He had been prepared to board the armed schooner *Gaspée,* but now he turned. He had only forty regular soldiers to defend Montreal, but a force of four hundred citizens and Indians was raised that morning.

Ethan prepared his defenses. He was cut off from retreat by his own decision to stay with his men at all costs. It would go particularly hard with most of them if they were captured, for they were Canadians, not Americans. So Ethan walked among them, encouraging, examining the defenses, and waiting. When someone asked, he spoke with his usual assurance to tell them that help must be coming along soon from Brown or from L'Assomption.

The Carleton force was some hours in getting assembled, and it was two o'clock in the afternoon before they attacked. The Allen force was disposed around pilings, ditches, and buildings—anywhere that cover could be found for the riflemen. Ethan ordered a Canadian named Richard Young to take a detachment of nine men and guard the flank on the bank of the river, to the left of his main defense line.

Carleton's troops attacked on the front, and this suited Ethan just fine. He was certain they would never dislodge him by such tactics. But then the Canadians sent flankers out to the right. Ethan ordered John Dugan and fifty of the Canadians to repel the flank attack. Disaster! Dugan on the right and Young on the left decided to save their own skins instead of fighting, and they made off in the canoes. As the British and their allies moved in along his flanks, Ethan was reduced to a force of forty-five men, some of them wounded by this time, and was in danger of being surrounded.

Ethan ordered rapid retreat, hoping to use his knowledge and experience as a guerilla fighter to advantage. His men began to move back swiftly through the brush. But his attackers followed, maintaining the pressure on flanks and line. After a mile of retreat, Ethan decided on a stand. He was certain that there would be a price on his head because of his spying and propaganda work among the people and the Indians, and he determined to sell his life as expensively as he might. He stood fast. One of the British officers rushed forward and fired a musket at him, but missed because he was out of breath and quivering from the run he had made. Ethan fired back and missed. Then, with only a few yards separating them, Ethan shouted that he would surrender if he and his men could be assured of decent treatment. The officer said they would be treated as prisoners of war, not rebels, and Ethan then surrendered his force of thirty-eight men, seven of them wounded.

The British officer ordered the American to come forward with his men. Ethan did, and handed over his sword, hilt first. Just then, an Indian brave, head shaved for war and feathers in his hair, came whooping toward Ethan.

"As he approached near me," Ethan wrote later, "his hellish visage was beyond all description; snakes' eyes appear innocent in comparison of his; his features extorted; malice, death, murder, and the wrath of devils and damned spirits are the emblems of his countenance; and, in less than twelve feet of me, [he] presented his firelock."

Ethan had just handed over his sword. He grasped the red coat of the British officer and whirled the officer between himself and the murderous Indian. The Indian flew around to the other side and leveled his gun again. Ethan swung the officer about, using him as a shield, and as the Indian brave turned, Ethan turned, interposing the Indian's ally between them.

Up came another Indian equally bent on the destruction of the American commander. Ethan whirled his officer around and back again, until finally an Irish soldier came up, swearing that by Jesus he would kill the savages if they touched the prisoner, and drove them off with fixed bayonet.

Ethan let go of the officer, who shook himself and regained composure enough to remark that he was happy to see Colonel Allen.

"I'd be a damned sight happier to be seeing you in Montgomery's camp," said Ethan.

They walked two miles, Ethan between a British officer and a Frenchman, until they came to the military barracks of the garrison, where they waited upon General Richard Prescott, commander of the British forces.

Prescott asked the captive his name, and Ethan told him he was Colonel Ethan Allen of the Green Mountain Boys.

Was that the Colonel Allen who took Ticonderoga? asked the general.

The same, said Ethan.

That admission sent General Prescott into a fury. His face reddened; he stood up and raged. He waved his cane above Ethan's head and dressed him up and down, calling him a damned rebel and many other names.

Ethan's temper was never very long. When someone insulted him he took a very great risk. The general had better stop waving that cane around, Ethan warned as he shook his fist at the officer. If Prescott touched Ethan with it, he was damned well going to meet his maker at that moment.

Captain McCloud, the general's aide, pulled him by the skirt of his jacket and whispered that it was most unseemly to strike a prisoner.

Quivering with rage, Prescott then turned his attention to the Canadians who had been with Ethan, and ordered his sergeant's guard to come up.

"Shoot those men," he ordered.

Ethan was aghast. He had bargained for decent treatment for all those with him. Now he stepped forward, opened his shirt, and told General Prescott to thrust his bayonet into the Allen breast before he killed anyone else.

The guard waited before taking action. General Prescott stood still a moment, rage and thought clouding his face. Thought won the day. He made a signal to desist, and looked Ethan in the eye coldly.

"I will not execute you now," the general said to his prisoner, "but you shall grace a halter at Tyburn, God damn you."

Pirates or Patriots?

THE word that Ethan Allen had been captured by the British in a virtually singlehanded attempt to take Montreal reached the American camp at St. John's through Colonel Seth Warner of the Green Mountain Boys, and in his laconic way he had little to say about it. Major Brown, who had fomented the whole affair, had nothing at all to say, and drifted away lest he take his part of the blame.

For blame there was. The British were delighted to have taken so big a fish—the man who had outraged British sovereignty by capturing His Majesty's fort at Ticonderoga. They were not slow to send their own propaganda waves throughout Canada. See, said the Loyalist reports, he who goes against the king gets his comeuppance. It was widely rumored that Ethan Allen was going in chains to London to be hanged.

Ethan was in chains. General Prescott, still red with rage, ordered one of his officers to take his captive to the *Gaspée* and to confine him there in irons. His handcuffs were standard, but the irons they put on his feet weighed thirty pounds and the shackles were attached to a bar eight feet long. The British were taking no chances that this prisoner might escape them. Ethan was taken deep into the ship's hold. There he was confined in a dark hole with only a chest on which he might sit or sleep. Because of the irons, he could rest only on his back.

Captain Royal, commander of the *Gaspée*, was embarrassed at the treatment he was giving his prisoner, but he informed Ethan that he had been ordered to be unusually severe and that the general was watching to see that his orders were carried out. One guard was detailed to watch Ethan at all times, bayonet fixed, so he had no privacy. He did manage to persuade a guard to give him two little blocks to put under the ends of the bar on his leg irons so they would not press against his ankles as he slept.

After a few days Ethan asked that his irons be loosened so he might lie on his side. The request was refused. The captain had no options. But the captain and the officers of the ship could take pity on the poor prisoner in the matter of food, and Lieutenant Bradley, in particular, saw that Ethan had a drink of grog every day and food from the officers' mess.

For the next six weeks, Ethan was confined aboard the *Gaspée*. He wrote letters to General Prescott asking for better treatment. They were not answered. Then he wrote to Sir Guy Carleton, the governor, and neither was this letter answered. Ethan gave better than he received: the air of his prison cell was blue with his curses as he called down the wrath of Jehovah on his enemies. In his own wrath, according to some accounts, he bit off the head of a tenpenny nail that was used as a fastener in his handcuff, and the alarmed British captors replaced it with a stout padlock. A Dr. Dace, who had lived for some time in New York, often came down into his cell to abuse him and laughed that this great scoundrel, who should have been punished by Governor Tryon, was now headed for the gallows in London. Ethan spat and snarled and challenged Dace to a duel, but the doctor begged off: he did not duel with criminals.

In October, the Americans began to move against Canada on two fronts. Montgomery attacked St. John's, threatening Montreal. Farther to the east, Ethan's old acquaintance Benedict Arnold was moving against Quebec. He intended to link up with Montgomery on the St. Lawrence, between Quebec and Montreal.

When the Montgomery attack on St. John's began, Ethan was shipped downstream to a vessel off Quebec. His escort was Captain McCloud, whom he had met earlier on the field above Montreal. McCloud was very decent to Ethan; his irons were removed and he was treated as an officer for the first time. Ethan was given over to the charge of a Captain Littlejohn, with whom he became so friendly that Ethan offered to act as the captain's second in a duel with an officer from a British man-of-war. The duel never came off, but Ethan had won the respect of Littlejohn.

In November, General Arnold and a handful of his men managed to reach the St. Lawrence opposite Quebec, after a dreadful trip through the wilderness. The British immediately decided they must make new arrangements for their important prisoner, and Ethan was moved to the dispatch carrier *Adamant,* commanded by Brook Watson, the former merchant and Lord Mayor of London who had tried to trick Ira into captivity a few months before. Watson was delighted to have in his power the brother of the man who had escaped him, and he now proved that he was every bit as malicious and untrustworthy as Ira had suspected. Watson and the Tories with him contrived to make the lives of the American prisoners dreadful indeed. For Ethan was no longer alone. All the prisoners taken with him at the battle above Montreal were on board this prison ship. All were subjected to the full spite of the American Tories, who hated no one so much as the men who were rebelling against king and country, and who had seized their property and driven them out of the American Colonies.

Thirty-four men, Ethan among them, were assigned to a compartment 20 by 22 feet, with two tubs for their excrement. That was where they lived on the voyage to England.

The other men were confined, and then Ethan was led to the tiny door that opened into this horror chamber. He refused to enter. Brook Watson insisted that the place was good enough for a rebel.

One Tory went too far. He stood up next to Ethan and said that the leader of the Green Mountain Boys ought to have been executed for his rebellion against New York. Then he spat in Ethan's face. That was a mistake. Ethan was handcuffed. Nonetheless, he pushed aside his captor soldiers with their fixed bayonets and sprang on the Tory. He knocked him down and then went after him, but the Tory scrambled between the legs of the soldiers, and they prodded Ethan back with their bayonets. Otherwise he might well have killed the miscreant.

Ethan stood there and challenged the Tory to a fight. The man blenched and trembled until Brook Watson stepped in and ordered Ethan driven by bayonet into the filthy hole.

Watson was determined to torture these men as much as he could. He dared not starve them to death, but he did do something almost equally effective. He made sure they had full allowance of food, primarily salt pork and beef—and then he refused them all but a minimal quantity of water. Ethan asked for more water. The guards sneered at him. The men pleaded; they were cursed as rebels. But they were given a gill of rum per man each day, and bad as life got during the forty days of the voyage to England, Ethan was certain that the rum saved their lives. They were half crazed with thirst. They developed diarrhea and fever. Lice swarmed over them and the stench of their hole grew almost unbearable. But not a man among them died, and finally they arrived at Falmouth in Cornwall on December 22, 1775.

The poor, filthy scarecrows of men were then marched a mile through the streets to Pendennis Castle. A huge crowd watching the American rebels became so unruly that the officers had to draw their swords to force their way through the mob.

Ethan and his men were ordered confined in close arrest, by the demand of Governor Carleton of Canada. Brook Watson, the American-hater, hied himself off to London, hoping at least for a knighthood for his harsh treatment of the King's enemies— only to discover that he was very coldly received. Indeed, instead of being honored for his treatment of the prisoners, he was chastised. Change was in the air in London.

Meanwhile, the other Allens were carrying on their affairs as best they might. Levi had returned to Salisbury not quite sure where his loyalties lay, awaiting the outcome of the negotiations. There were many at that time, including members of Congress, who still hoped for a reconciliation between the Colonies and London, and Levi was among them.

Heman was with the Green Mountain Boys at the siege of Canada, which was to continue until the spring of 1776. And Ira, who this fall had reached the ripe old age of twenty-four, was serving as a scout for Montgomery in the initial phases of the Canada campaign.

Ira was hurt and furious when he learned that Ethan had been captured. Colonel Seth Warner had been with Brown at LaPrairie when Ethan was approached to move on Montreal.

Ira felt that Warner had deserted his brother under fire, and he spoke bitterly of the commander of the Green Mountain Boys ever after. As October moved along, Warner and a majority of the Green Mountain Boys lost their taste for sustained action, as was their way, and without an Ethan Allen to inspire and harangue them, they began to head for home. Montgomery was so irate with them that he complained to Schuyler about the regiment. "The rascally Green Mountain Boys have left me in the lurch," he wrote his commander in Albany.

But not Ira. He was committed, and his commitment was strengthened by the capture of his oldest brother. He became Montgomery's most trusted messenger. The Green Mountain Boys drifted home as winter closed in, but Ira was called upon more and more often. He carried a message to Sir Guy Carleton, who was then aboard the *Gaspée:* Ethan's prison ship was now the governor's refuge in the siege of his city. The letter demanded Carleton's surrender. He did not surrender, but escaped in an open boat down the St. Lawrence to Quebec to lead the defense against that other American commander, Benedict Arnold.

On the night of December 31, 1775, General Montgomery planned to assault Quebec City. He sent Ira and Captain Robert Cochran of the Green Mountain Boys to lead a feint attack on the side of Cape Diamond, a great jutting rock that protects the city and the Plains of Abraham. Diverted by the feint, the British were to be outflanked and beaten. Cochran, Ira, and their men would set off rockets and make a good deal of noise that night while Montgomery led the main attack below with the forces of Arnold.

Somehow, their French guide led Ira and Cochran astray and cost them valuable time. They put him under guard and then went off alone to try to repair the damage, but they were late. The night was black and cold, and a heavy snow was falling as they clambered up the steep sides of the rock and made their signals, drawing attention to the extreme eastern point of the place.

Below, General Montgomery personally led the attack on the

British palisade, until he was killed by a cannon shot. The night's action ended in disaster. Montgomery was dead, and over three hundred Americans were taken prisoner.

Deprived of the commander who had trusted him, Ira saw little more important action in the long days of delay and forlorn hope that remained in the Quebec campaign. By February he was relieved and he headed home, alone and on horseback, for the Onion River country that now seemed so lonely with the death of Remember Baker, his best friend and cousin, and the capture of Ethan.

The Canadian campaign, failure though it was, made one vital change in the struggle between the redcoats and the men in buckskin and homespun. The struggle had become a real war. General Prescott, who had waved his cane so threateningly above Ethan's head and then threatened him with death at the end of a rope, was captured at Montreal. When his treatment of Ethan Allen became known he was clapped in irons, thrown into a filthy cell, and threatened with death—just as he had done to Ethan.

Sir Guy Carleton and General Prescott had regarded Ethan and the other Americans as no better than pirates. That was in the fall of 1775, when Britain's leaders still did not understand that they had something more on their hands than the machinations of a few malcontents. But as Ethan languished in his irons, Congress reconvened in Philadelphia. All thirteen colonies were represented for the first time. Within a few weeks Congress had authorized the creation of a navy and was sending envoys abroad to seek aid from other nations. An outraged King George declared the Colonies to be in open revolt, even though Congress indicated that it would remain loyal to the Crown if Americans were allowed to manage their own internal affairs. So to call Ethan Allen a mere felon, as many had done, was an oversimplification that bothered many men in Parliament. As it turned out, had Ethan and his hundred men marched on Montreal without the help of the elusive Major Brown, they might have captured the place, and instead of being a British prisoner Ethan would have been an American hero.

[PLATE 1] No authentic, drawn-from-life portrait of Ethan Allen has come down to us. This lack is especially remarkable in the case of a figure like Ethan, who was hardly one to shun celebrity. He must have posed for portraits, but if he did they are lost. What likenesses of Ethan we have are conjectural; this engraving, which appeared on the title page of an 1853 Allen biography, is typical. (*Courtesy Vermont Historical Society*)

Lives of Great Americans.

Published Monthly.   Number Four.

Ethan Allen.

BEADLE AND ADAMS, 98 WILLIAM STREET, N. Y.

[PLATE 2] Ethan appears on the cover of a periodical dating from about 1861.
The artist, having no idea what Ethan really looked like, has given him a marked
resemblance to George Washington—an ironic choice of model in view of the
sometimes strained relations between Ethan and the Father of our Country.
(*Courtesy Vermont Historical Society*)

Of these two heroic military statues of Ethan, the one below [PLATE 3] can be seen today at the Vermont State House in Montpelier. It is the work of the celebrated nineteenth century sculptor and architect William Rutherford Mead. Above it is the famous "lost statue" of Ethan [PLATE 4]. Made before 1853 by the sculptor Kinney, the statue disappeared some years later and has not been seen since. Men who knew Ethan during his life stated that Kinney's statue was a good likeness of the hero. (*Courtesy Vermont Agency of Development and Community Affairs; Vermont Historical Society*)

[PLATE 5] Of the seven brothers and sisters of the Allen clan besides Ethan, Ira is the only other of whom pictures exist. This portrait was made sometime around 1795, in the period of Ira's European adventures. (*Courtesy Vermont Historical Society*)

Almost at the moment Ethan arrived in England in chains, matters were coming to a head. In London, it became very clear to Parliament that if Ethan Allen and the other rebels in Pendennis Castle were tried as criminals and hanged, then something less than pleasant was likely to befall General Prescott and the several hundred other British officers and men who had been captured in the battles so far. As the Duke of York warned in the House of Lords, the result of it all might be dreadful.

Immediately on arrival, therefore, Ethan could sense a changed attitude toward him and the other prisoners in England. Food and wine were sent to Ethan every day from the castle kitchens. Ladies and gentlemen came from fifty miles around to see the notorious prisoner, and several times he was taken to a garden in the castle where groups waited. Ethan then made speeches, at which he was very expert, and joked with the ladies and gentlemen about public affairs.

What had been his occupation in life before he became a state criminal? asked one.

He had studied divinity but was a conjurer by profession, said Ethan, his eyes crinkling.

Ha, said the Englishman, he had certainly conjured himself into a fix.

Right, said Ethan, but he had also conjured the British out of Ticonderoga.

The whole party laughed.

Another day, Ethan made a long speech to these gentry about the impossibility of Britain's ever conquering the Americans. When he finished, his throat was dry, so he asked one of the men to order up a bowl of punch from the servants. The gentleman was surprised at Ethan's temerity, but he did so and when it came directed that it be given Ethan.

Ethan turned it aside with a lordly gesture. He would take it only from the hands of his gentleman friend, he said. So the gentleman gave it to him. Ethan offered him the first drink, but the Englishman said no, he could not drink with a state criminal. Ethan picked up the bowl and downed the whole in a few gulps, amid the gasps of the shocked ladies.

If they wanted a show, Ethan would give them one they would not forget. He was an immense figure of a man, big, beefy, and red-faced. He was dressed in a short jacket of fawn-skin, homespun breeches and worsted stockings, a heavy pair of nailed shoes, and a red woolen cap—clothing the gentlemen of England had never seen before.

One young dandy claimed to know the Americans very well. Ethan might as well quit talking, he said, because he knew for a fact that Americans could not bear the smell of gunpowder.

Ethan challenged the gentleman then and there to a duel, but was rebuffed. The dandy sniffed and said he would not lower himself to fight a criminal.

Then he should treat the Americans with more respect, said Ethan, particularly if he was afraid to fight them.

So it went. Two clergymen came to see Ethan, and he delighted in baiting them with phrases from the Bible. Then they got down to a philosophical discussion, in which Ethan absolutely reveled; he played his role of Deist and philosopher and kept turning the reverend gentlemen into corners.

Meanwhile in London, the debates as to the fate of the captives raged through Parliament and the press. Ethan and his companions waited anxiously. Suddenly, early in January, the Americans were removed from their prison and taken to the frigate *Solebay*. They were told nothing. Perhaps they were being taken to be hanged. Ethan was prepared even for this. He wrote:

I could not but feel inwardly, extremely anxious for my fate. This I however concealed from the prisoners, as well as from the enemy, who were perpetually shaking the halter at me. I nevertheless treated them with scorn and contempt . . . Such a conduct, I judged, would have a more probable tendency to my preservation than concession and timidity. This therefore, was my deportment; and I had lastly determined in my own mind that if a cruel death must inevitably be my portion, I would face it undaunted.

But their transfer did not mean death. Quite the opposite, it represented the direct intervention of King George III, who put an end to the whole debate about the Americans by ordering that they be returned to America and held as prisoners of war. Ethan's protests, the rough treatment handed General Prescott, and the realization that the "incident" in America was far more than a simple matter of criminal rebels, suddenly struck home in London. Ethan was no longer a common criminal, but an honorable prisoner of war.

The Long Voyage Home

CAPTAIN Symonds, the commander of the frigate *Solebay*, had been brought up in the iron tradition of the quarterdeck, and he had no use for rebels, patriots, criminals, or whatever they might be called.

Symonds had his orders from the Admiralty regarding the motley human cargo that he was called upon to transport, and it was not his place to question orders. But he would be damned if he would have anything more than necessary to do with his pile of flotsam that had been foisted upon him. And he wanted to make his position clear.

So on the afternoon of January 8, 1776, when the freed, unshackled prisoners were escorted to the frigate, Captain Symonds ordered all prisoners and crew on deck. It was the custom of the Royal Navy that before the beginning of a voyage the crew should be read the Articles of Command and be reminded of the awesome power of the Navy and its captains. Having done this duty, the captain turned on his heel, looked coldly at the prisoners, and announced loudly that he did not want to see any of them on deck.

"And that particularly means you sir, Colonel Allen, for this is a place for gentlemen to walk."

Whereupon Ethan was taken in hand by a young lieutenant, who, aping his captain, strode stiffly down to the cable tier in the guts of the frigate and announced that this was to be Ethan's quarters while he was aboard.

The damp had settled deep in Ethan's bones during the stay in the musty Pendennis Castle, and he was suffering from a severe cold. So he did not argue or insult the young lieutenant as would have been his normal response to such treatment. He made himself as comfortable as he could in the close and uneven quarters and tried to get a little rest. But his sleep was disturbed by worry: what if the British government had taken this easy way out to rid themselves of unwanted trouble? It would be a simple enough matter for some "accident" to deprive the world of Ethan Allen and his companions while, remarkably, the captain and crew of the frigate were saved. The more Ethan considered, the more he believed he was the victim of a very clever scheme to murder them all. For two days he brooded. Then, on the third day he bathed himself and shaved as best he could in his wretched surroundings, and went up on deck. There he encountered Captain Symonds, striding along the quarterdeck in his long coat of blue.

"Did I not order you never to come on deck?" demanded the furious captain.

"And at the same time you said it is the place for gentlemen to walk," rejoined Ethan. "I am Colonel Allen. I don't believe we have been properly introduced."

Symonds turned pale with rage.

"God damn you, sir, be careful not to walk on the same side of the deck that I do."

Ethan knew that he had been wrong, that the captain was more afraid of him and his men than he could ever let on. Ethan walked the decks then as he chose, except that when the captain was on deck he stayed on the opposite side of the ship from him, and when Symonds occasionally ordered Ethan below in one of his fits of rage, Ethan always complied, only to reappear as soon as the captain had gone.

The Americans and their Canadian allies were befriended by some members of the crew. Ethan, in particular, drew the attention of an Irishman named Gilligan, who was master at arms. Gilligan offered Ethan space in his stateroom. It was a tiny affair, between decks, and walled off from the crew's quarters only by canvas, but it was far better than the sloping sides of the cable tier, and Ethan was pleased to accept the offer.

The frigate put in at Cork after a wicked storm that made some old sailors believe the ship was going under. There Ethan and the others were befriended by a number of Irish merchants, some of them showing their disapproval of Parliament's high-handedness, others simply looking to the day when the American trade might again be restored. They provided clothes for every prisoner: an overcoat, a suit of clothing, and two shirts.

For Ethan there was more—eight fine Holland shirts and stocks, enough fine broadcloth for two suits, silk and woolen hose, two pair of shoes, and two beaver hats, one of them trimmed in gold.

The merchants also sent aboard whiskey and Geneva gin, wines, turkeys, a round of pickled beef, many other stores for Ethan and his men, and fifty guineas for Ethan.

All this provender came aboard during the absence of the captain, who was off on private business. When he returned to the ship he was furious to see that the Irish had outfitted Ethan better than he himself was provided. He took away all the wines and liquors. "Those damned American rebels are not going to be feasted by the damned rebels of Ireland," he announced loudly.

There was some commotion over the captain's arbitrary action. The second lieutenant, who had received the stores for the prisoners, was a young man named Douglass, son of an admiral, and he spoke up on behalf of the prisoners. He only gained the enmity of the captain, and the prisoners were further deprived as the commander insisted on showing his authority.

At Cork the prisoners were divided among three different warships, after Symonds saw how well they got on with the crew and the people of Ireland. He may have been concerned lest the thirty-five men arise, persuade the crew to mutiny, and seize the frigate. In any event the Americans had plenty of company on the voyage home: the *Solebay* awaited a large convoy of forty-five ships, five of them warships. On February 12 the convoy sailed. They moved down to the Bay of Biscay, where they encountered a dreadful storm that sent spindrift mast-high. Not a man could remain on deck in the pitching and crashing of the waves unless he was lashed. The ship of the line *Thunderbomb* sprang a leak and had to limp back to the English coast.

After the storm, Ethan noted a certain relaxation in the behavior of even the most devoted enemies of the Americans. Captain Symonds granted him the right to have the ship's tailor make a suit, which much improved Ethan's morale and appearance. Considering the reasons for this leniency, as was Ethan's manner, he came to the philosophical conclusion that the captain and his officers had been terribly frightened during the storm. Considering their sins, they had realized how foully they were using the prisoners; they were not prepared to meet their maker and face such charges.

"Imminent danger would have a tendency to relax the iron hand of oppression when the breast is otherwise sealed against entreaties, or a view of the excess of human suffering," wrote the homespun philosopher in his canvas-lined stateroom on the frigate.

They put in at Madeira and another Irish merchant offered Ethan food and wines, but Captain Symonds bollixed that gesture by sailing before they could be put aboard.

Madeira behind, the storm forgotten, the captain and his minions cracked down again. Ethan had money and could have purchased stores, but the purser would not sell them. Ethan fell ill and wanted to buy some medicines. The purser refused. His answer was that the sooner Ethan was dead the better. He had no interest in saving the lives of rebels.

Ethan was never one to walk away from an argument. He went to the captain to complain about the treatment and the attitude. In the first place, he said, if England did not treat him as a criminal, what right did a mere ship's captain have to do so? In the second place, the policy was foolish, for if Ethan lived he might be exchanged for some important officer—such as General Prescott. If he died, he was of no use to the English.

The captain was a fool. He needed no directions from a prisoner as to his behavior, he said loftily. The British would win the war, conquer the rebels, hang the Congress and such men as Ethan who had promoted the rebellion, recapture their own prisoners, and bring order again to America. Ethan's life was a matter of no consequence to them.

"Before you hang me, I'll die of old age if you're waiting to conquer America," said the rebel.

Such remarks did little to endear Ethan to the captain, and in fact it was a wonder that he did not "fall overboard" on the voyage. But he did not. He put up with the inconveniences, complaining all the while, and never let the captain forget his behavior. He reminded him that American captors were treating their British prisoners much better, as the Irish papers had reported. But that was because the Americans were afraid of the British, said the Captain. They expected to be reconquered and hoped to buy their souls if not their lives by lenient treatment of prisoners.

The voyage west took nearly three months; it was May 3 when the fleet anchored in the harbor at Cape Fear, North Carolina. The ships had separated, some going north, but *Solebay* and one ship of the line, *Sphynx,* remained to guard fourteen transports carrying reinforcements for His Majesty's army in North Carolina.

From his ship's perch, Ethan saw a little of the war and heard more. A detachment of soldiers, sent up the Brunswick River to clear the area of rebels, was ambushed by irregulars. They came back next day minus thirty-one men, damning and cursing the rebels who fought in so unseemly a manner. If Ethan had listened before to those who advocated an adjustment with Britain, he was becoming disabused of the idea.

Ethan was closely watched and had no chance to escape. One prisoner did get away, however: Peter Noble jumped overboard from the *Sphynx* and swam several miles to hide in the coastal forest. Eventually he reached New England and gave the first word of the prisoners.

At Cape Fear all the captives were put aboard the frigate *Mercury.* Ethan hoped that Captain James Montague would be an easier captor than Captain Symonds, but he was disappointed. Montague was far worse.

A fortnight after anchoring off Cape Fear the *Mercury* set sail for Halifax, Nova Scotia. The prisoners and the crew of the ships had been for months now without fresh provisions, and scurvy broke out. Even Ethan got a touch of it, and many prisoners fell very sick indeed. But Captain Montague flatly refused them any assistance. The purser was forbidden to sell or give them anything.

Ethan went on deck one day to complain to Montague about this treatment, and was greeted by a storm of abuse. He would be hanged as soon as he reached Halifax, the captain threatened.

Ethan already knew that he was not going to be hanged, or he would have been hanged in England. So he tried to reason with this captain, but Montague was so incensed against disloyalty to the Crown that there was no reasoning with him. Ethan began to think fondly of the days when Symonds had been his captor, for Symonds was at least quixotic enough that he might be touched by some gesture or statement. Not Montague. He was as inflexible as an iron bar.

On behalf of the suffering prisoners, Ethan approached the ship's surgeon, but he was as deaf as the captain to their pleas. Only the young midshipmen were decent to the prisoners, and they had to conceal their sympathy and help from the others.

Early in June the *Mercury* came to anchor at the Hook, off New York, and Ethan was home again for a moment. But only for a moment. His destination was Halifax. In New York the ship was visited by Governor Tryon and former Attorney General Kemp, two of Ethan's oldest enemies. The pair came aboard and walked on the windward side of the deck with the captain. Ethan walked the leeward side with the midshipmen, and the captain and his visitors looked straight ahead and paid no attention to the old Green Mountain Boy who had caused the Yorkers such pain in days past.

Captain and visitors went below, and then later went back aboard another ship of the blockade. What they said to one another was never known, but the treatment of Ethan and the other prisoners became worse thereafter.

By the time the ship reached Halifax in mid-June, scurvy had attacked the crew and they were taken ashore. But the sick prisoners were kept in the cable tier, not allowed any medicine, and finally moved to a sloop in the middle of the harbor, where they were ignored except for a guard—and half starved. Ethan sent letters to Captain Montague. They were ignored. The ship's doctor came by in a boat so close the oars grazed the sloop, but refused to acknowledge a hail from the ship. A canoe-load of Indians came by selling strawberries to the men of the ships, and one prisoner spent all he had on them. They so quickly caused him to lose his scurvy symptoms that the others tried, but vainly, to get fresh fruits. The only relief they had came from a surgeon's mate who sneaked a vial of ascorbic acid aboard the sloop. This medicine was doled out by Ethan to the worst cases, without doubt saving their lives.

Some of the guards became outraged at the inhumane treatment accorded their charges, and one of them finally was persuaded to smuggle a letter to Governor Arbuthnot of Halifax. When he got the letter the governor sent a boat with a surgeon in it, and when that officer confirmed the sad plight of the prisoners and spoke harshly against the cruel treatment given them, the governor took action. Ethan and the others were removed from the ship and taken to Halifax.

The sick were taken to the hospital for treatment. And the long voyage came to an end.

CHAPTER NINETEEN

The Dilemma of the Grants

THE people of the Hampshire Grants found themselves in a strange situation in the beginning of 1776. They seemed to be surrounded by enemies, and they had lost their most important leader, Ethan Allen, to the British. No matter what the old settlers might say about Ethan and his aggressive, godless ways, he was the one who had held the Grants together in the difficult times of the early 1770's.

Now the British were threatening them, itching to attack and divide the Colonies along the Hudson-Champlain Valley. On the west the Grantsmen were faced by New York, with whose government they had been quarreling for years. On the eastern border stood New Hampshire, whose new government had declined to get into the quarrel begun by Governor Wentworth so many years ago.

In Ethan's absence, new factors had complicated life in the Grants. The settlers who had wanted to make peace with New York to guarantee their holdings were now talking openly. The area east of the Green Mountains was filling with people who were willing to recognize New York's authority.

All these matters came to a head in January, 1776, at a convention held in Dorset to determine what course to take. Heman, Heber, and Ira Allen were there. Levi was not; he was back in Salisbury, trying to make up his mind again whether to follow the Revolution or his personal proclivity for British rule. He was concerned about Ethan, for in spite of many differences the members of the family had always been close. Levi volunteered to go to London, and even wrote General Washington about Ethan, saying he hoped to be able to do something for his brother. Levi did not know that Ethan was then already on his way back to America.

But the other Allens were in Dorset, where Heman saved the day against men of small spirit. It was a close call. The Yorkers had been busy on the evening of the Dorset convention. In fact they had instigated the whole meeting, and the first order of business was to be a resolution to see if the people would accept New York rule and "suppress all schismatic mobbs." The majority of people at this moment probably felt the only solution to the problems of the Grants was to join New York. They had wanted earlier to join New Hampshire, but that colony's government had turned them down. There were too many elements of New York control in the Connecticut Valley, and at Portsmouth the colonial fathers decided they had more important things to do than to quarrel with the powerful colony to the west. So by default, and knowing the British were restive on their northern frontier, the people of the Grants saw no other way out than to join their old enemies.

But Heman was there and was able to speak up as a major landholder. He and Joseph Bowker of Rutland soon discovered that the convention was loaded against the people who wanted to remain independent of the Yorkers. Heman used every wile— he cited the past and appealed to such men as Dr. Jonas Fay, the son of the owner of the Catamount Tavern, and James Breakenridge, on whose farm the whole fight had begun seven years earlier. In the end Heman carried the day with his eloquence. He and Fay and Breakenridge were chosen to go to Philadelphia and petition Congress for a solution to the difficulties in the Grants.

Ira Allen and Thomas Chittenden joined Heman and Fay at Heman's place in Salisbury and discussed the future. They agreed that some sort of government must be established immediately in the Grants if the people were to carry on the war and do the things necessary to save themselves and contribute to the common American good. Whatever they did, they must be careful not to let the Yorkers use the war as a pretext for seizing control of the lands that Ethan and others had fought so hard to retain. That was the only point on which they were agreed, for there was plenty of room for difference about the future. Some wanted an independent colony. Some wanted to join New Hampshire. But no one wanted to join New York.

Heman and Ira wanted to establish a separate colony, for this would be a source of pride to the people of the Grants. They had been let down badly by New Hampshire, whose governor had made the grants in the first place and whose successors had refused to support the people who bought them.

Ira marshalled the arguments. He did not want any connection with a colony that had consented to a policy under which the people were exposed to "the evil intentions of the colony of New York." He wanted to perpetuate the name of the Green Mountain Boys and the honor of their leaders. And a new colony would settle once and for all any question about the validity of the Grants.

The next few months were spent preparing the way for such a government, and as the men worked, the need became more important every day. Congress had severe financial problems. Part of the difficulty in the Grants could be resolved by selling off, in the interest of the new state government, all the undivided lands of the area. That would be an argument to sway Congress in favor of supporting the new government, the men thought, for at this moment the war was going very badly. In Quebec, Montgomery was dead and Colonel Benedict Arnold was laid low by a bullet in the leg. The siege of Quebec continued through the winter, but by spring it was apparent that it could not last much longer, for the moment the ice went out of the St. Lawrence the British would begin reinforcing their garrison. In fact, the very convoy that had brought Ethan home to America in the frigate *Solebay* also carried a large force of redcoats to prosecute the war in the Colonies. The fleet arrived in the beginning of May, and on May 6 the Americans began to retreat from Quebec. They were in a dreadful state. Many had caught smallpox, and General John Thomas died of the disease at Chambly, during the retreat. The withdrawal became a rout—General John Sullivan tried to stem the British at Trois-Rivières, but was defeated. He moved back to St. John's, where he met Arnold and the remains of his army, and headed south toward the safety of Crown Point and Ticonderoga, which the Americans still held.

All this activity was occurring as Heman Allen rode down to Philadelphia in May to present to Congress the petition drawn by Ira, Dr. Fay, and himself. The petition cited the whole history of the Grants, and asked for the help of Congress. The people of the Grants, it said, were not willing to put themselves under the jurisdiction of New York as had been earlier suggested.

The petition languished in the press of more important business. General Sullivan, retreating raggedly with his exhausted force, reached Crown Point early in July and was met there by Ira, who wanted to hear all the news. He learned that conditions were as bad up in the Onion River country as he feared. The retreat of the American force let loose the suppressed rage of the Indians against settlers, and many people on the west side of Lake Champlain had been scalped and murdered by Indians.

Ira sent out letters to settlements all along the lake, warning of the state of affairs. The best thing to do, he advised, was to bring in all families in the outlying areas so the settlements would be secure, and then to keep scouts out at all times to warn of approaching Indians.

Ira had approached General Sullivan for help, and had been assured that the American army would do all it could to protect the people of the Grants. He was heartened to learn that the Americans proposed to build a line of forts in the north country and maintain a fleet that would fight against the British and retain American control of Lake Champlain. With this information, Ira came to Dorset on July 24 for another convention of people from the towns of the Grants.

From Philadelphia, Congress advised the people of the Grants to make their peace with New York for the present, leaving the land squabble until later. Heman, on learning this, quickly withdrew their petition for Congressional help. Events had changed the minds and hearts of many people in the Grants, who now favored the Allens' plans for independence from Yorker rule. At Dorset were forty-nine representatives from thirty-two towns. All the old talk about divisiveness and godless people was stilled. The forty-nine were unanimously agreed on one point: under no conditions would they join with the Yorkers and let those land grabbers steal the very soil on which they trod. They declared all who associated with New York government to be as great enemies as the British, and they called for the people to form a new state of their own. Heman, Jonas Fay, and William Marsh were appointed to travel about the area and proselytize. That summer Ira was asked to do the same.

Ira went off into the Yorker-named counties of Gloucester and Cumberland on the east side of the Green Mountains, where there were many settlers who favored New York. He tried to persuade them that they needed a government of their own. Results were disappointing. In November the convention met again at Westminster in the heart of the Connecticut River country, and Ira and Heman had to report that the biggest obstacle to their plans was the strength of the Yorker party in the eastern part of the Grants. The convention sent Ira and William Marsh back to work harder and to report again in January of 1777 to see if matters had changed for the better.

Ira was manager of this convention. He was sly, a politician to the core, and he did not hesitate to rewrite the minutes of a meeting to support his own position.

Now Ira, Heman, Fay, Marsh, Chittenden and a handful of others set out to persuade inhabitants of the area to create the new state. They were careful to call it a district, and to avoid wherever possible opening any old wounds. But they were moving steadily toward the formation of a new government.

By fall a committee was considering the ways in which they could raise a militia to help in the war against Britain. They planned to adhere to Congress and its orders, and to send delegates to petition Congress to unite the Grants area under one rule and, above all, to proclaim it independent of New York. The trouble was that the people of Gloucester and Cumberland Counties had accepted New York law, were living under New York rules, and their officials reported to New York. This state of affairs had to be ended.

Ira went over to the east side of the Grants to bring his powerful and persuasive personality to bear on the people. He soon realized that it was going to take a little time.

The convention kept meeting and adjourning as its members ran hither and yon trying to strengthen support. But it was never out of the control of the Allen faction. Indeed, Ira's biographer, James Benjamin Wilbur, states flatly that not a single paper or decision, then or any time in the next ten years, passed without Ira's scrutiny, and that he had a hand in writing most of them. The Allens were building an empire.

The Low, Low Time

ETHAN was sick. He had survived treatment that might have killed an ordinary man, and he was seemingly indestructible, a point that annoyed many of his captors. But even as the prisoners were moved to Halifax jail, Ethan's health began to decline. His once robust body began to weaken. He was still a young man, not yet forty, but nearly a year's imprisonment had begun to tell on his constitution.

The Halifax jail seemed a benefaction at the time, but it was a matter of comparisons, for the jail was old-fashioned and designed for confinement, not comfort. Ethan and his men were kept with another twenty prisoners in one great common cell, whose principal furniture was excrement tubs. He immediately petitioned for the removal of the sick men to a hospital, but this was denied.

Ethan met James Lovell in the jail. Lovell was a member of the Continental Congress from Massachusetts. He and Ethan prepared petition after petition for the sick, against mixing private soldiers and officers, in demand of better food, but all went for nothing.

With Lovell, Ethan could discuss politics and philosophy, and they whiled away the summer days of 1776 doing so. As the days rolled on and the plight of the American captives became known throughout Halifax, the gentlefolk took pity on them. A Mrs. Blacden brought them fruit and meat and wine. Even so, Ethan and many others fell ill with fever; he claimed he cured himself and his men by feeding them raw onions.

High authority now remembered that Ethan Allen and his men were alive, and issued orders that they were to be moved to New York. Two of Ethan's men were too sick to be moved (one of them later died) but the slender remnant of the force that launched the brave attack on Montreal was herded into boats and moved to the H.M.S. *Lark*, a British frigate bound for New York harbor. There, on the twelfth day of October, 1776, Ethan was ordered to the quarterdeck. He went, half expecting another confrontation with British authority. Instead, he met Captain Smith, who welcomed him to his ship, asked him to dine that very day, and assured Allen that he would be treated as an officer and a gentleman while aboard this vessel. Ethan was dumbstruck. He wrote, "This was so unexpected and sudden a transition that it drew tears to my eyes which all the ill usage I had before met with was not able to produce. Nor could I at first hardly speak, but soon recovered myself and expressed my gratitude . . ."

Captain Smith said gravely that he expected no returns of favor, but it was a changeable world, and one day perhaps Ethan Allen would be able to do him a good turn.

The frigate was not designed to accommodate passengers, but Captain Smith rigged up a place between decks where each man had his little canvas-lined stateroom. From time to time Ethan dined with the captain or with the other officers, but usually he and Lovell and the other gentlemen prisoners stuck together and ate in the gunroom. They had provisions—Mrs. Blacden and others had made sure the gentlemen were provided with food and drink for the voyage—so their lot was suddenly changed as from night to day. The freshness of it all brought hope that they would soon be exchanged for British prisoners, and that was a prime topic of conversation on the voyage south.

Another prisoner, a Captain Burk, joined them. He urged that they rebel, seize the frigate, and turn her into the service of the American cause. Ethan would have none of it. He threatened that if Burk tried to murder the captain and the officers, Ethan would stand with the British. With Congressman Lovell, Ethan talked the conspirators out of their plan. Ethan had no love for the British, nor did Lovell, but they refused to become involved in a plot of this kind against the only man who had so far befriended them and made their lot a bit less miserable.

In New York, Ethan went to a transport ship commanded by Captain Craige. This captain shared his cabin with Ethan, a favor prompted by the arguments presented in Ethan's favor by

Captain Smith. Lovell was with him for a time, but he was soon exchanged for Colonel Philip Skene, who had been captured early in the war.

Although Ethan and his captors were enemies, he talked freely about the war with them and struck up a friendship with several British officers. He met a half-dozen Tories, too, including an obnoxious Sergeant Hoyt from Connecticut who kept boasting of all the emoluments he would receive when King and Parliament had conquered the damned rebels. In this encounter Ethan was impressed by how Tories seemed uniformly to be bent on personal profit. Ethan had known loyalists before —the hated Yorker officials in the heart of the Green Mountain country. Now he turned irrevocably against Tories and Toryism, and vowed that he would take the estate of any Tory and make sure that rascal received nothing but trouble.

The British would have been wise to parole all the prisoners who had suffered so much since those days in Canada, but they paroled only four—Ethan and three of his officers. Ethan and the officers were set free on their word that they would not try to escape the confines of New York City. How Ethan lived in New York he never said, but it was obviously off loans and gifts from citizens sympathetic to the Revolution, for he had not a copper in his pockets by the time he was paroled.

Life ashore, surrounded by friends and friendly acquaintances did marvels for Ethan's health. It also strengthened—if that were needed—his resolution about the Revolution and independence. He was confined to lower Manhattan when the wounded and prisoners of the battle of Long Island were brought into the city, and he saw how miserably they were treated, confined to the churches under guard and given little medical care and little food. Ethan saw and grew to hate the Hessians with their strange ways and foreign language. But his real fury was turned toward the Tories, who seemed to exult in the misery of their revolutionary opponents more than anyone else.

The winter of 1776 was a low point of the Revolution, and even in New York Ethan could sense the despair that gripped many in the Colonies. The British were not unmindful of the situation, and the wise among them sought ways to capitalize on the worries of the rebels.

General Howe, one of the British high command, sent a high-placed officer to talk to Ethan about joining the British. The officer brought promise of a colonel's commission to lead a band of Tories. They would send Ethan to England, he would consult with the Colonial Secretary, Lord Germain—he would be given the highest and finest treatment as a loyal subject. He might even be granted a royal audience in London. Ethan would be paid in guineas, he would be given uniform allowances and materials. Then he was to join with General John Burgoyne in the northern campaign. Clearly, someone in the British army had considered the military problem and had the good sense to see that the man who was most capable of re-taking Ticonderoga for the British was the one who had taken it for the Americans: Ethan Allen. When all this was done and the war was ended, Ethan was to have a huge tract of land in the Hampshire Grants or in Connecticut.

Ethan listened carefully. How simple it sounded to declare loyalty to a crown under which he had grown up. He listened and then he answered.

"If by faithfulness I recommended myself to General Howe, I should be loath by unfaithfulness to lose his good opinion. Besides, I view the offer of land to be similar to that which the devil offered Jesus Christ."

This turning of the talk to Biblical reference was a typical Allen ploy. It was also very telling, and the officer turned away from Ethan with a frown and accused him of being a bigot. That was the end of the conversation. Ethan did not hear again from General Howe or his staff.

In the winter of 1777 Ethan and a number of other American prisoners were moved to Long Island. They were provided with housing and food and were still on parole; they could move about, but they had to report back to their quarters at night. Ethan lodged with a Dutch farmer at New Lots. Heman and Ira managed to get money to him, and he was able to live well.

Ethan took command of almost any situation with his over-powering presence and his very real experience and knowledge of frontier warfare. The parolees gathered at one or two tav-erns, and every day Ethan was there, telling of the capture of Ticonderoga, his battles against New York authority, his fight in Canada, or his imprisonment. He told a story well, even if some of the others did tire of hearing it three or four times running. But he was the outstanding military figure among the captives, and who could blame him if he lorded it over them a bit? How many of them had been offered a baron's ransom and audience with His Majesty if they would turn their coats?

The year 1777 was difficult for Ethan. Before, he had been pressed by the simple problems of survival. Now his captivity became a boring and loathsome thing. He smuggled out letters to the Connecticut Committee of War complaining of his dreadful lot. Somehow he hoped for exchange and release. But the weeks went by and nothing happened. He had bad news from home in the late spring. His only son, Joseph, had died of smallpox in Sheffield. He grieved in letters to others of the fam-ily, particularly Heman, who was dividing his time between service with the Green Mountain Regiment and the business in Salisbury.

Early in July, the sad news of the death of Joseph was com-pounded by the almost equally desperate news of the fall of Ticonderoga to the British under Burgoyne. It was a personal blow to Ethan, for he had comforted himself often with the fact that if he had done nothing else during the war, he had given his countrymen control of Lake Champlain and the waterway of the north. Now it was lost.

The war was going badly. Burgoyne was on the march in the Grants. The British blockade of American ports was proving effective. Howe was moving very successfully, it seemed, against Philadelphia, and there the very heart of the American nation was threatened. Here was Ethan paroled in western Long Island, unable to turn his tremendous energy to any program of assistance for his fellows, unable to do anything but walk about, talk, drink, eat, and worry about what was going to become of him and the nation.

He grew restless, and New Lots was too small to hold him. He wandered into the edges of New York, finally, and took to traveling to New York City and walking the streets in open defiance of the conditions of his parole. He was cross and belligerent in his old fashion. He was looking for trouble, as if somehow trouble would relieve the situation of his fellows.

CHAPTER TWENTY-ONE

The Price of Independence

IRA Allen had spent cold and sometimes thankless days in the saddle during the last weeks of 1776 and the early part of 1777. He had been trying to persuade the people of the Connecticut River valley that their best hope lay with their fellows of the Hampshire Grants and not with the Yorkers.

By January 15, 1777, when the convention of the Grants settlers had met again to consider their pressing common need, Ira, Joseph Bowker, and other leaders had carried out a master stroke. Twenty-two delegates had come to the meeting, thirteen of them from the lands east of the Green Mountains. A year earlier such a division would have swung the convention for New York, but Ira's proselytizing had borne fruit. A special committee had reported that three-quarters of the people in the eastern counties were in favor of the creation of a new state. It is highly doubtful if there were that many so enthusiastic, but the important matter was that the people in favor of the idea were at the meeting.

As clerk of the convention, Ira had been in charge of preparing most of the documents. When it ended, he had headed for Hartford to put the declaration of the convention in the Hartford newspapers and be sure it was printed for all the world to see. For the convention had taken the giant step. Soon all America knew of the intention of the people of the Hampshire Grants to form a state, which they wanted to call New Connecticut.

A committee that included Jonas Fay, Thomas Chittenden, and Heman Allen had assembled to carry the declaration to Congress in Philadelphia. They had headed south on horseback, avoiding areas of British control. Philadelphia had been a big disappointment, however, for the New York delegates were outraged by the idea that those upstarts on the Grants could use the Revolution to steal New York's rightful property. Heman and his friends had been rejected. But they had gotten a new idea.

At the tavern where they were staying, the committeemen

encountered Dr. Thomas Young, the philosopher from Amenia, New York, who used to talk philosophy half the night with Ethan in his Salisbury days. Dr. Young had been tempered, hardened, and gentled by experience. Although he and Ethan had parted in some strain over the manuscript of the book they were supposedly writing, Dr. Young had none but kind words to Heman for Ethan, and sympathy over his plight as a captive. Asked for advice on the state business of the Hampshire Grants' representatives, Dr. Young insisted that the committee had but one course: go home, draft their own declaration of independence, and become a sovereign republic. Then, having thrown off the chains of the Yorkers, they could come back to Congress as a truly independent state, seeking admission on equitable terms with all the rest. And one other thing, said Dr. Young. They could not use the name New Connecticut, for there was a place in Pennsylvania by that name; nor was the name very striking or original. Reaching into his store of classical knowledge, Dr. Young produced a better name for them. Why did they not call their new state *Vermont*, from the French words that mean "green mountains"?

Taken with the brevity and descriptiveness of the term, the committeemen had headed home, musing over all that they had learned and seen. It was apparent that Dr. Young's point was valid. The Yorkers would never allow them to come into Congress as long as they petitioned in this way. They had to go it alone for a little while. Later, an accommodation could be reached in which the old claims of the Yorkers would not figure.

Ira made public what had occurred in Philadelphia, and he urged settlers on the Grants to establish the independent republic of Vermont. His enthusiasm was catching, for on June 4, 1777, when the convention was meeting at Windsor, there were seventy-two delegates, more than at any previous meeting. They came fresh from farm and village, knowing that just a month earlier the Yorkers had met in convention and done just what Ira warned they would do: reaffirmed the New York sovereignty over the Grants' land.

The Windsor delegates listened to what Heman and the others had to say about their trip to Philadelphia. Dr. Young's suggestion for a name created a discussion, and Heman and other Green Mountain Boys suggested that the name Vermont would perpetuate the memory of the militiamen who had sacrificed so much to keep the Yorkers out of their homes. So the convention voted to form a new state and to call it Vermont. They would form a Committee of Safety and elect delegates to wait on Congress and seek admission to that body. They appointed officials to take over the public offices held by Yorkers and sent word to New York to vacate public places, for they had been taken over by Vermonters. All this business was to be finished and ratified later in the year.

In July Ira went to Saratoga to call on General Arthur St. Clair and discuss the defense of Vermont against the British. He discovered that St. Clair was woefully ignorant about what was going on to the north. Two days later General Burgoyne's southern attack unit arrived from Montreal at Crown Point, just a few miles from Ticonderoga. Burgoyne was on his way down to the strategically vital Hudson valley. His plan for Ticonderoga was to flank the fort on the Vermont side by sending a war party out along Otter Creek.

Ira and Seth Warner and a handful of Green Mountain Boys set out to rouse the settlers. They raised a force of militia, and for the next two weeks scoured the countryside, advocating a program of removal and destruction. The Americans could not stop the British yet, but they could drive their cattle south and burn their fields so the oncoming enemy army would have nothing to eat.

Confident, as was nearly every one else, that Ticonderoga was the bastion of defense and that the British would never pass that point on the lake, Ira headed to Windsor for the renewal of the convention.

On July 2, 1777, even as the solemn little band of Grantsmen convened in Windsor to worry over the problems of establishing their new state, one of General Burgoyne's officers discovered the weak point of Fort Ticonderoga—it was vulnerable to cannon fire from a small eminence nearby that the British christened Sugar Hill. Two days later the place was fortified. The British were ready to attack the fort itself.

Vermonters were now in the majority among the defenders of the fort. General St. Clair had placed Colonel Moses Robinson in command of the troops, and Major Heber Allen was second in command. As the night of July 5 fell, the British mistakenly fired one of the cannon on Sugar Hill. St. Clair called Seth Warner and other commanders for a quick session and then decided to escape. The impregnable fortress had become a trap.

St. Clair sent the sick, wounded, and some others under heavy guard south on the lake toward Skenesboro, but the majority of the troops headed across the lake over a wooden bridge, into the area the convention in Windsor was just then naming Vermont. Major Heber Allen rallied his men and followed Seth Warner. The Americans headed toward the road that Ira and Remember Baker had laid out years before, the road that headed for Hubbardton and then Castleton and south. The British gave chase.

Seth Warner, Heber, and the other Green Mountain Boys were in the rear, guarding St. Clair's troops from ambush or surprise by General Simon Fraser and General Friedrich von Riedesel, the British and Hessian commanders who were behind them. Late the next afternoon Warner decided to make a stand at Hubbardton to protect the American rear, and he told Heber and his other officers to dispose themselves in the woods along the high ridge to the east of the road. Below them was the plain, a deserted farm, and Sucker Brook, on which Ira had camped so many times. Soldiers from New Hampshire were on Sucker Brook and a number of Massachusetts men were around the old Sellick cabin in the clearing.

Early the next morning, General Fraser's men burst into the clearing, and the New Hampshiremen panicked and ran into the woods. This desertion of a vital position made the tasks of Seth Warner and the others much harder, but the Green Mountain Boys stayed down behind felled trees and fired away at the advancing enemy. The British split—the majority went after the Massachusetts men, but another group pressed up the hill. Seth Warner, Heber, and the others fell back in the fashion in which they fought so well, contesting every foot of the ground. Colonel Francis and the Massachusetts men bore the brunt of the British assault after the failure of the New Hampshire regiment to fight effectively. As the sun rose Seth Warner saw that the day was lost; he told his Boys to retreat in the way they knew best, drifting off singly and in pairs. Warner's men were to meet him later in Manchester.

Many of the Americans escaped the enemy that day, but the New Hampshire regiment was captured nearly intact. Colonel Francis of the Massachusetts regiment was killed in the battle, but the majority of his men escaped down the road to Castleton, covered from the hill by the retreating Green Mountain Boys. Then Heber and the others vanished from the field, leaving the British in control.

Meanwhile in Windsor, the convention members were considering the adoption of their Declaration of Independence when word came that Ticonderoga had fallen to the British. The convention almost erupted in panic. President Joseph Bowker's family was right in the line of advance and he wanted to head home. As they gathered their papers and their guns, the men of the convention were delayed by one of Vermont's famous thunderstorms, and while they waited for the lightning and thunder to cease, they were persuaded by those who were not directly threatened to stay and finish the job.

So the task was done and the machinery of government was set up temporarily, pending elections to be held in December. The delegates even set up a loan office so that the state might borrow money. Ira was trustee. The only loan he could get was one for twenty-seven pounds from Heman—hardly high finance. But at least Vermont was now an entity of sorts and had a constitution. That instrument was in its way the most advanced of the time: slavery was prohibited, and all men over twenty-one were permitted to vote without reference to personal condition or property.

It was July 8 when the delegates finished their work. Ticonderoga had fallen and Burgoyne was at Castleton in the heartland of their new state. Seldom has a government come into being under such inimical conditions.

The Struggle

IRA was not pleased. General Schuyler, that old enemy of the Green Mountain Boys and their Hampshire Grants, now American commander of the northern district, was giving the people of the new state of Vermont a bad name with General Washington and others in the south who did not know the true situation. Von Riedesel and his men had moved down to Castleton where they quartered themselves. A contemptuous and resentful Schuyler wrote Washington that the Vermonters were giving up—helping the British and seeking their protection. Ira knew it was not true, and so did General Burgoyne and his lesser commanders.

The British had hoped that when they got away from the supply line of Lake Champlain they could live off the country-side. They were discovering in Castleton and thereabouts that the local farmers would not supply them. Although Burgoyne had offered amnesty and protection to the people of the Grants if they would succor him, the independence movement was strong and deep. Had it not been, it might easily have failed then and there. The British attack could not have come at a more embarrassing time for the new Vermont patriots. They had declared their independence, but they did not yet have an effective government. On July 10 Burgoyne announced to the inhabitants of Castleton, Hubbardton, Rutland, Tinmouth, Pawlet, Wells, and Granville that they should appoint representatives to come and meet with the Tories and the British. If they resisted they would be killed and their property taken.

The answer of the revolutionaries was to hasten to Manchester, where Ira and the other members of the new Committee of Safety discovered that Seth Warner's regiment had been badly mauled at Hubbardton. "Thus in a few days," wrote Ira, "the inhabitants for near a hundred miles on the west side of the Green Mountains were left without protection by the American army."

Something must be done, and quickly. Three quarters of the people on the west side of the Green Mountains were moving out rather than stay under British control. A Council of State was immediately organized, with Thomas Chittenden as president, Jonas Fay as vice president, and Ira as secretary. The first thing to do, with money or without it, was to raise some troops to drive the British out.

The brash Ira had only until sunrise of the next day to complete a plan of organization, but he worked all night, and by dawn he was ready. First of all, said Ira, let the Council form a Commission of Sequestration. The commissioners would go about the countryside and discover who had sold out to the British. The property of those disloyal persons would be seized and sold at public auction, the proceeds going to raise and support a Vermont regiment to use against the British.

Ira had names and numbers with him to indicate that with all the defaults there would be a considerable amount of property available for the purpose. His fellows agreed, and that very day the Council commissioned Samuel Herrick colonel of the new regiment and sent him out with Vermont's blessing to find troops. Thus to Ira goes the honor of having been the first to use the seizure of Tory assets as the solution to the Colonies' problems of defense and resistance.

Herrick lost very little time. Ebenezer Allen, one of the cousins of the Allens, soon enlisted and was made a captain. He went out forthwith from Manchester to scout the enemy in the north and find some men at the same time. One of his soldiers stopped off in Danby to talk to a settler named Irish, who turned out to be a Tory. Irish caught the soldier at gunpoint and prepared to march him off to Castleton to deliver him to General von Riedesel and collect a bounty. But Herrick and his men surprised Irish in the act and killed him.

This move infuriated a number of residents of the Danby area who were wondering which side they ought to jump to— and they jumped the wrong way. They fled north to the arms of von Riedesel in Castleton, whereupon Herrick collected their farm animals and valuables to take back to Manchester for sale to support the regiment.

As Secretary of the Committee of Safety, Ira was entrusted with the responsibility of making contact with other colonies for the common defense. He wrote to the governments of New Hampshire and Massachusetts, informing them of the fall of Ticonderoga, the plans of Burgoyne, the general military situation, and the desperate need for troops. So disorganized was the Colonial effort at this moment that these words were the first Massachusetts and New Hampshire received of the situation.

The Council of State moved to Bennington, the site of the Green Mountain Boys headquarters, and the largest and most useful place for organization. There Ira and his friends waited. If Vermont was to survive, and if Burgoyne was to be stopped, they would have to get the help they had called for.

Three days after Ira had written his desperate pleas for help to New Hampshire and Massachusetts, action began. The assembly of New Hampshire met and voted to raise a brigade to fight on the edge of the Hampshire Grants. Brigadier General John Stark was appointed to raise the troops and move immediately. In farms and villages all around, New Hampshiremen picked up their muskets and began to move.

At Bennington, Ira and the other members of the Council puzzled over a communication they received from General Schuyler, the chief of the northern Colonial army. Schuyler had heard of the defense efforts of Vermont, and he now demanded that Colonel Herrick's regiment and any other troops that came into Vermont should be placed under his command. Ira could not hear the name Schuyler without thinking "Yorker," and his fellows were equally suspicious of the arrogant, patrician general.

Schuyler's orders produced grave resentment in Bennington. It was true that Congress had ordered all American forces to be placed under unified command, but Congress still had not accepted Vermont and, Ira argued, had no sovereignty over Vermont until it did. Heman had told him how badly the Yorkers had behaved when the delegates from Vermont went to plead for Congressional help in establishing a new state. Heber had told Ira of his suspicion that the Yorkers at Saratoga had tried to throw the Green Mountain Boys to the wolves during the retreat to Hubbardton. Heber claimed then and forever after that he and Warner and the rest had not gotten the word to retreat until almost the last moment; it had seemed to him that a deliberate effort was afoot to sacrifice them and thus get rid of a disturbingly independent element of the army.

Ira and his fellow Council members then rejected General Schuyler's orders and told Colonel Herrick to stay right where he was rather than march to Saratoga to join Schuyler. Schuyler protested and repeated the order. The Council gave a flat dictum to Herrick that he must not put himself under the command of General Schuyler, who in turn fired off a letter to Congress. Congress complained bitterly that Vermont was acting against the common interest, but Ira and his fellows would not be distracted. They did not answer the charges from Congress, but sat to await developments. They were certain that putting themselves at the mercy of Schuyler would be suicidal, for his history of opposition to the people of the Grants was clear. Ira and his friends believed Schuyler would be only too eager to sacrifice Vermont as a way of eliminating the new government of the new state.

If Ira needed support in his view, it came from General Stark, who had nothing but contempt for Schuyler and the men who were running the American army. Stark had seen military service and had fought well early in the war. But in Massachusetts he felt he had been passed over by Washington for lesser men, and he had repaired to his New Hampshire home and refused to budge. Now he was coming down to fight for the people on the Grants and the common cause, but he was damned if he was going to put himself under the control of Schuyler.

Stark's attitude created a fuss in New Hampshire. The Assembly ordered him to report to Schuyler. Stark refused and offered to resign if they insisted. The Assembly gave in and left it to General Stark to decide under whose command he would fight.

Stark then moved to Charlestown on the Connecticut River, while his recruiters gathered the brigade together from the hills. He wrote to Ira in Bennington, where Ira was carrying on a furious spate of activity, sending out agents and spies to determine the strength and attitude of the enemy, and scouring the countryside for men and information. He felt the situation was growing every day more serious, and he urged Stark to move.

Ira's intelligence was accurate. General Burgoyne was itching to move down the Hudson, but his basic problem was a shortage of draft animals to haul the big brass cannon he was bringing with him. As long as they stayed on Lake Champlain and Lake George they could use water transport. But from this point on the army must take to the road, and that meant horses. Burgoyne was making ready to send a force east into the Connecticut valley to seize horses and supplies for the march south.

Ira lost no time in informing General Stark that he should march to Manchester by the direct road. There he would have the services of Colonel Herrick and his Rangers and could link up with Colonel Seth Warner's Green Mountain Boys.

General Stark came to Bennington to consult with Ira and the other members of the Committee of Safety. On August 9 Ira had intelligence that the Hessian Colonel Baum was leading a British unit heading for the town.

Heman was in Bennington, too. He was a member of the Committee of Safety, but he was also an active commander of a company of Green Mountain Boys, and as the orders to get ready for battle came, Heman donned his uniform and picked up his sword.

Britain's Colonel Baum marched toward Bennington, delayed by rain and rearguard actions of the American backwoodsmen. The British and the Hessians had the idea that the Americans would not stand and fight. They had seen them melt away into the woods at Ticonderoga when outflanked. They had seen the New Hampshiremen surrender in confusion at Hubbardton, and others (Warner's Green Mountain Boys) run away and disappear. The Hessians thought the Americans were cowards.

But at Bennington General Stark decided that they would smash the British-Hessian force. For two days after he reached Bennington and made camp, it rained down in sheets. The Germans advanced to within a few miles and waited in the mud near the Walloomsac River. Heman Allen was with his troops up on the hill in Manchester, shivering with fever and a bad cold he had caught in the rain, and waiting, along with the New Hampshire volunteers.

The Germans marched on the morning of August 16, 1777, determined that they would fight this day, rain or not. Their powder was growing wet and they were soaked through the thickness of their heavy woolen uniforms.

Ira and the other members of the Committee of Safety were not averse to picking up a gun for this battle, but they had other tasks before them. The Committee functioned as supply force, intelligence agency, and general staff of the American force. Ira was busy day and night sifting messages and making sure his men had powder and food. On the night before the battle he had learned that Colonel Skene, the old English army officer who had once hoped to be governor of the new state, was marching to Baum's aid with fifteen hundred men.

That night, General Stark decided that he, too, would fight next day, regardless of the weather. The word was sent to Colonel Seth Warner to bring the Green Mountain Boys down from Manchester—the fight would be at Bennington, not up north. A shivering Heman Allen struggled from his cot into his dank uniform and prepared to march.

Next morning the attack came. Ebenezer Webster, the father of Daniel Webster, led a force that attacked the Tories and Germans down in their swamp and then up on the hill. Flankers went out to get the Tories, whom the patriots hated as much as the Tories hated them. The battle lasted two hours, with Colonel Baum holding the top of a hill (later named Hessian Hill in his honor) and the Americans attacking. The Germans fought bravely, but their position was wrong and they faced men with much more at stake. They ran out of ammunition, slung their carbines, and tried to hack their way out with their swords and gain the road back to New York. They failed. Colonel Baum was shot through the stomach and fell to die. His dragoons were routed and sent scurrying through the woods in disorder.

Meanwhile Colonel Warner, Captain Heman Allen, and the

Green Mountain Boys came from Manchester and began the pursuit of the Germans and the Tories. They very nearly caught Colonel Skene, and they did kill his horse. Back along the road into New York territory they fought until they reached the Walloomsac. After the rain the sun had come out and turned the woods into a steaming jungle thick with mosquitoes and flies. Darkness neared, but still the Americans pursued. Warner, Heman, and their men captured some seven hundred prisoners on the road and most of the cannons and equipment of the expeditionary force. Heman caught a more serious cold because of his exertions that day. He was confined to bed, and when he arose days later, he was thin and wan, racked by a choking cough. He could no longer fight with the Green Mountain Boys and headed back to Salisbury to try to recover his health.

CHAPTER TWENTY-THREE

The Hero's Return

IN New York City the British were more than a little concerned about the way the war was going. In this summer of 1777 the Americans had proved that they could defeat an impressive military force of highly skilled soldiers. The battle at Bennington had marked a new wave in the war, and even those British officers who would say little about this change were vaguely worried. All the more reason that the cocky behavior of Colonel Ethan Allen was galling. He had been paroled to Flatbush on Long Island. The condition of parole was that he would not try to escape. He did not try to escape, but neither would Colonel Allen stay where he belonged. He was forever popping up at some coffee house or tavern in Manhattan, in the most annoying fashion.

He was a hard man to dislike, even for an enemy. His open face, his ready smile, his impressive physique made him an object of attention wherever he went. Thanks to the materials given by the Irish merchants, he had a very respectable blue suit, and his gold-trimmed blue hat gave him a striking appearance. When he sat down in a tavern to discuss the affairs of the day and show his self-garnered erudition, he was even more impressive. It was not hard for the British to learn that their bird would not stay in his proper cage.

During the early months of war, the British had shown contempt for their country cousins, and the disgust the loyal felt for the disloyal surpassed all else. After two years of struggle, however, a real battle and siege at Quebec, the naval fight at Valcour Island, and now a major defeat by the Americans at Bennington, the British were beginning to regard the unpleasantness involving the Green Mountain Boys as something like a war. The violation of war's rules by Colonel Ethan Allen was not something to be taken lightly, and on August 25, 1777, as he sat in a New Lots tavern whiling away the afternoon telling tales and worrying about his family, the British descended on him. In spite of his protests, the redcoats carried Ethan off to Manhattan, where they slapped him in the provost jail.

Although his admiring brother Levi sent him money, it did not do any good now, and although publicly he complained that he had been mistreated by the enemy, privately he admitted cheerfully that he had been playing a game with them. It was better to be caught and be a prisoner, in a way, than to be in the limbo of parole, where he was neither fighter nor a noncombatant. Parolees, he said, "were mere ciphers exempted from both danger and honor."

Ethan made many acquaintances in prison. He met a Captain Travis of Virginia, who occupied the dungeon cell beneath him, by boring a hole through the floor with a pocket knife. He met other officers, members of Congress, and patriots, and they shared the feeling that they were somehow all together, and they helped one another as they could. Ethan helped Captain Travis get out of his cell. He learned that John Fell, another prisoner, was about to die from pneumonia, and he wrote the British commander of New York. In a few days Fell was removed to private lodgings and recovered.

Ethan had small use for most of his jailers, but his particular enemy was Joshua Loring, the commissary of prisoners, who was a Tory. How Ethan detested Tories! He wrote,

This Loring is a monster! There is not his like in human shape. He exhibits a smiling countenance, seems to wear a phiz of humanity, but has been instrumentally capable of the most consummate acts of wickedness, which were first projected by an abandoned British council, clothed with the authority of a Howe, murdering premeditatedly in cold blood near or quite two thousand helpless prisoners, and that in the most clandestine, mean and shameful manner at New York. He is the most mean spirited cowardly, deceitful, and destructive animal in God's creation below, and legions of infernal devils, with all their tremendous horrors, are impatiently ready to receive Howe and him, with all their detestable accomplices, into the most exquisite agonies of the hottest region of hell's fire.

The quotation above, from Ethan's own account of his imprisonment, is a fair example of Ethan's literary style, very plain and outspoken for its day, even shocking.

Ethan stayed on in jail as the war raged, and he became impatient, but it did him no good. He amused himself by writing letters and carrying on communication with other prisoners. Although he could not fight, he could write, and he wrote spiritedly.

Ethan had begun life a loyal servant of the British Crown. By the winter of 1777 he declared himself Frenchified. He studied the French writers and thinkers. He undertook to learn French in his prison cell, and recommended that Americans study that language before any other, even Greek or Latin. So he passed the dreaded months of captivity in study and correspondence and conversation.

Finally, in May, 1778, Ethan was exchanged for one Colonel Archibald Campbell. The jailers came to his cell one morning and took him out under guard. He was escorted to a sloop in the harbor and kept there in very loose confinement. In fact, he was the guest of the ship, and ate with the officers. Ethan was his old self. While drinking wine with the officers on the second night, he could not suppress the indignation he felt over his previous treatment, and launched into the tale of the vicious captains who had brought him across the Atlantic. Well, he said, grinning, at the end he could give the British a little credit. General Prescott had threatened him with a cane. Captain Symonds had suggested he would dangle at a rope's end. But at least, Ethan said expansively, the British should have credit for two days of good treatment of Colonel Ethan Allen, and he would not forget it.

Ethan was still seething with resentment at all he had seen in those months of torture. The useless deaths and the wicked denial of the most simple necessities to the Americans was not to be forgotten. On the following day he was exchanged for Colonel Campbell, who was brought to the sloop by Mr. Boudinot, the American commissary of prisoners. Boudinot and Ethan greeted each other warmly. Ethan then whiled away the remaining hour of his captivity by telling Boudinot loudly in the presence of his former captors of the horrors of British captivity, suggesting that the Americans should really begin treating their enemies the same.

"I assured them that I should use my influence that their

prisoners should be treated in future in the same manner."

Cocky to the last, Ethan left his enemies and was taken by an American boat across the Hudson to Elizabethtown. He had been a captive of the enemy for nearly three years. His plight had been the subject of almost constant negotiation; General Washington and Congress had spent many hours trying to have him freed, and now finally he was able to fight.

Ethan was greeted as a hero. A Colonel Sheldon of a light horse regiment accompanied him to Valley Forge, where General George Washington was in headquarters. Ethan arrived there on May 8 to grimace visibly at the sight he saw. Washington and his men had just come through the terrible long winter of 1777–8, and signs of suffering were still about them—men with emaciated faces, sickbays filled with bodies.

Ethan wanted to get back into military action, but Washington was very cautious. The generals in whom he trusted had ill things to say about Ethan Allen. Schuyler had never liked Ethan; he did not like any of the Allens or anyone who had fought the battles of the Grants. Benedict Arnold, who had Washington's confidence at this time, always spoke harshly of Ethan.

In fact, Ethan was not so much a military commander as he was a political figure. True, he had been the head of the Green Mountain Boys during the fitful days before the war. The Green Mountain Boys, however, did not ever consider themselves to be an army, but rather a committee of militia whose basic job was to influence settlers and keep the Yorker enemies off the Grants without spilling any blood. They were expert woodsmen and brave fighters, but they were guerillas, not organized soldiers. And much of Ethan's time had always been spent in writing, speaking, and propagandizing for the cause at hand.

Still Ethan was quite humble. He did not suggest that Washington make him second in command. He simply asked to be employed again in the war against their enemies. Washington was much taken by the character he saw before him. He advised Ethan that his best course was to write to Congress for a commission. Washington himself wrote a recommendation that Congress do something for this returning hero: "He appears very desirous of rendering his services to the States, and of being employed, and at the same time he does not discover any ambition for high rank. Congress will herewith receive a letter from him; and I doubt not that they will make such provision for him as they think profitable and suitable."

Ethan sent off his own letter telling of the evils of his incarceration, thanking Congress for getting him out of prison, and again offering his services, even as a private with a musket and bayonet. Then, after three days, Ethan started for home.

Home was now Sunderland on the Hampshire Grants. Ethan had sold off the Sheffield property, and Mary and the children had gone up to a small house in Sunderland to be among friends during his captivity. Ethan started for home in company with General Horatio Gates, whose star was very high at the moment after Burgoyne's surrender at Saratoga. Gates and Ethan got on famously, for Ethan admired this kind of general. Granny Gates was as full of homilies as Ethan himself, and they shared an animosity to men like Philip Schuyler, with his lordly ways and body servants.

Ethan and Gates rode together northward. They spun yarns and thoroughly enjoyed each other's company. At Newburgh on the Hudson Ethan left Gates and his entourage. They were traveling north to rejoin the army. Ethan was going to Salisbury to visit Heman and Levi, then up north into the Grants to see his wife and Heber and Ira.

But when Ethan arrived in Salisbury, he found the big house clothed in mourning. Heman had died just a week before his oldest brother arrived. That cold and fever he had contracted in the Bennington fight had never left him; he had worsened over the winter, and died as spring began to come.

Ethan rode northward past Sheffield, which no longer meant a thing to him, through Pittsfield, the home of the strange Major Brown who had caused him so much trouble, and then on to Bennington. He was thin and tired from the long journey when he arrived in the end of May. After a little time at the tavern, talking over old days, he headed for Arlington, where Mary was living with Ethan's three daughters, Loraine, Lucy, and Mary Ann.

Ethan found wife Mary no more compatible than she had

ever been, for she was given to complaint about her life, her health, and her husband. Ira had taken them in when Ethan had been captured and Mary moved north; she kept house for him at the Arlington place, where he had a gristmill and a sawmill. Of course, Ira was not there often and he was more malleable, or at least more patient, than Ethan.

After two days Ethan could bear home no longer, and he and Ira went to Bennington, where the Vermont Assembly was going to meet. Ira had to go, for he was treasurer and secretary of the state government, one of its half-dozen most important figures. Ethan insisted on going, for he was the returning hero, as he already knew well from an incident that had occurred while he was at home.

During the stay at Ira's place, one of the settlers at Sunderland came by to report a terrible tragedy. His two daughters, aged seven and four, said Eldad Taylor, had wandered off in the woods and were lost. In the wilderness country of Vermont no man ever failed another in such an hour, and Ethan and Ira were soon out with a hundred others in the area, combing the woods around the Taylor place for the little girls. As hours passed and they were not found, the searchers lost heart. All night long they looked, and the next day, and the next. In the middle of the afternoon of the third day someone questioned whether the little girls could have lived so long. They must have been eaten by a cougar or fallen in a stream and been swept down and drowned. They could not be alive. The search was futile, and it was time to get back to haying.

Ethan listened. He saw the men before him, collapsed against logs and tree trunks, and could sense that they were getting ready to give up and go home. He mounted a stump and insisted on being heard.

This was no time to quit, said Ethan. The little girls were out there. They had not been eaten by anything and they had not died of exposure, for it was a warm spring and this just could not be. It was not right to quit. He, Ethan, would not leave the place until the little girls were found and if he had to search alone he would search alone, by God, but he would not have it on his conscience that he had left two starving little girls out in the woods to die when all that was needed was a little more manly effort.

The tired men looked at one another. Blasted by Ethan's bombast, not one dared to quit. They dragged themselves back into the woods again to beat and call and cry out. In a few more hours the little girls were found, safe, hungry, and frightened, and returned to their parents unharmed.

So as Ethan and Ira rode into Bennington the latest bit of weaving in the legend of Ethan Allen had preceded them, and the people were turning on the street to see the greatest hero Vermont had and to wave and cheer him as he came. On the outskirts of town they met Tom Chittenden, who was president of the Council of Vermont. He rode along and talked about affairs since Ethan's departure. Chittenden had lived up in the Onion River country—he had been the first to buy land from the Allens. He had been driven down to the Bennington area as Ira and Remember Baker's widow and children had, when the British and their Indian allies moved south toward Ticonderoga.

Ethan's arrival had Bennington buzzing. The town was alive with delight. Too bad about Heman, a fine fellow and worthy citizen. But he was not the hero of Ticonderoga. That night people began to flock into Bennington from the towns and countryside around. There were two attractions—the meeting of the Assembly and, far more interesting in its way, the chance to see the famous Ethan Allen. The old folks knew him, but many of the children had heard of him only in tales of the dreaded Yorkers and how they had been driven from the Grants by Ethan and his band of mighty Green Mountain Boys.

So the bar at the Catamount Tavern was busy, serving rum punch and sherry flip and whiskey by the gallon. Under the influence of Ethan and God knows what else, the militiamen of Bennington unlimbered their three old cannon and hauled them up the hill to fire them off in honor of the returning hero. Next day Sam Herrick put on his colonel's uniform and ordered a fourteen-gun salute, thirteen guns for the Union, one gun for Vermont. The whole extravagant show was in honor of the returning hero. If they couldn't waste a few charges of powder on the day Ethan Allen came back, then to hell with the war.

Ethan had a long session with Dr. Jonas Fay, who was now running the tavern as his father's deputy. They talked over old times and new, for Jonas was a founder of the new state and a member of the Governor's Council. Then, the next day, Ethan went down the hill to the meeting house where the Assembly was getting down to the business of running the new government, and he was greeted by rounds of applause and cheering as he entered the hall. Right there the men—some of whom he knew and some of whom he didn't—unanimously voted a resolution congratulating Ethan on his safe return from captivity.

So it was a great homecoming and just the kind that warmed Ethan's heart. And yet, even as he came home, the question was arising What place would Ethan Allen find in the new scheme of things in Vermont?

The Republic

ETHAN Allen was never one to stand on ceremony, or to expect gratitude to take the place of common sense in men's dealings with one another. He had served his state and people well, and they were properly grateful to him. But the future lay before them all, and Ethan, now past forty, still had to make his place in the fast-moving society around him.

Congress had been suitably cognizant of Ethan's service in the past. It gave him back pay as a lieutenant colonel for all the time he had been a captive of the British, and a commission as a brevet colonel in the army. That meant that when time came to go into the field and soldier, Ethan would have some official rank and would not have to argue with the Benedict Arnolds of the world.

What would he do now? Although Mary was living at Arlington, not very far away, it was unthinkable that he should share his life with her, so he took a house down the hill, a little walk from the Catamount and from the center of town. This would be his home for the next few years.

Just as Ethan arrived in town, Bennington was buzzing with an event that mirrored the temper of the time. A new Vermont settler named David Redding had been caught sending powder and ball from a public arsenal to the British. The Tory Redding had been captured, confined, tried, found guilty, and sentenced to hang. He was to be executed on June 4, just a few days after Ethan's arrival in town.

Ira, Tom Chittenden, Jonas Fay, and Ethan had exchanged many a tale about the Tories. Ethan's views were so strong that they could hardly be expressed in polite company, and the others had come around very much to his point of view because of worrisome events of the recent past.

The founders of the new state had been very busy in those months after the battle of Bennington. Ira had been the principal pamphleteer and writer of documents, and had spent a good deal of his time traveling to Hartford, the regional printing center and a hub of New England communications, to see that the Vermont constitution was printed and various documents gotten out to other governments.

The surrender of Burgoyne had brought a new sense of importance to the Colonial cause. The British could be beaten in battle, and they had been. But the matter of divided and uncertain loyalties remained. It was asking a great deal of people who had grown up loyal to the king to suddenly divest themselves of an entire heritage, and many of the people of the American Colonies were slow to be convinced of the need for absolute separation from the home country. For example, Colonel Peter Olcott reported to the Council that several of his men had deserted, but then had reconsidered and come back. They had gone over to the enemy and found the British less to their liking than their American companions, so they had returned. What should be done with them?

Ira and the others debated. There was no good answer—but they had to be punished for disloyalty. The punishment was either to pay a fine or to accept the confiscation of their property. If they would do that, then all would be forgotten. But if they refused, they would be treated as outlaws.

These were harsh decisions, but they had to be made, and as Vermont struggled for its very being, the decisions continued. There was the complicating matter of New York's efforts to hang on to power over the Hampshire Grants. Governor Clinton issued a proclamation staying all prosecution of anyone in the Grants who would accept New York authority, and threatening anyone who would not. And over on the eastern side of the new state, disloyalty seemed rampant. The west side of Vermont was represented by six counselors, as was the east side, where New York influence had been so strong before the war.

Even as Ethan had been sitting in jail in New York awaiting his exchange in the spring of 1778, Ira and the others had struggled with the Tories. President Wheelock of Dartmouth College and his associates were leading an element that was doing its best to overthrow the new state government of Vermont and perhaps set up an independent state that spanned the Connecticut River. And Tories were everywhere.

When David Redding was sentenced and about to be hanged there was great anticipation in Bennington, and hundreds came to town from all around to see the affair. But when the fathers of Vermont, Ira and Heman among them, had been forming the state constitution and the laws, they had been careful to protect the liberties of all men. They realized that government must be controlled to preserve liberties of its citizens. Now David Redding's lawyer claimed that there had been irregularities in his trial. As the jurists and men of the Council examined the record, they found it was true. So the execution was called off and a new trial was ordered.

All this happened in the first week of June, right under Ethan's nose. The gallows had been put up in a field across the road from the Catamount. The people who had come for the purpose of seeing Ethan, seeing the legislators, and seeing the hanging were still about the town. And they wanted that hanging. There was talk in the Catamount about having it anyhow, without regard for Ira and Tom Chittenden and the rest of them. When the word came that Tom Chittenden had sat down in his president's chair and signed a reprieve, the Green Mountain Boys got mad. They began milling around in the field by the gallows, and threatened to hang Redding themselves. Ethan heard the racket and went down to the field. Since he stood a good half-foot above most of the bunch, and had a strong pair of shoulders to work with, he was soon in the middle, holding up his arms and shouting down everyone around.

Finally he had the quiet he wanted.

"Go on home and come back here in a week," he shouted. "By God, you shall then see somebody hung at all events, for if Redding is not hung I will be hung myself."

There was irrepressible Ethan. He got a laugh and the crowd began to break up, the men nodding and shaking their heads. They believed him. Ethan had been expounding about Tories, and he was never one to sit by and watch the world move.

Ethan was as good as his word. He headed straight down the

street, found Ira and the others, and got the Council to appoint him prosecuting attorney for the state. The fact that Ethan had no legal experience did not make much difference, for neither did anybody else. Heber's judicial authority was being exerted without more experience than that gained as town clerk of Poultney. In the backwoods, men of good sense were the lawyers; there was not much else that could be done.

The new trial was held to preserve the dignity of the law and whatever rights defendant Redding had. The result was a foregone conclusion: it was quickly proved that Redding had stolen muskets and turned them over to the British, and that he had spied for the enemy. That was enough. A second jury took little time to convict him. And on June 11, the people from the villages flocked back to the big field down the hill from the Catamount. The Assembly recessed for the afternoon so the legislators might enjoy the spectacle. Everybody turned out while poor Tory Redding was brought forth, escorted solemnly to the field, and hanged just as Ethan had promised he would be.

In a way it could be said that Captain Symonds of the frigate *Solebay*, jailer Joshua Loring, and all the other cruel men into whose hands Ethan had fallen were responsible for the harassment of American Tories in the new state of Vermont, where the most stringent policies were adopted in 1778. For Ethan could never forget what had been done to him, nor that the Tories among his enemies had been the worst of all. Now he had a chance to repay them in kind.

The new government of Vermont had a great need for money. Since the founding of the new state, the estates of 158 Tories had been taken, but almost all of these represented abandoned property. They had been sold to meet expenses before Ethan reappeared on the Vermont scene. When he learned of the fiscal problem, Ethan had a ready solution that was soon adopted by the Vermont Assembly. Ethan talked it over with Ira and Tom Chittenden, and the Assembly passed the Banishment Act, which established confiscation boards in various counties. Ethan suggested that if they used the confiscation method they would be able to meet all the needs of the state from the sale of property of "banished" Tories. And to him Tories meant not just those who abandoned their property to join the British, but also those who favored the Yorkers, or who objected to the Republic of Vermont, or who spoke favorably of the enemy.

Ethan undertook the organization of the whole confiscation structure. He was appointed a judge of the Bennington Board of Confiscation, and he chose the other four judges, who were approved by the legislature. He then rushed into confiscating the property of people he knew to be enemies. He rounded up eight old foes of the Green Mountain Boys, declared them Tories, stripped them of their property, and personally escorted them to Albany to turn them over to General John Stark, with the laconic announcement that they should be shoved through the lines into the hands of their British friends.

But word of the banishment reached Governor Clinton of New York, along with the whisper that these eight were not Tories at all but loyal New Yorkers who had the misfortune of running afoul of Ethan Allen in the matter of the Hampshire Grants and property rights. If there was one animal that Ethan hated as much as a Tory it was a Yorker, so there may have been some truth in what the whisperers said to Governor Clinton.

Clinton, understandably, was angry. Here were citizens of his state being deprived of property and liberty by a blackguard of the illegal Republic of Vermont. Furthermore, the depriver was none other than the most notorious enemy and criminal in the history of New York's struggles to maintain the historic boundaries bestowed upon it by a benevolent monarch. Clinton could not possibly let the matter pass once it had come to his attention; to do so would be to recognize the sovereignty of Vermont over the Hampshire Grants, which New York *did not.*

Clinton ordered General Stark to give up the prisoners. But Stark was a New Englander, and shared the deep distrust of New York and its officials. He ignored Clinton and sent the prisoners to General Gates, also a New Englander and not inclined to believe men like Clinton, particularly when his friend and riding companion, Ethan Allen, had just addressed a letter to him describing these "atrocious villains." Ethan cheerfully admitted that his primary charge against the eight was their advocacy of New York government, but that was enough. Anyone who was fighting Vermont was her enemy, and thus a friend of the British.

Gates was about to drive the prisoners across into the British lines when General Washington sent a letter. The politicians had been at Washington, and he could see the outline of a great argument shaping up. Being a pretty good politician himself, he entered the case and ordered the eight offenders sent to West Point, the fortress prison.

So, in essence, Ethan had his way and the Yorkers were confounded. The bitterness in New York City and Albany would be hard to describe. The jubilation in Bennington took the form of visits to the Catamount, where many a cup was quaffed to the confounding of Yorkers and all other enemies of Vermont.

In the east, it seemed there was new trouble. Sixteen towns on the New Hampshire side of the Connecticut River petitioned to join Vermont. The towns' affinities were much closer with Vermont than with the New Hampshire government in far-off Exeter, but the Allens recognized that admitting the towns would infuriate New Hampshire. And they were right. New Hampshire, which had hitherto been friendly to Vermont's aspirations, erupted in indignation and threatened to call on Congress to destroy the Republic of Vermont unless the towns were given back. Vermont's government, initially warm to the idea of annexing new lands, cooled as Ira, Ethan, and the Boys realized that their hold on Vermont politics would be loosened if that many eastern towns were added.

Ethan, as a respected citizen, was sent to Philadelphia to assess Congress's reaction; he returned to report only that Congress was disturbed by the grab. The struggle continued during all of 1778, with Ira journeying back and forth from west to east and even to New Hampshire to explain the Vermont position. In the end it worked out. The dissidents in the east who would rule or ruin were brought under control, and Vermont survived the crisis of government with the Allens very much in the fore.

CHAPTER TWENTY-FIVE

Family Rupture

ETHAN'S bombastic attacks on Tories and Yorkers, delivered in his time-honored fashion at the top of his lungs or in writing with remarkable expletives, created a rift in the Allen family about which nothing could be done during the war. The split began in 1778, and involved Levi.

At thirty-three, Levi apparently lacked the ambition and singlemindedness of his brothers. He had gone out west and learned trade and tanning from the Indians and the western traders. He had come back to help Heman with his business and had been sent out as a traveling salesman most of the time. This occupation suited his character, giving him chance for adventure and very little responsibility. But as he saw his brothers prosper he became envious, and he determined to make his own fortune.

The war years were not very good for that. Foundations were being laid for some fortunes, perhaps—Ira was a good example of that. He would be surveyor general of the Republic; his gristmill and sawmill would provide for the people of Arlington and Bennington; his Onion River lands would increase in value. But for these ventures to be successful, constant sacrifice and attention were necessary, and Ira was spending his total time these days in behalf of the new Republic of Vermont, not in behalf of Ira Allen.

Ethan was equally involved in the struggle, concentrating very much on New York and Governor Clinton, who was trying to subvert Vermont. In the summer of 1778 Ethan produced another of his powerful pamphlets, *An Animadversory Address to the Inhabitants of the State of Vermont: with Remarks on a Proclamation, under the Hand of his Excellency George Clinton, Esq; Governor of the State of New York.*

The title is wordy and difficult for the twentieth century, but in its day it was another of the Allen bombshells—an attack on Clinton and New York for following the same old land policies and playing into the hands of the British enemy. The pamphlet was really designed for reading by Congress, and it was to strengthen Vermont's case at a time when many a hand was being raised against the Green Mountain State and the Allens, Tom Chittenden, and other leaders, who had cause to worry lest they not only have to go it alone, but face military action by Colonial as well as British enemies.

The trouble in the Allen family began with some Vermont lands owned by Levi. He had sold his rights in the lands to Ethan and Ira, but when it came time to transfer the titles, the papers were muddled and Levi did not appear at what Ethan thought was the proper time. The brothers quarreled, causing tension that was not relieved when Levi went south to Connecticut and Long Island.

Ethan in particular owed a lot to Levi. It was Levi who had first sent him money when he was held prisoner in New York, and Levi who had kept up a constant badgering of Washington and Congress in Ethan's behalf. So had Heman, of course, but Heman was dead. Heman had been the great steadying force among the Allen brothers. He was the one who kept the big house in Salisbury that was headquarters of the clan, and the one whom they all came to when they needed a loan or some advice. With Heman gone, the family ties were weaker.

So when Levi began acting badly—by Ethan and Ira's standards—there was no one to cool them down. In Connecticut, Levi learned of the great business opportunities over on the Long Island side of the Sound, where everything was in short supply. So he took a vessel across and traded with the enemy. He somehow got involved in the circulation of counterfeit Continental money when he returned to Connecticut, and was clapped in jail for six months when he got back to New London from his trip to Long Island.

Word of Levi's trouble came to Salisbury, where Ethan and Ira were trying to settle the affairs of Heman, who had left his shares in the Onion River Company to his widow and his brothers. Heman's affairs were complicated, because like many a general storekeeper he had a long string of unpaid accounts that had to be collected, and sometimes this took time and effort.

When Ira heard what Levi had done, he was mildly concerned, but Ethan was infuriated and began shouting and fulminating around the house. That attitude was completely understandable, given Ethan and his position on public affairs. Levi must have known how strongly Ethan felt about Tories and trading with the enemy. Ethan's was not just a position in favor of the war against Britain; it went back to the whole quarrel with the Yorkers, now complicated by a quarrel with the New Hampshiremen. The whole of the family's fortunes were at stake in this matter—or so Ethan saw it, and his fury raged unabated against the younger brother who had shown such family disloyalty.

"A God damned devilish Tory," Ethan shouted when the news came of Levi's activity. "An accursed rogue."

Levi tried to explain in letters. He said he did not boast of loyalty to any government, and that he had never worried about politics or the revolutionary principles that seemed to drive Heman, Ethan and Ira. King or president were all the same to him.

Well, growled Ethan, he would see about that. And so when he came back from Salisbury, he appeared in the court at Bennington and charged that his own brother, Levi Allen, was dealing with the enemy—was a Tory, by God, and deserved nothing better than to have every bit of his land in Vermont confiscated and sold to help the common cause of the battle against the enemy. The court listened respectfully when Ethan spoke, for although he had stepped down from the bench to take on other duties for Ira and his friend Tom Chittenden, Ethan was still a very influential man whenever he spoke on any subject. Soon the court acted and announced the confiscation of all Levi Allen's land in Vermont for the purpose of furthering the war, accusing Levi of trading with the enemy. The notice was duly sent to the Connecticut *Courant,* the journal the Vermonters used regularly to further their official and unofficial views. In time it was printed in the paper and circulated throughout the Colonies.

Levi read it in Virginia after he had been released from the New London jail and was seeking farther afield for the fortune he wanted. He was furious. He came back to Vermont, but for some reason or other no action was taken while he was on this visit, and the quarrel among the Allens continued.

Levi countered Ethan's denunciation of him as a Tory: Ethan was a Godless adventurer, Levi said.

Levi moved over into Dutchess County, New York, safely out of the hands of roisterous Vermonters, and began an argument with his brother. He had the idea that the whole matter was a plot within the family to deny him his property, and he suspected that Ethan was the innocent pawn of somebody else. But innocent or not, Ethan could not be allowed to speak so libelously without answer.

Levi began with ridicule, and this verse soon appeared in the Connecticut *Courant:*

ETHAN: *Old Ethan once said over a full bowl of grog*
        Though I believe not in Jesus, I hold to a God,
        There is also a devil—you will see him one day
        In a whirlwind of fire take Levi away.

IRA: *Says Ira to Ethan it plain doth appear*
        That you are inclined to banter and jeer,
        I think for myself and I freely declare
        Our Levi's too stout for the prince of the air.
        If you ever see them engaged in affray,
        'Tis Levi who'll take the devil away.

LEVI: *Says Levi, your speeches make it perfectly clear*
        That you hath been inclined to banter and jeer,
        Though through all the world my name stands enrolled,
        For tricks, sly and crafty, ingenious and bold,
        There is one consolation which none can deny
        There's one greater rogue in this world than I.

ETHAN AND IRA: *Who's that? They both cry with equal surprise.*

LEVI: *'Tis Ira, 'tis Ira, I yield him the prise.*

To some, who had experienced Ira's weighty hand in land dealings and in his efforts to form and help control the infant government of Vermont, these words about Ira rang truer than any ever uttered about the Allens. To others, the claim that Ira was slippery as an elm twig was hard to understand. It all depended on how well one knew the youngest of the Allen clan.

The struggle soon became a *cause célèbre* in Vermont. If some did not know about it, Ethan was not slow in enlightening. One day a friend came back from Dutchess County and said pleasantly to Ethan that he had run into Levi.

"Seen Levi?" said Ethan. "Well, how was he? God damn his lukewarm soul."

So it went, with Ethan making public and noisy attacks on his younger brother, until finally Levi answered again in print.

How was it, he asked in a letter to the *Courant,* that he could be accused of disloyalty to his family and his people? He cited some of the record. Did his accusers know that when brother Ethan was held in London, Levi had written to General Washington offering to go to England and try to extricate Ethan? Did they know that when Ethan was brought back to Canada and confined in prison at Halifax, Levi had made a long and dangerous trip to that place to see the military governor and the prison officials and try to get Ethan set free? Did any of them have any idea how much money he had spent in entertaining officers, traveling, and supplying Ethan with cash at Halifax, in New York, and on Long Island when Ethan was prisoner and parolee? Did they understand what it was like to travel between the lines and cross them? Did anyone know these things?

Ethan did not like Levi's account. Its import was to put him at a disadvantage as one who might not have survived had it not been for the help of this Tory brother.

"God damn it all!" he said. "Under cover of doing favors for me, when I was prisoner in New York and Long Island, he was holding treasonable correspondence with the enemy."

This was the most blatant charge yet.

It was a damned lie, said Levi, and it had to be answered in only one way. He challenged his oldest brother to a duel.

Ethan received the challenge. He ignored it. He would not dignify any Tory by fighting a duel with him, he said—quite forgetting how he had offered to fight duels in prison and on Long Island with Tories and others when he was at a disadvantage.

The quarrel raged. Ethan calmed down, however, because friends convinced him that Levi had gone out of his mind and could not be held responsible for his actions. They continued to trade insults in print, but nothing more came of it. Levi, having secured more bad publicity than he liked, decided to leave the region. He traveled to South Carolina, crossed through the British lines, and joined the large numbers of loyalists who were flocking into that area in response to British victories in the region. There he decided to spend the rest of the war, as far as possible from Vermont and his ornery brothers.

CHAPTER TWENTY-SIX

The Future of the Republic

IN 1779 the British were watching very carefully the course of events in Vermont, particularly the quarrel between Vermont and New York that seemed to grow more formidable month after month. The British interest was in division and conquest: if they could persuade Vermont to come back into the imperial fold it would deal a serious blow to the American uprising.

Governor Clinton had been outraged by Ethan's latest pamphlet—the *Animadversory Address*—and had spoken gruffly of treason. In Congress the representatives of New York had indicated their unalterable opposition to accepting the independence of Vermont. There was a very good reason for this: Governor Clinton was one of the largest holders of lands under the New York patents instead of the New Hampshire Grants, and he was certainly not going to give up a part of his personal fortune if he could avoid it. So in the spring of 1779 Clinton was party to a movement in the eastern section of Vermont that threatened the life of the young Republic. Eleazer Patterson, a Yorker of Cumberland County in eastern Vermont, had raised a force of five hundred troops, ostensibly for defense against the British. Instead of defending, Colonel Patterson began using those troops to create trouble on the eastern side of the mountains, and finally wrote Governor Clinton to ask what mischief he might perform in behalf of the Yorker cause. Governor Clinton urged caution, but gave his backing to Patterson. That worthy gentleman then began squabbling with the officials of the Vermont Republic.

The issue came to a head in Putney when the Republic tried to raise a militia force there. Sergeant William McWain, the draft officer, was told to go to the devil when he tried to get Yorker men for service. Vermont law said they must serve or pay a forfeit for the hiring of substitutes. The men said they would do neither.

Sergeant McWain went to the house of James Clay, one recalcitrant, and took possession of a cow. He went to the house of Ben Willson and captured another cow. He announced publicly that a week later he would sell the cows to raise money for substitutes for the two unwilling soldiers. On the day of the sale, a hundred men—sympathizers with the unwilling ones—took the cows away from Sergeant McWain, who then went to President Chittenden in Arlington to warn the Council.

The hundred soon spread throughout Putney, Hinsdale, Brattleboro, and other nearby towns, forming committees that stated their outright opposition to the "pretended state of Vermont." At Brattleboro, the committee sent a letter to Governor Clinton that was obviously a "show" letter for Congress—it charged that Vermont was an outlaw state stealing New York lands, and it demanded action. Governor Clinton replied that he was about ready to send in New York troops.

It was time for strong action by Tom Chittenden and the Council, and they turned to the one man who could settle such an affair with the greatest dispatch—Ethan.

Ethan could not have been more pleased. Here was a chance to ring up the glory of the past. He sent out the word, and a few days later he marched in front of a hundred of the old Green Mountain Boys. They were not going to waste any time in quelling this insurrection.

Ira was along—a mature Ira who had the greatest respect for his brother's ability as an organizer, but who also wanted to be sure nothing went wrong legally. Representing the Council, Ira wrote out the warrants for the arrest of Patterson and the others, and Ethan arrested them.

This great giant of a man, with his foghorn voice and ready smile, was frowning this day as he came charging into Putney. He rounded up the offenders, and whacked them soundly across the buttocks with the flat of his huge sword.

Colonel Patterson and forty-three others soon found themselves in jail at Westminster, and Ethan encouraged them to write to New York and complain. There was nothing he would have liked better than a fight with Governor Clinton and all those Yorkers who bedeviled honest men. While he waited for the trial of the miscreants, Ethan snooped around and seized a horde of gunpowder and weapons secreted by the disloyal. He ringed the courthouse and the jail with guards to prevent other disloyal citizens from helping his charges out the window.

The New York adherents wrote Clinton for help, and their friends also wrote, complaining that unless Clinton stepped in with the power of New York, all the people in the Connecticut Valley would be "at the disposal of Ethan Allen, which is more to be dreaded than Death with all its Terrors."

Governor Clinton was growing rash. He complained that matters were coming to a head, and he threatened that unless Congress did something about upstart Vermont he was going to send a thousand militiamen to seize the land, which belonged rightfully to New York, and destroy the government.

Ethan, given his way, would probably have had all the offenders flogged and sent packing off to New York, as he had done with Yorkers before. But Ira was of more cautious disposition, and he prevailed on the old Allen friend, Judge Moses Robinson, to take a different view. Ethan could have had his way: Vermont law provided for thirty-nine lashes for anyone who opposed it. But Ira and Robinson had a longer view. The defendants were represented by counsel, and at their trial in late May they were only slapped across the wrists, fined, and ordered to pay the costs of the trial. On June 4, a general amnesty for such crimes was handed down.

This canny device was Ira's contribution to solving the problem. The offenders had recognized the jurisdiction of the Vermont court—and this destroyed their arguments about being citizens of New York. The amnesty had established the power and law of Vermont over the people of the area. For if one was given and accepted the amnesty of a state, then one must accept its other laws. It was as much a master stroke as any Ethan had ever carried out in his brash manner.

In a way, Ira was the most powerful figure in practical politics in the Republic of Vermont. He was treasurer, which was no sinecure but a very important post. He was a member of the board of war, and a member of the ruling Council. In effect he was the government's envoy to every part of the state. With his various powers, Ira often was the law itself.

The prompt settlement of the Connecticut Valley troubles indicated how this situation could be put to the use of the infant Republic—as long as Ira did not make any dreadful mistakes.

Ethan did not understand such niceties. He got up in court to curse the proceedings and harangue Defense Counsel Stephen Bradley for using artful quirks to defeat the ends of justice and prevent his criminals from getting the punishment "they so richly deserve." He shook his finger at Judge Robinson, his old friend, and shouted, "Let me warn your Honor to be on your guard lest these delinquents should slip through your fingers."

Then Ethan strode out of the room to sit in the tavern and lament that the prisoners got off with only a handful of fines. The fine—£1,477 18s.—could not have seemed very lenient to the defendants; it was just about what Ira assessed as the most he could charge and still maintain his point that Vermont *was* the law. Ethan did not appreciate that, though. This is why Ethan was the darling of the people, who had not yet cottoned to Ira. Young Ira was the manipulator. Levi had certainly hinted at the convolutions of this young man's character. Ira could see far, he could appreciate the turns that must be taken in the road ahead far better than Ethan, who always considered a straight line the most reasonable approach from one point to another. But when Ethan sat in his tavern and grumbled, everybody in Vermont heard, and laughed or cursed or cried, depending on his proclivities.

Ethan and Ira went up to Windsor on the river, to attend the opening spring session of the Vermont Assembly. The men of Colonel Patterson were riding, too, to describe the dreadful proceedings at Westminster and to urge the choleric Clinton to an outright attack on Vermont.

The word of what was on the Yorkers' minds reached Windsor before long, and the Assembly listened as Ethan reported on his suppression of the troubles in Cumberland County. The legislators then shook his hand and gave him a vote of thanks, and before long the Boys adjourned to the local tavern where the thanks were more effusive and more liquid.

Before the week was out they had elected Ethan brigadier general and commander of the Vermont militia.

Meanwhile in New York, Governor Clinton was writing furious letters. He wrote to John Jay, the new president of Congress and a New Yorker born and bred, to the Congressional delegation from New York, and to Washington. Clinton reiterated all his old threats and complaints and added half a dozen. It appeared that New York was finally going to move to crush the infant Republic of Vermont and take back all the territory James Duane and the other landowners had claimed for so long.

Privately, Ethan felt that Ira and his constituents were going much too far to appease the Yorker crowd. Hang a handful of them, he believed, and the effect on the rest would be most salutary. The Assembly agreed with him in part, for although Tom Chittenden and Ira dreamed up this idea of amnesty for crimes past, there was a catch: anyone claiming Vermont justice had to recognize the authority of the state. Those who denied the rights of the state were to be fined the first time, given forty lashes the second, and on the third time there would be real punishment. To these offenders, Vermont law promised, "His right ear shall be nailed to a post, and cut off. He shall be branded in the forehead with a capital letter C on a hot iron." With laws like this, and men like Ethan only too eager to enforce them, most Vermonters breathed a sigh of satisfaction. They did not care what the Yorkers did. Ethan had shown the Yorkers for years what they could do—and what he *would* do.

But Vermont's land troubles were still far from over. Another worry was from Congress, where anything but unity prevailed except on the subject of prosecuting the war against Britain. Virginia and other colonies had difficulties about lands, too. They claimed the lands extending west of them as far as the mind could conjure. Yet men and women on the frontiers of the west already were restive, feeling that the people of the old-established seaboard districts neither knew nor appreciated their problems. There were a number of movements—in Virginia, in the Carolinas, in Pennsylvania—for creation of new colonies or states, and the powerful landowning group was worried. Thus when New York complained vigorously about the Vermont situation, she had allies who did not give a fig for New York or Vermont. And New Hampshiremen were still uneasy and sore over the attempt by sixteen towns on the east bank of the Connecticut to join the Republic. They would never believe that the whole thing had not been fomented by Ira Allen, Tom Chittenden, and the Arlington gang.

Congress decided to investigate. It formed a committee of five members and sent two of them up to Vermont to see what was happening. Congressman Witherspoon of New Jersey and Congressman Atles of Pennsylvania came to Bennington to confer with President Chittenden and see how matters stood in the Hampshire Grants.

Chittenden was blunt enough with the gentlemen. He did not even have to call in Ethan to make the speech. Let it be known to Congress, he said, that Vermonters were sick and tired of interference in their affairs by New Yorkers, and sick of the general disloyalty of the Yorkers who lived in Vermont. As to Governor Clinton's claims—why, the people of Vermont would just as soon live under Great Britain again as under New York.

The two Congressmen then went off to see Governor Clinton at Albany, the capital ever since the British held New York City. While they were visiting the wrathful governor, they had a message from Chittenden: he had just issued an order seizing the property of those who refused military duty. That was what he had been talking about the day the Congressmen called, and he wanted to be sure they understood how matters stood.

So the two Congressmen listened to Clinton's fulminations, and headed mournfully back to Philadelphia, having accomplished nothing.

In the meantime, Ethan and Jonas Fay had been in Philadelphia pressing the Vermont case for admission to the Union and damning the Yorkers up and down. Ethan had fine welcome, as always—his personality attracted people of all views. But nothing happened, and he and Fay came home. When Fay and Paul Spooner went back to Philadelphia in July, Tom Chittenden kept Ethan home, wondering if maybe he was not a little rich for the Philadelphia blood. The result was the same, though. New York and New Hampshire were fighting against Vermont, and their efforts were enough to prevent the Congress from coming to its senses and realizing the dangers of the course it pursued. Vermonters were getting sick and tired of hearing of the machinations of those politicians down in Philadelphia.

How Wise the British . . .

LONDON was still watching and waiting, and the brighter officials of the foreign and colonial offices rubbed their hands as they learned of the growing dissension in the northern part of the rebellious Colonies.

In the fall of 1779, Congress, trying to be neutral, resolved that Massachusetts Bay, New Hampshire, and New York should try to come to terms in the matter of their various claims in the New Hampshire Grants, and that pending a settlement, the people of "the separate jurisdiction which they call the state of Vermont" should not try to enforce Vermont laws over those who professed to adhere to New York, New Hampshire, or Massachusetts Bay.

Anyone can understand how *that* resolution was greeted in Bennington.

John Jay then entered the intrigue on the part of his New York friends. He began by trying to push Congress into meddling in the Vermont affair. As he wrote Governor Clinton, "if they once interfered ever so little they might with more ease be led to a further and more effectual interposition."

By the beginning of winter, events in Congress were moving in ways that made the people concerned with the matter in New York wonder whether they ought to share the Vermont territory with New Hampshire or hold out for all of it.

Up in Vermont Ira Allen saw these dangers and began talking about them. Vermont was now struggling for her very existence, he said, and the next few months would tell the tale. When the Assembly met in October, so dispirited were the Vermonters that many delegates wanted to stop selling lands and wait for New York to put the yoke around the necks of the people of the Green Mountain State. But before that Assembly adjourned, Ira and Chittenden and a handful of fighters had turned the thinking about, and the Assemblymen were eager to go forward with the Republic.

Ira's power continued to increase. He was again chosen treasurer and a member of the Governing Council. He was also
surveyor general, which meant that no lands could be sold until
he saw them—and also meant that he could approve the sale of
lands. Ira was thus in charge of Vermont's purse strings and her
source of income.

Ethan and Ira were chosen to go off to visit other legislatures
and argue Vermont's case. Ira went to New Jersey, Pennsylvania, Delaware, and Maryland. Ethan went to Massachusetts
and also to Philadelphia, where he waited on Congress again.

John Jay had recognized one abiding reason for Vermont's
demand for independence: economics. The Hampshire Grants
were held by various powerful figures like the Allens, who
would be wiped out if the New York view prevailed. Ira and
Ethan were still deep in speculation and feathering their own
nests. The Assembly this session voted to sell the two Hero
islands in Lake Champlain to Ethan, Jonas Fay, and other investors for £10,000. That was one mark of their continued
interest.

Vermont had come to mean much more than Jay knew,
though. Ethan and Ira might easily have worked out an arrangement to cast their lot with New Hampshire in exchange
for surety of their land holdings. But independence had a life of
its own apart from economics, and the Allens were bitten by a
bug that would prevent them from compromising on this issue.

Ethan and Ira both continued pamphleteering this year; the
substance of the pamphlets was well illustrated in one done by
Ethan and Jonas Fay—*A Concise Refutation of the Claims of
New Hampshire and Massachusetts Bay to the Territory of Vermont; with Occasional Remarks on the Long Disputed Claim of
New York to the Same.* That title told it all. But what it did not
tell was the chill sense of foreboding under which the Vermont
patriots lived and worked in these months. The war was at
stalemate; the British were making slight progress, but Spain
was entering the war against Britain. Negotiation was in the air
as Congress worked over a set of peace terms. Vermont seemed
to be swallowed up in inaction.

At this point Ethan's fire may have saved his state, for in his pamphlet he went very far, stating flatly that Vermont would fight with arms any attempt by Congress to impose a settlement. These were strong words coming at a time when the Vermont issue was troublesome but not that important. Consequently, although Governor Clinton and his friends had been hoping in the fall of 1779 for a quick end to the dispute, in the first few months of 1780 it appeared further away than ever, with the added factor that Vermonters were hardening their demands.

If that was to be the way Vermont would act then Congress would respond accordingly. Congress arbitrarily cut off all military supplies for Vermont troops—it was to be "go it alone." This fed the fervor that began again to rise in Vermont. When it came to standing up in an assembly of men and waving his hands and speaking his heart, no man could surpass Ethan and few could withstand his blandishments. Everyone agreed that winter that Ethan had kept Vermonters from knuckling under to Congress. Now Ethan felt he must turn to the military side of affairs.

He took his appointment as general of the Vermont militia very seriously, as indeed he should, for Tom Chittenden and the rest depended on him. For years Ethan had adopted a dog's head as his symbol, and his big flat sword was so decorated on the end of the pommel. This winter, on a trip to Boston to visit the Massachusetts legislature, he secured a military uniform and dog's-head buttons to match his sword. On his return, he established his military headquarters at Rutland. From that base he wandered about the Republic, visiting troops and moving his garrisons around constantly to give the illusion to British and Yorker spies that he had many men.

The banning of supplies for the Vermont militia was a real shock. It meant that Congress would not accept Vermont as a state or as an ally—Congress had thrown down the gauntlet. Vermont was either to submit to Congress or to die. And everyone in the Green Mountain State knew what submission meant—they would be lost in the quarrels of New York, New Hampshire, and Massachusetts over the booty.

Tom Chittenden called a quick meeting of the Council at his place in Arlington, and Ira, Ethan, and the others devised some plans. Ethan was furious. He let his views be known, and then in typical fashion he got onto his horse and rode down into Connecticut and Massachusetts and personally bought £5,000 worth of gunpowder and lead for his Boys. Continental currency was virtually worthless, and few in these states were eager to take Vermont's paper, but Ethan gave his personal notes, and such was his reputation that no one failed to accept them.

In Bennington the Council had been acting. On February 29 Tom Chittenden, Ira, and the rest gave stern warning to Congress: Vermont prohibited the export of wheat, flour, pork, and all other provisions. The Vermonters were determined, and they were prepared, to go it alone.

In March at Westminster the gravity of affairs was explained to the Assembly, and for the most part the Assemblymen reacted favorably to what had been done. Ethan, though never elected, functioned as a member of the Assembly and was chairman of various committees at different times—moving where he was most needed. He kept their spirits up with speeches about the need to fight.

There were a handful of dissenting votes. The first of the New Jerseyites ever to invade Vermont was a gentleman named Isaac Tichenor, known also as the Jersey Slick. He tried to take over the finances of the Republic, thereby becoming Ira's undying enemy. Tichenor managed only to confuse the treasurer's report and create some suspicion before he had to go down to Massachusetts to face a court-martial ordered by General Washington for stealing from the Continental army. But he began working against the Allens. Tichenor was one of three informants who let it be known that Ethan Allen had made a secret trip south to confer with Sir Henry Clinton, the British commander in New York. Washington was so alarmed that he ordered General Schuyler to investigate and, if he found the story to be true, to arrest Ethan at once as a traitor.

Schuyler couldn't prove that Ethan had met with the British. In fact, Ethan might well have done so, and with the blessing of Tom Chittenden and all the other governing members of the Council of Vermont. The Council was sick of the shilly-shallying and double-dealing of Congress. Vermonters were sure of one thing only: there was going to be an independent Vermont, no matter whether it existed in the United States, the British Empire, or alone.

Chittenden laid it all out for Congress in a letter he and Ira composed at Chittenden's house on July 13. President Chittenden stated Vermont's case for independence within the framework of the American Union. He also gave clear warning: Vermont was not going to stand by and watch its own destruction, and if Congress did not accept Vermont, it must remember that the people of Vermont "would still have in their power other advantages, for they are (if necessitated to it) at liberty to offer, or accept terms of cessation of hostilities with Great Britain. . . ."

Let them be warned, the gentlemen of Congress: ". . . For on proviso that neither Congress nor the Legislatures of those states which they represent, will support Vermont in her independence but devote her to the usurped government of any other power, she has not the most distant motive to continue hostilities with Great Britain, and maintain an important frontier for the benefit of the United States, and for no other reward than the ungrateful one of being inslaved by them. . . ."

There was no question about it, Vermonters were thinking very seriously about their future. They would once more offer Vermont as a state to the American Union. They would then offer union with various of the states who might want to make common cause—and then they would "take such other measures as self preservation may justify."

The letter was clear and cool. If Congress and the thirteen Colonies did not want Vermont, then Vermont might very well rejoin England.

England would have liked nothing better. Months earlier, Lord Germain had written Clinton fron London suggesting that Vermont be singled out for special attention. Clinton could promise Vermont, said Germain, that it would be given the status of a separate province and that the land policies of the Vermonters would be accepted.

The first serious contact between the Vermonters and the

British came through Ethan. He, after all, was known in London as the wild man of Vermont; the king himself knew the Allen name, for had not Ethan taken away Ticonderoga at a time when the Crown's counselors were warning that the fight in America was nothing to worry about?

One day late in July Ethan was stopped on the road in Arlington. A man he did not know, dressed in the usual homespun, handed him a letter. Ethan opened it and discovered the missive came from Colonel Beverly Robinson, a Virginian who had joined the British and now commanded a Tory regiment known as the Royal Americans.

How odd! Never had there been a man in all America who hated Tories with so grinding a determination of the soul as Ethan, and yet he could look at this letter, read its contents, and smile, not frown, as he hurried to Tom Chittenden and Ira to tell them about it.

The letter offered a way of treating with Sir Henry Clinton and rejoining Britain. And Ethan, the Tory-hater, the lover of freedom, was ready to consider such a course. His unpleasant encounters at Congress and in the legislatures he visited, the stalling and backing of the American leaders, the outright attempts by New York and other states to subvert Vermont, had finally convinced Ethan that there was no place for Vermont in the Union if she wished to remain independent.

Colonel Robinson had given all sorts of assurances that if Ethan did not work out something with the British, all the discussions that went between them would be secret. Robinson, like his British master, believed that Ethan was the sole power in Vermont and that he could sway the state.

Ethan had no secrets from his brother Ira or their old friend, Tom Chittenden, and within a matter of hours the three were together, heads over the letter, planning the best way of dealing with the British. Not one of them saw much wrong with the offer—indeed, all Vermont's leaders were growing disaffected from the stumbling Congress. Nevertheless, they decided to wait. The letter had taken four months to arrive. They could save it and see what came of their warnings to Congress. It would be better, all things considered, for Vermont to join the other American colonies. But if those colonies simply refused to listen to reason, here was one of the new avenues about which President Chittenden had already warned.

The British ploy had come at the right time for the Vermonters. It gave them an ace in the hole in dealing with their enemies, New York and New Hampshire, and with faint hearts elsewhere.

The Haldimand Affair

GENERAL Frederick Haldimand was the British commander of troops in Canada, and it was to him that Tom Chittenden, Ethan, Ira and the rest of the Vermont Council turned when they were first approached by the British. Ethan told him Vermonters would rather hide in the mountains and live on "mousemeat" than submit to the rule of those damned Yorkers, but from everything Ethan and Ira could see, the Yorkers were about to win the struggle for control of the land Vermonters called their own.

Historians have suggested when Ethan and Ira and Tom Chittenden decided to deal with the British, treason was in the air. That is a harsh word, but looking back at conditions in the early 1780's it is possible to say that treason was indeed in the air, everywhere. General Washington was complaining that unless something were done to better conditions and meet the needs of the army, all the soldiers might well desert to Vermont. So many Continental Army deserters came there—men who were dissatisfied with Congress but still not ready to join the British again—that Vermont kept a special fund for paying and feeding them.

Still, nobody was doing anything for Vermont, and the slight of Congress in halting supplies for Vermont soldiers who were defending the northern borders still rankled with all the other injustices, wrongs, and abuses of the Yorkers and others. The struggle against the Yorker crowd was still the central fact about the existence of Vermont.

Discontent was in the air when the Vermont Assembly met in October. A battle scare was on and at one point some members went home because of a rumor that the British were marching against the state. Chittenden was persuaded to keep his office; Ira held his posts. Ethan was still the military commander, and he was in his headquarters at Castleton, rather than at the meeting. The approach of the British was real, and he kept writing Chittenden and Ira about it.

In a way this was all part of a plot among them. Chittenden had suggested that the first approach to Haldimand should be through a prisoner-of-war exchange, and this idea was adopted. Ethan handled the negotiations in the beginning, largely because of his experience as a military commander. It was certain by this time that Britain was not going to sacrifice Canada in the American struggle no matter what, and Ethan and his friends reasoned that they could jump either way, depending on which side would have them.

There was some attempt made at secrecy in the negotiations with the British, lest the Congress take umbrage. Before anything was done, Ethan wrote General Washington complaining about the treatment Vermont prisoners of war were receiving at the hands of the British. Since Ethan had already written a book on his own sorry experiences as a prisoner, and had told Washington personally about some of them, this was not a surprising communication. Washington answered it as Ethan knew he must, by saying that the Vermont prisoners of war would simply have to await their turns for exchange along with others.

It certainly appeared that the Vermonters had been abandoned by Congress and the Colonies. Congress had withdrawn its troops from the area along the border, leaving General Ethan Allen with a force of fewer than three hundred men to defend the whole state.

Meanwhile, from Canada, the British had been reinforcing Lake Champlain. A thousand men had been sent to garrison Ticonderoga and Skenesboro. If the British confined themselves to raiding, they could keep the Vermonters off balance for years. If they decided to attack, they could go where they wished. And rumor held that other British troops were soon to come and that the Americans would do nothing to help Vermont.

Late in October, a small party came across the woodland from Lake Champlain. One of the party detached himself and made for Castleton. He was a woodsman and he carried himself as though he was walking in familiar territory. He was careful,

however, and as he came into Castleton, where Ethan maintained headquarters, the young man brought a flag of truce.

He came straight into the headquarters and addressed Ethan
by name. The commander of the Vermont troops squinted and
then grinned. By God, it was Justus Sherwood, one of Ethan's
old Green Mountain Boys. In a sense Sherwood typified Vermont's dilemma. He had been as active as any man in defending his holdings and his friends from the Yorkers. But when the
rebellion came, he had flatly refused to fight against the king,
and had moved up to Canada where he could be a loyal citizen.
Loftily and contemptuously, Ethan and the others had stripped
Sherwood's place and then sold it off to further the war effort.
Now here came Justus Sherwood, in the uniform of a captain of
the Queen's Loyal Rangers, on commission from General
Haldimand to treat with Ethan.

Well, times had changed a lot, and Ethan was no longer
fulminating about Tories every time he saw someone who
would not fight on his side. Justus Sherwood had been a great
loss—he had been a leader of the Green Mountain Boys that
winter day when the Yorkers, led by Squire Munro, kidnaped
Remember Baker and tried to hustle him off to Albany to stand
trial. Justus Sherwood and the others had rescued Baker and
saved him to fight again.

How long ago it seemed. After a bit of fencing in which
Sherwood outlined what General Haldimand had on his mind,
the two of them went for a long walk in the woods, and Ethan
said tiredly that he was sick of the war.

This was the opening for which the younger man was waiting. First noting that these were delicate matters, he suggested
that Governor Carleton and General Haldimand knew all
about Vermont's mistreatment by Congress. Britain wanted
Vermont back. The king would make Vermont an independent
province of Canada, and Ethan would be given command of a
regiment. . . .

Ethan stopped Sherwood right there. He would never agree
to some kind of "damned Arnold plan to sell his country and
his honor or be betraying the trust reposed in him." He did not
want anything for himself.

No, it was not an Arnold plan, said Sherwood, referring to the plan offered by the British Major André to Benedict Arnold, which had called for the general to betray his fellow soldiers for personal gain. What Sherwood was talking about was Vermont, which had no status in the eyes of the Americans, and when Ethan referred to his country, he was not talking about the United States of America, but about Vermont.

Ethan had slept on the matter, as he said he would, and the next day he outlined his plan. The people of Vermont must be made to understand the problem they faced, and he, Ethan would undertake their education, as he had done so many times before. The first thing was to begin public denunciation in Vermont of Congress's attitude toward the Green Mountain State and its people. He would do that. In due time General Haldimand could send another emissary, and the Vermonters would talk with him again. All Haldimand had to do was slow down any military effort and give Vermont a bit of time.

Here was diplomacy fitting a Richelieu; Ethan and Ira and Tom Chittenden were playing for time with both sides, waiting for the offer that would preserve the integrity of Vermont. All things equal, they would have preferred to continue with the thirteen fighting colonies with whom they had cast their lot in the beginning of the war with the capture of Ticonderoga. But the promises and assurances of olden days were so much dust; the harsh reality was the constant, insistent demand the Yorkers made for return of the territory on both sides of the Green Mountains to Yorker jurisdiction. They would never live under the Yorker yoke, the revolutionaries of Vermont insisted, and they meant it. Far better to return to the king.

Ethan and Sherwood agreed on a truce. Prisoners would be exchanged. The British would withdraw from along the Vermont border. The Vermont militia was to be disbanded. Armed with this agreement, Sherwood went back through the woods to Ticonderoga and reported to General Haldimand.

He told Haldimand he was not convinced that Ethan was doing any more than playing both sides. Sherwood had hoped that Ethan would now be ready to embrace his Britannic Majesty's knees, but he had been disappointed to learn that

Ethan still did not give a fig for the king's shilling or for the honor of becoming a British colonel.

Haldimand snorted. He had expected no more. "I am assured by all," he wrote Lord Germain, "that no dependence can be had in him—his character is well known, and his Followers . . . are a collection of the most abandoned wretches that ever lived. . . ."

Haldimand was angry because he believed Ethan Allen was trying to use Britain to force Congress to recognize the Republic of Vermont and take her in as an equal partner in the Colonial war against the king. An intelligent man, a statesman, would have contrived somehow to meet Vermont's self-interest to match Britain's. But Britain was governed and served by short-sighted men in the American War of Independence.

The Most Dangerous Game

HISTORIANS have puzzled long over the negotiations of what they call the Arlington Junto with the British and the Congress, and they have used the word *treason* almost as much as the British used the word when Ethan took Ticonderoga at the outbreak of the Revolution. But treason was a meaningless word in the context of the rebellion of the American Colonies. Of what treason could any Vermonters be accused? Of treason against a Congress that would not recognize their state, withdrew its military assistance, and refused to send troops to defend Vermont's borders? Treason against a king who had set up two different sets of property titles? The Vermonters felt a loyalty to the state they had created out of the wilderness. They could be accused of being speculators—and they were. They could be accused of being rebels—and they were. But they could not be accused of treason to the ideal of their statehood, and nothing else meant anything to them. They had dealt with the Clintons and the Jays and the Haldimands of this world long enough to know what they might expect if they followed anything save their own self-interest. So anyone who declared that after 1780 the Allens and their friends were dipping their pens in treason was quite right, if he used a simplistic definition. They were traitors to New York, and had been since they refused to accept its jurisdiction. They were traitors to a Congress that had abandoned them, if a man can be a traitor to an authority that ignores him and will not defend him. They were traitors to the king. But they were fiercely loyal to the Green Mountain State.

All this negotiation had not been done as secretly as some have indicated. The Vermont Assembly had wind of it, although the facts were obscure, and the same old group of troublemakers on the east side of the state was instantly up in arms. In October, when the Assembly met, Chittenden sensed the opposition to his policy and resigned. The Assembly quavered and refused to accept his resignation, for even the opponents to the Arlington Junto knew very well that there was no other group in Vermont capable of governing. So the whole of the negotiations was approved, including the discharge of the militia, and Vermont alone among the American revolutionary states was in a condition of truce with Mother England.

William Hutchins got up in the Assembly in the last days and complained loudly that Ethan had been dealing with the enemy. When the Assembly calmed down, Ethan insisted on resigning because of the questions raised. It was a typically neat Allen trick—the militia was out of business anyhow, and this gave Ethan an honorable out, as well as a dramatic one. The Assembly accepted his resignation and gave him and his associates the town of East Haven in recognition of their services.

Ethan then began the publicity campaign he and Ira and Tom Chittenden had decided to wage. Its object: to force the hand of Congress one way or the other, and thus to settle the affairs of Vermont. It seems very evident that if Congress had insisted on the Yorker position, Ethan and his friends would have lead Vermont back into the arms of Great Britain. There was no very great mystery about it.

Ethan wrote to Colonel Alexander Webster of the New York militia, telling him of the truce. Ethan also wrote to General John Stark, a sympathetic man, although a Hampshireman, telling him the truce with the British was real and had drawn much public attention, and making vague allusions to new and startling developments that might be forthcoming. Ethan's precise intention was to begin the rumor that Vermont was about to rejoin the British.

Ethan then wrote to Congress.

He picked up an idea or two from the letter Ira had drafted for Tom Chittenden, and then went on in his own inimitable style:

I do not hesitate to say I am fully grounded in opinion that Vermont has an indubitable right to agree on terms of cessation of hostilities with Great Britain, provided the United States persist in rejecting her application for a union with them, for Vermont, of all people, would be the most miserable, were she obliged to defend the independence of united claiming states, and they, at the same time were at full liberty to overturn and ruin the independence of Vermont.

I am resolutely determined to defend the independence of Vermont as Congress are that of the United States, and rather than fail, will retire with hardy Green Mountain Boys into the desolate caverns of the mountains, and wage war with human nature at large.

That was Ethan. By God, if necessary he was going to declare war on the whole damned world and fight it out all the rest of his life.

All these events took place in October and November, and mid-November saw Congress and the nation seething with anger and overcome with worry lest Vermont upset their whole applecart.

Rumor had it that Ethan had joined the British, raised a force of six hundred Green Mountain Boys and was going to attack New York. In Albany, where Ethan was regarded as the devil's own brother, this was not too much to believe.

One must admire the Arlington Junto for their thorough planning. As Ethan was publicizing the Vermont position, Tom Chittenden was giving it hardness and life through his executive acts. Colonel Udney Hay, commissary general of the Continental Army, wrote the governor asking permission to buy supplies in the New Hampshire Grants. Chittenden told the Assembly and secured its angry refusal to deal with an army that did not recognize Vermont's existence.

So the pressure was on. Ira's part in it was totally in keeping with his diplomatic abilities and proclivity for what others might call scheming. Part of the plan was to annex territory out of New Hampshire and New York both. That, plus the threat to join the British, would give the Hampshiremen and the Yorkers something to think about. As far as New Hampshire was concerned it was not a real problem to stir up enthusiasm; that had already been done several years earlier, when the first annexation of lands east of the Connecticut River had been tried and had failed.

But New York posed a different case. How sly they were, the

men of the Arlington Junto, in their approach to the Yorkers. In the agreement for a truce with the British, they had insisted that General Haldimand include the Yorker land bordering on Vermont. Thus they had relieved the pressure on their neighbors as well as themselves, and they lost no time in informing the people of the eastern border of New York of the fact. Ira's job was to secure the annexation of the New York towns east of the Hudson River by spring of 1781.

What a plan! Even the weather played into their hands that year. Ira set forth for St. John's to work out the prisoner exchange. But winter came early to the lake, and when Ira got to Crown Point the ice was already two inches thick, which put the use of a bateau out of the question. A scout was sent to the British to report on the difficulty and extend the truce until the next spring. It could not have been better planned to excite and keep excited the level of interest and worry down in Philadelphia.

Ethan had now taken a house in Sunderland, five miles north of Arlington, and this became the headquarters of the Junto that winter. There were mysterious comings and goings, messages from St. John's and Ticonderoga—all kinds of trading with the enemy, conducted cheerfully and with the end open and in view: securing the independence of Vermont. The land was *not* going back to the Yorkers; Vermonters would *not* knuckle under to New Hampshire; Massachusetts Bay could damned well keep its sticky fingers to itself.

Ethan was not unwary of the dangers this course offered; he *was* trading with the enemy. He knew that Washington was worried about it, Schuyler and Clinton were furious, and Congress was puzzled. He knew that over in the east side of the state his enemies would cheerfully chop off his head given any chance, and a conviction of treason, if it could be managed, would be just what they wanted. He warned Haldimand to be careful with the dispatch of agents, for Haldimand was sending a virtual stream of them on the road down to Sunderland, 150 miles by snowshoe through the frozen forest.

The game of the Arlington Junto was risky. All they had going for them was their own determination and ability to control the destiny of Vermont. If they lost either—and public opinion might quickly turn against them if they made a wrong move—then they would indeed be cast as traitors to an American republic to which they did not belong, and quite possibly hanged.

By mid-December, 1780, Ethan and the others had news that their plan was working better than they had dared hope. Connecticut and Rhode Island delegates to Congress were beginning to urge the admission of Vermont to the United States with a real fervor.

Ethan sat at the house in Sunderland, dealing with the British agents. Ira rode off into "the oblong"—that strip of New York land bounded by the Vermont border and the Hudson River—to seek converts to the idea of joining Vermont. Tom Chittenden in Arlington wrote friendly but firm letters to governors and legislatures of other states, imploring them to work for the admission of Vermont to the Union before it was too late. He even wrote Governor Clinton, urging him to forget the land claims and help Vermont. He dispatched a special delegation to Congress to plead again for admission—but also to let it be known that something definitely was up with the British.

This stick-and-carrot approach seemed to be bearing results in the winter of 1781. The Connecticut and Rhode Island legislatures met in February and asked for a convention of commissioners at Providence in April to consider the admission of Vermont to the Union. Dr. Benjamin Gale, a prominent Connecticut doctor and patriot, stated the problem in a letter to his friend Ben Franklin: "If Congress still continue to refuse them admission, there is danger, I apprehend, of their throwing their weight into the opposite scale . . . to which measure I apprehend they have not the least disposition unless forced into the measure." So Congress was warned. Dr. Gale suggested that Franklin be serious in his consideration of what Gale had just said.

But the real rub was a secret agreement between New York and New Hampshire to divide Vermont between them. It had been planned by men like James Duane and accepted by men like Governor Clinton, and it was very hard for any of them to

give up the thought of the wealth it would generate for them
and their friends.

For a time, it seemed as though Vermont's plan was working.
The individual states were being approached to see if they
would override their Congressional delegates. In New York,
there was a ground swell against the movers and shakers who
controlled the state's economy. Early in the year their senate
voted to recognize Vermont's independence, and the house
seemed about to do the same. Furious Governor Clinton, seeing
all that land drop away from beneath his fingers, stepped in and
threatened to disband the legislature. He would *never,* he said,
permit New York to give up the territory of the Green
Mountains.

It was apparent that unless Governor Clinton died or was
removed from power, Vermont would not be allowed into the
Union. If New York could not be conciliated she would be
defied. And conditions were ripe in the New York oblong for
rebellion against Albany. The government had abandoned
these people, most of them Yankees by birth and inclination.
There was no money for aid, no money for defense. And Vermont was keeping the British off their backs and offering them
defense and well-being. Ira let it be known that it was through
the efforts of Vermont that the British had included those
neighboring portions of New York in the truce. Ethan made
frequent trips there and promised the people that the British
would not bother them, while Ira went east to console and
cajole the people on the east side of the Connecticut River.

The governments of New York and New Hampshire reacted:
New Hampshiremen screamed, threatened to leave the war entirely and invade Vermont; Governor Clinton threatened to
send five thousand men to crush Vermont and hang Ethan Allen
and those other rogues.

Ethan and Ira had heard this talk for years from Yorkers and
they paid no attention. Town by town the people of the oblong
and the New Hampshire counties began to vote to join Vermont, while in Concord and Albany governors fumed. Ethan
began in a lordly way to describe the state as "Greater
Vermont."

Washington was worried. He disbanded Seth Warner's Vermont regiment on a pretext, but the real reason was the hatred of the Congress for what was occurring, and his own fear that under certain conditions Warner's regiment could become a liability, if not a unit of treason. This unfortunate act only weakened the ties that bound Vermont to the American Union, and created a new surge of distrust in Vermont itself.

Deserters from the American ranks were now openly welcomed in Vermont, and even Tories were invited to come home. When General Schuyler learned this he began agitating with Clinton against Ethan and the others. They both kept dossiers on Ethan, and now they began trying to get Congress and Washington to declare him a traitor for dealing with the enemy. How nice it would be if Washington would not act at all unless they could seize Ethan and offer incriminating papers. In fact, Washington advocated just that: get the goods and kidnap Ethan Allen, he said, and he would have him tried and disposed of. Ethan was aware of the feeling. He continued to be careful.

Still, he and Tom Chittenden and Ira never let up the pressure for a moment. Chittenden fired off a letter to Washington in January, expressing Vermonter's confidence in Washington and hoping "they could be assured at the end of sharing equal privilege with the United States." He asked for British prisoners he could exchange for Vermonters.

Washington was wary. He said he could not guarantee anything about Vermont's future, and he refused to send any prisoners for exchange. Washington's coldness only worsened the relationship, and Vermont's leaders grew increasingly disaffected from the United States.

This winter of 1781 was the most severe in years. A bad spring had given Vermont a short growing season and grain was scarce. Ira was moving about everywhere in his capacity as treasurer, trading off Vermont land grants for loans and supplies to keep the Republic going.

In the spring, Ira set out for British territory, accompanied by a lieutenant of the militia and sixteen privates. He traveled in his capacity as colonel of the militia, and he carried papers from President Chittenden. They traveled overland and then by boat up the lake to Île-aux-Noix, where they were greeted by Major Dundas, the British commandant. Captain Justus Sherwood came down from St. John's to meet them. The negotiations were protracted and difficult. One problem was that Vermont had sent all its British prisoners to United States prison camps and had none to exchange for Vermont prisoners.

Instead of understanding the problems Vermont faced, Haldimand became more suspicious. Ira did the best he could. He explained the situation: it seemed most unlikely that the United States would give Vermont state status, but it was going to take some time to prove this to Vermonters before they would be ready to join Britain again. The British must bear with Vermont and they must not attack. He would also like some help in case the Americans tried to overwhelm Vermont by force—perhaps the British could feint an attack and draw them off.

The result of Ira's mission was the extension of the truce with the British. Ira started home on May 25 to attend the coming session of the Vermont Assembly and take steps to prepare the people for a union with Britain once again. He went down the lake and stopped off in Castleton and then in Poultney to see Heber, who inquired whether or not he ought to dust off his major's uniform. No, said Ira, things were jut fine as they were going. The next step was to take over those towns in Vermont that had belonged to New Hampshire and New York.

In Albany and Concord there was real consternation. Part of New Hampshire was disappearing into the maw of Vermont. At Ticonderoga, on the other side, General Schuyler was astonished to learn that if he took his headquarters out of Saratoga, all his followers would leave and that place would fall into the hands of Vermont.

When the Assembly met in Bennington in the middle of June it voted in all those Yorkers and New Hampshiremen who represented the new towns, and suddenly Vermont was a larger territorial entity. If they could hang onto the new territory and join the British they would have a province of impressive size.

There were some tense moments when Ira explained his mission to the legislature—for among the Vermonters were some who were intensely loyal to the United States cause—but Ira explained that he had dealt openly with the British and he emphasized the matter of Britain's desire for peace. It was never improper to talk of peace.

The pressure on the United States continued. Would Congress permit Vermont to enter, or not? By midsummer Congress was at least beginning to realize that it must do something. In its ponderous way, it created a committee.

There was a big new issue now: the new territories annexed by Vermont. Ethan, Ira, and Tom Chittenden conferred with other members of the Council, with the result that Ira went over to Skenesboro, ostensibly to arrange for some prisoner exchanges, but actually to deal indirectly with General Haldimand. What he wanted now was a declaration from the British that they would accept the new territories as part of the deal if Vermont became a Canadian province.

In October, General Haldimand prepared a proclamation admitting Vermont into the British league. American armies were gaining on the British in the southern colonies, a fact that the Allens knew, for they were very careful observers of the political and military scene. The French had not only come into the war, but now they had committed ships and troops to the American cause, giving Washington his first chance to win a major engagement and perhaps settle the war. Washington then was marching against Cornwallis at Yorktown.

The Allens figured it this way: if Washington lost then the rebellion was probably lost; Haldimand's proclamation could be accepted by Vermont immediately and she would enter the Empire again under reasonable conditions, without penalty. If Washington won, that was another matter, and the negotiations with Britain might be abandoned. They would see.

The Vermont Assembly met in Charlestown, which was part of the "captured" New Hampshire territory. The first important matter to be considered was Congress's demand that Vermont dissolve her new unions with New York and New Hampshire territories before Congress could consider admitting her as the fourteenth state.

It was too late. Nobody in Vermont was ready to give up the new lands, and the people who had voted to join Vermont were not willing to go back. But, if Vermont was admitted first, she would be willing—as an equal party—to discuss land disputes with Congress and the other states.

As the Assembly convened, the British were moving on the lake. They had the Haldimand proclamation ready, and twelve sloops with troops were heading for the Champlain forts. Ira and the others knew that this was part of the overall plan: the British would seem to be threatening just as the offer to join Britain would be made public. The moment of crisis was upon them all.

Ira delayed it a bit. On October 20 he wrote Justus Sherwood telling him the proclamation must be postponed in view of the British defeat at sea by the French naval commander, Admiral De Grasse. Cornwallis was cut off in Virginia. It was not time for such a proclamation; the people of Vermont were in no mood to listen.

A serious British error very nearly upset the whole scheme just then. Colonel St. Leger, the British commander at Ticonderoga, wanted to send a message to Governor Chittenden and the Allens, and he ordered his men to capture a scout. They did capture a Sergeant Tupper and nine men, but these Vermonters resisted so stoutly that Sergeant Tupper was killed in the struggle. St. Leger wrote a letter of sorrow and sent it with Tupper's clothes and valuables to Governor Chittenden.

Unfortunately the letter was intercepted by the public. The messenger, Simon Hathaway, told everybody as he came up to the governor's office that he had a letter from the British. A huge crowd followed him into the governor's office. Chittenden opened the letter, coughed and excused himself.

The crowd grew very suspicious—and well they might have, had they read the opening lines of the letter: "Not meaning hostilities against Vermont, while they choose to continue inimically disposed to the King's troops as well as to evince the friendly inclinations of his Excellency, General Haldimand, towards them in the strongest manner, I have the honor to send back a scout of yours, surprised by one of mine . . ."

Well, Tom Chittenden and Ira sat down together and rewrote the St. Leger letter leaving out all that. Then they reappeared and the new letter was read to the people, who never were quite able to understand just why a British colonel was sending the effects of a Vermont scout to Tom Chittenden.

There was a heated debate in the legislature about the matter. A suspicious Major Runnals demanded that Ira explain it.

"Good men are sorry when good men are killed," said Ira, airily. That only began the fracas, and the words became more and more heated until finally Runnals left the place.

In a way it was a lucky encounter. Runnals had been so vehement and insulting that the argument had drawn attention away from the facts. For this was a tense moment. The British army was poised to take over Vermont. If Haldimand's proclamation was issued and accepted, then it would be a case of His Majesty's troops coming in to protect the territory. But if the Americans won, perhaps it would be foolhardy to join the British—and *then* if the British insisted on moving those troops on the lake toward Castleton, there would be hell to pay.

The Lone Republic

THE surrender of Cornwallis at Yorktown on October 19, 1781, changed everything for Vermont. The British, having so long confidently assumed an offensive position, were now on the defensive. Washington was talking about a strong move against New York and would have made it then and there except that Admiral De Grasse pleaded a previous engagement in the West Indies, and the French could not give the Americans the support they needed.

Ira was in a quandary, one shared by Tom Chittenden and the other members of the Council. They simply did not know which way to jump. Congress now offered Vermont admission to the Union if she would discard her claims to the new territory she had annexed in New Hampshire and New York. The Assembly refused, and that put an end to that overture. Vermont was very definitely on her own.

By December Governor Clinton was making very loud noises, and Ethan was summoned in a hurry. He had spent the last few weeks in Sunderland composing a new pamphlet that discussed the state of the struggle for territory between Vermont and her neighbors. He hurried in December to the New York "oblong" between Vermont proper and the Hudson, dressed in his splendid uniform, his troops toting one small old cannon to emphasize their strength. It might have been effective to reduce an outhouse, but not much more.

Clinton was so mad that he ordered several hundred troops of the New York militia to quell the rebellion in the oblong. Ethan marched straight for them, and the forces came to a confrontation on the banks of the Walloomsac River, where they sat and glared at each other while Clinton and his friends tried to persuade Congress and General Stark to intervene. Congress was busy with other matters. General Stark, who knew and respected the Vermonters, did not choose to get involved in picking Clinton's chestnuts out of the fire.

Ethan rounded up more volunteers and put them with the force at the river. He rode on his great horse, wearing his impressive uniform with the dog's-head buttons. His huge dog's-head sword swung by his side. Ethan doffed his tricornered hat and smiled his weather-beaten smile at the troops as he reviewed them. The fifes and drummers played, the troops marched, and they even fired the cannon without any regard for waste of shot and shell. Seeing how matters stood, the Yorkers decided to go home.

But the matter was far from settled. If New York was backing away for the moment from confrontation, the men of New Hampshire were growing ever angrier—and with good reason. The towns that Ira had annexed on the east side of the Connecticut comprised much of the land mass of New Hampshire. Without them the state was almost as small as Rhode Island. Naturally, the New Hampshiremen would fight if threatened, and Ira was sensible enough to understand that they meant business.

As the British military position eroded to the point of weakness, all the negotiations with Haldimand were so much waste matter. Britain would have had to guarantee the frontiers of Vermont to make a change of allegiance worthwhile, but Britain could no longer do so.

In their enthusiasm of the summer and fall the Vermonters had been taking some strong actions. When officials from New Hampshire came into the new towns to protest, they were thrown in jail. The tensions grew so great that at year's end an observer of American affairs for the French foreign office wrote home that "these excesses seem to point to civil war among the eastern states."

Ira, sensing all this, went to Exeter, learning en route that there was no joking here: the people of New Hampshire were enraged at Vermont, and a militia force was being raised to march to the Connecticut River. Over many years of travel to and from New England towns, Ira had cultivated his friendships carefully, and he knew perhaps half the members of the New Hampshire legislature. But now they would not even talk to him in private. What he wanted desperately to know was the real intention of New Hampshire. He even engaged a woman spy to help him, but all she could find out was when the New Hampshire legislature would act. He was getting nowhere.

Ira hastened back to Arlington to confer with Tom Chittenden and other members of the Council. He reported that the situation was indeed very serious, and that Vermont must be prepared to fight on her eastern borders. What was needed now was time, and the assurance that Vermont would be accepted as a state if she gave up her new territory. Congress had agreed to that months earlier, but circumstances alter cases. Nobody knew that fact better than the Allen brothers and their friends, who had been jumping from one hot pot to another for years.

Knowing how difficult affairs had become, Ethan, Ira, and Tom Chittenden collaborated in writing a letter to General Washington laying out all the history of Vermont's efforts in the common cause, good-naturedly referring to the failures of Congress to live up to its words and commitments in the past, and admitting that Vermont had adopted power politics as her only line of defense.

They sent this letter down to Washington, Ira even lending the rider his own horse, so important did they all regard the matter.

But before they had an answer to Washington's letter, Congress began worrying over the Vermont problem. In the early winter of 1782, Ira and Jonas Fay went to Philadelphia to present the Vermont case. On the way they passed unknowingly the messenger who was bringing Washington's reply.

When Ira and Fay arrived in Philadelphia they were greeted by some ugly rumors. New York's delegation was preparing a strong statement accusing the Allens of treason against the United States for dealing with the British. Ira was in a poor position. Had he remained in Vermont, he would have been a statesman of an independent nation, but in Philadelphia he was an entreating colonist. He was in much personal danger at the moment. However, he weathered the storm, speaking endlessly about Vermont's very real services to America at Ticonderoga and Bennington, and preventing any action against Vermont.

Imagine Ira's shock when, on arrival home in Bennington, he discovered that the legislature had just adjourned and that Tom Chittenden had persuaded it to give up all the towns in New Hampshire and New York that had been annexed at such heavy cost in work and emotion. The reason was the letter from Washington to Chittenden, which virtually promised in behalf of Congress admission to the Union if Vermont gave up this territory.

Ira was furious. He had no faith at all in Congress's willingness to abide by a promise. Further, in his absence, Isaac Tichenor, the Jersey Slick, had wormed his way into the confidence of enough legislators to secure a considerable amount of power, and even as Ira came home, Tichenor and a new group of commissioners were on their way to Philadelphia, confident that they would secure prompt admission of Vermont as a state, having done what General Washington asked.

Ira's anger was based on his feeling that Vermont had destroyed her own case. By showing weakness, she had given Congress the upper hand.

And, of course, this was precisely what occurred. Congress knew that the British would not prosecute the war further. In the end Congress did not seat the Vermont delegates, although Tichenor had been sure they would. One important outside factor was the growing agitation in Kentucky to break away from Virginia rule. Virginia and other southern states thus hardened completely against Vermont, hoping that admitting only Kentucky would swing the balance of power in Congress to the South. The issue of Vermont statehood was disregarded.

Had the Congress accepted Vermont's latest bid for statehood, Tichenor and his friends might have seized control of the state's government; this was obviously their intention. But the attitude of the men at Philadelphia immediately brought Ira, Ethan, and Tom Chittenden back into a strong position, because they had always warned that Vermont must be prepared to go it alone.

At the Catamount Tavern, Ethan damned the Congress and drank confusion to the United States. As for the people living in the Hudson strip and east of the Connecticut, this second rejection was to be permanent. There simply did not exist any more emotional ammunition to ever again take over outside counties and towns that really believed they belonged with Vermont.

Altogether the timing had been wrong for what the Allens tried to do. The enemy had been defeated in America. The Vermont Assembly itself was growing more independent of the Allens, and could not be relied upon to do the Arlington Junto's bidding as it once could; the Allens were, quite naturally, losing some of the political power they had exerted for twenty years. But Ethan and Ira knew very well that once the pressure was off New York and New Hampshire, the old arguments would begin again and Vermont would once more have to defend herself.

The trouble did not wait long—it began in the fall of 1782 when Yorker sentiment erupted again in Brattleboro. A Yorker mob had risen there to create trouble. When the word came, Ethan was off in Hartford negotiating with a publisher for his philosophical and anti-church book *Reason the Only Oracle of Man*. But he hurried home, put on his uniform, called out the troops Tom Chittenden had authorized him to raise, and headed for the little town of Guilford, on the east side of the mountains, where those damned Yorkers were raising hell again just as Ethan knew they would.

The Troubled Days of the Republic

NOT counting Lucy, who had drifted out of the world of the Allens, there were only three of the tribe left in the fall of 1782. Heber had died in the spring of that year. Yet of the three who survived, two almost completely dominated the young Republic of Vermont, while the third was as far from them as he could get, in every way. Ethan was marching against the riotous and disloyal of Guilford in the east. Ira was backing him solidly as one of the counselors of the Republic. Levi, the Tory, was living in the South and would soon go to England for solace. But the word Tory no longer had any power to stir emotions in Ethan's broad breast. He had exhausted his political fervor on the war between the Colonies and England; now he had no faith left in any government body save that of the Republic of Vermont itself.

Ethan, riding with the fears of dissolution that troubled him and Ira these days, headed for the scene of yet another rebellion against Vermont authority. He knew full well the danger his little Republic faced. The Yorkers would not give up. Curse the men who persuaded Tom Chittenden to dissolve the ties with the New Hampshire and New York counties, for if those states knew but one real deity, it was strength and force. Vermont had shown herself conciliatory and thus weak, and it would take a marvelous show of strength by Ethan to keep the Yorker harpies off Vermonters' backs.

Ethan was on his big black horse, moving swiftly through the countryside and telling his friends he was off on a wolf hunt. Two hundred men rode behind him, many of them old Green Mountain Boys, and all of them safe, sane Grantsmen from the Bennington area.

Down below Brattleboro in the hilly corner of southeastern Vermont nestled the traitorous little town of Guilford. It had a bad reputation with Ethan that went back ten years. The town had been patented by New York, and its people had always

preferred New York's rule to Vermont's. This year they were up
in arms, taking matters into their own hands. They got themselves a sheriff with a New York commission, Timothy Phelps
by name, and they supported this loud-mouthed, uncouth man
who went about beating respectable Vermont officials with a
pitchfork handle.

As they rode on September 7, Ira joined the troop. It was
only thirty miles across the mountains, but Ethan took his time.
At the end of the first day he called Ira to him and asked him to
take twenty men and move ahead as an advance guard and
scouting force.

"Colonel Allen," Ethan said, "while you are about it you
might arrest that eternal Tim Phelps who has been calling himself sheriff."

"Yes, sir," said Colonel Allen, saluting General Allen, and he
spurred off.

Ira this day again proved himself more politician than sol-
dier. On the second day of the march he was ambushed. The
Guilfordites were very clever. They let Ira march right into
town and gave no indication that there was any trouble at all.
Of course, when Ira asked the whereabouts of the pesky Tim
Phelps, he got evasive answers. There was absolutely no trouble
in Guilford: the word had come swiftly enough that Ethan
Allen was marching again, and the fear that this always sent
through Yorker hearts had apparently done the job. But outside
Guilford, when the farmers and Tim Phelps's men learned that
they apparently had only Ira to deal with, they set a trap. Fifty
men concealed themselves in the brush along the road, and
when Ira and his troops came up they opened fire.

Ira's men panicked at the sound of so many more guns than
they had themselves, and they hurried back to Guilford. Ethan
was just arriving. When Ira told him about the ambush, Ethan
gave a mighty shout of rage, spurred the big black on vigorously, and in a few minutes reached the site of the ambush,
sword in hand, standing tall in the saddle, his men hurrying
along to keep up with him.

Ethan halted at the roadblock and danced his black horse
around a little to give a show. Then he lifted that great re-

sounding voice and boomed across the land: "I, Ethan Allen, do declare that I will give no quarter to the man, woman, or child who shall oppose me, and unless the inhabitants of Guilford peacefully submit to the authority of Vermont, I swear that I will lay it as desolate as Sodom and Gomorrah, by God."

The people listened, and they shuddered, for Ethan had often caused it to be trumpeted throughout Vermont how he had beaten and flogged Yorkers in the past. As everyone well knew, the Vermont miscreant law called for the nailing of an ear, forty stripes, branding, and other miserable punishments, so when Ethan bellowed and threatened, people listened. Guilford was tamed and cowed.

They captured Tim Phelps and brought him before the general. Ethan was resplendent in his blue tunic, gold epaulets and dog's-head buttons. Phelps was brought in without a scratch and without a rope on him. What he should have had, it was apparent very quickly, was a gag. He berated Ethan, calling him outlaw, rioter, and usurper. He stood on his dignity as Governor Clinton's man and ordered Ethan to leave Guilford.

Phelps cursed and raised his fist and threatened; Ethan just sat there on the big black stallion and said nothing. Finally, as Phelps began to run down a bit and note that he was drowning in the noise of his own voice, Ethan unlimbered the great long sword and swung it with a mighty blow that cut Sheriff Phelps's hat off his head. The hat came tumbling down to the ground, and Ethan boomed out, "Take the damned rascal out of the way." Then he spurred his horse, and was gone to lead his troops against Brattleboro, another sink of Yorkist iniquity.

Ethan rode briskly into Brattleboro, stepped down in front of the tavern, and went inside to hold court. In an hour he had the names of the ringleaders of the Yorker crowd, and men were moving out to find and arrest them. Ethan arrested about twenty men and moved them north to Westminster to stand trial on charges of "enemical conduct"—by which Ethan meant the conduct of all Yorkers. Ira went along and counseled the judge and prosecutor to take it easy, in the interest of unity. Most of the men got off with moderate fines and warnings to behave themselves. Half a dozen were singled out by Ethan as troublemakers he had met before, and they were dealt with in a different manner—they were stripped of their property and banished from Vermont. Before they left, Ethan spoke to them: "Damn your Governor Clinton," he shouted at the prisoners. "You have called on your God Clinton until you are tired. Call now on your God Congress, and they will answer you as Clinton has done."

And then he sent them packing, one of them to Philadelphia to tell the story to no less interested a listener than James Duane, the eternally optimistic Yorker land speculator. When the other ousted Yorkers showed up in Philadelphia, backed by the New York delegation to Congress and the usual strong letters from Governor Clinton, Congress responded by passing a resolution of censure against Vermont.

That did it. Any of the ruling party of Vermont who had maintained lingering respect for Congress now abandoned that allegiance. With the worsening of the affairs of the British armies, there seemed small chance that Vermont could just then join the British Empire. But her citizens were beginning to turn their attention to the north and away from the south.

CHAPTER THIRTY-TWO

The Happy Warriors

IN the winter of 1782–3, nearly everyone in Vermont, it seemed, was figuring out how to make some profitable contact with the British in Canada. Cousin Ebenezer Allen, still a captain in the militia, was thinking most unwarlike thoughts: he wanted to open a trading firm to do business exclusively with the Canadians. Brigadier General Roger Enos, whose daughter Jarusha had caught the eye of Ira Allen, was trying to raise an army, move into Canada, and get inducted into the British army before the excitement ended and he had to go back to work.

Tom Chittenden and Ira were keeping the Yorkers in line in the eastern section of the state, for Ethan had lost interest once he had made his point, and he was back working on his philosophical treatise. Ira was also busy; as the unmarried son of the Allen clan, he had taken in Heber's widow and four children. Ira was sick of government and wanted to get back to surveying and land speculation. He was particularly sick of a government that would encourage the Jersey Slick, Isaac Tichenor, and as he considered the matter, Ira became more and more rankled. He decided he would resign all his offices and say to hell with it. But the Assembly knew when it had a good man for low pay, and it would not let him quit. He continued on as treasurer and surveyor general.

Times were changing. The Allens did not have as much influence as they had enjoyed previously, partly because the Assembly was taking more power into its own hands and not letting the governor and the Council run the state as they had previously. For Isaac Tichenor and some others, it was a matter of business importance that they stand well with Congress, and they still hoped to secure Vermont's entry into the United States in some fashion. Ira more or less favored this course, too; Ethan was now almost unalterably opposed to it, feeling that Congress had mistreated Vermont too badly for too long. In the spring of 1783 he wrote: "I assure you that Vermont [is] deter-mined not to unite or confederate with Congress." That was his position, and it was made a good bit stronger by the news that the huge Congressional debt would have to be paid by the states.

Spring of 1783 brought an end to the war with Britain and an end to the uncertainty about Vermont's position. Although Ira and Ethan and some others still thought seriously of joining the British, the impetus was gone.

Relations between Vermont and the United States were bad. New York ships and boats would not carry Vermont goods. The Republic was in danger of strangling. Ira began trade negotia-tions with the British in Quebec, hoping to resolve the state's problems.

Ethan was slipping out of the public eye. His wife, Mary, died of tuberculosis, and a few months later his daughter Loraine died, too. Ethan turned inward, thoroughly sick of politicians and their weaseling ways. He turned to the manuscript of his forthcoming book, which would show the world how it ought to comport itself in the future. That became his abiding interest in these years of change.

If Ethan was becoming a less public figure, he was still most active in the business interests of the Allens. He was rejuvenat-ing the old Onion River Company. He wrote General Haldi-mand and friends that Vermont would welcome settlement in the north by Tories and other folk. What he meant was the Allens would welcome settlement of their huge land holdings there. And settlement was needed; the war had ended expan-sion of the Onion River land, and had brought desolation. There were no settlers now in the northern part of Vermont; the failure of the Americans at Quebec had given the Indians free reign in the region, and none dared defy them.

Ethan, Ira, Tom Chittenden and Joseph Fay reorganized the Onion River Company and planned to sell lands with a whoop and a holler as soon as life quieted down. With the end of war, the American farmers were beginning to pick up the threads of the old peacetime existence, and something had to be done with the Tories who had lost everything in the Revolution. Odd, but true—Vermont now took a most enlightened and conciliatory position toward the Tories.

In fact, some of those Tories were close to being the best friends of the Arlington Junto. One of these was Luke Knowlton, who had carried many a message from Ethan to Justus Sherwood and General Haldimand. For his adherence to the king and Canada, Knowlton was declared by Congress to be an enemy of the people, and George Washington had condemned him as a traitor and ordered his arrest.

One night in the autumn of 1783 a gang of Yorkers burst into Luke Knowlton's cabin in Newfane, Vermont, and took Luke prisoner, hustling him across the Republic's line into Massachusetts. They intended to ship him down to Washington for trial and probable hanging.

The kidnaping occurred at two o'clock in the morning. Before dawn riders were knocking at Tom Chittenden's door and before breakfast Chittenden and the others were at Ethan's place telling him of the desperate deed. Ethan listened, then grabbed his tricorn, his tunic with the brass buttons, and his big, long sword. He rode straight for the Catamount Tavern, and there announced in strident tones that he was marching again. This time General Allen would lead the Republic's troops down into Massachusetts to raid the jail and bring Luke Knowlton home. Who wanted to come on this new wolf hunt?

Ethan began taking names and men began sliding out of the tavern. One rode at breakneck speed down past the border and into the American territory to announce that the Vermonters were coming with blood in their eyes to rescue Knowlton, build a fire under any Yorkers they caught who had been involved, and possibly shed a little Massachusetts blood.

As fast as this word was whisked south, Luke Knowlton was whisked back safe and sound and released inside Vermont territory. Ethan did not have to march after all. Just the announcement that he was coming was still enough to make brave men quake, for Ethan never backed down.

*   *   *

Ira was occupying himself this year with the job of settling up Vermont's accounts. The Republic was prospering with the new trade that had developed between Quebec Frenchmen and Vermont Yankees. Timber, cattle, and hogs began to move north to be exchanged largely for British manufactures. In the fall, Ira and Tom Chittenden were re-elected, and things seemed to continue as before. But the old zest was gone. Gone were many of the fighters who had made the Republic. In their place were coming the Jersey men and other new Vermonters, far too many of them men like Tichenor, who had wormed his way up to become secretary of state.

Ira's heart was no longer in government. He and Ethan were immersed in business affairs. Levi, with the war over, came north and was mildly surprised to be greeted by Ethan as though nothing had ever happened and Ethan had not been prepared to hang his erring brother at the height of the Allen feeling against Tories. Soon Levi was in business with Ira, raising and trading in cattle, particularly to the Canadians. Their farms were prospering. Ira called his big place a "plantation," and said without boasting that he and Levi could supply as many cattle as anyone might need on as reasonable terms as anyone. A big statement, and one not lightly made to Canadians.

Since Ira was by this time the largest single landholder in Vermont, management of his property was beginning to be a full-time job. He had trouble with squatters who began coming into the territory. Levi, as usual, found that he would rather trade in goods than land, so he spent most of his time above the Canadian border, handling cattle sales and looking for new avenues for trade.

Ethan and Tom Chittenden were managing political affairs, Ethan from his lofty post without portfolio. There was a very good reason for Ethan's way of doing things: he was a professed Deist, and just as years before in Salisbury he had objected to the state's telling him he must not inoculate his body against smallpox, so now he objected to the religious oath that was required of public officials. He would not swear to the Congregational God, and so he could not hold civil office where that was required. He got quite out of the habit of holding office—as long as Tom Chittenden and Ira had power, Ethan could use theirs.

Besides, Ethan was bemused. In the course of his many visits to Westminster on the eastern side of the mountains, he had met a young widow, Fanny Montresor Buchanan, who lived there with her mother and stepfather. He needed a wife, for he was in the fullness of middle age. She, at twenty-four, needed a husband, and in all Vermont there was no more distinguished bachelor than Ethan Allen. She was bright and witty and very pretty, and she suited Ethan just fine.

As usual he took the citadel by storm. He came to Westminster in January to be sure that nobody tried to disturb the winter sitting of the courts. As far as anyone knew he had not met Fanny Buchanan before, but soon they were seen together everywhere that ladies might go. John Norton, the wag who kept the tavern on the green, remarked to Fanny one day that Ethan was quite a catch.

"If you marry General Allen you will be queen of a new state."

Bold Fanny, who did not like meddlers in her affairs, flashed her dark eyes and replied: "Yes, and if I married the devil I would be queen of hell."

That was Fanny—obviously a wise choice for the intemperate and blasphemous Ethan.

As the story goes, on the morning of February 9, 1784, Fanny was in the dining room of the house where she and her family lived, when in marched Ethan.

"Fanny," he said, "if we are to be married, now is the time, for I am on my way to Sunderland."

From her chair Fanny looked Ethan in the eye. "Very well," she said. All she wanted was time to get her coat.

Then Ethan walked through the house to the other side, where Judge Robinson, his old friend from the troubled days, was having breakfast in the rooms occupied by Stephen Bradley, the Westminster lawyer.

"Judge Robinson," Ethan announced, "this young woman

and myself have concluded to marry each other and to have you perform the ceremony."

Judge Robinson started. "When?" he asked.

"Now," said Ethan. "Right now. As for myself, I have no great opinion of such formality, and from what I can discover, she thinks as little of the formality as I do. But as a decent respect for the opinions of mankind seems to require it, you will proceed."

And then and there the judge did proceed. There was only one hitch, and that came in the civil marriage ceremony.

"Do you, Ethan Allen," intoned the judge at the proper point, "promise to live with Fanny Buchanan agreeable to the laws of God?"

Ethan erupted.

"Which God are you talking about?"

Ethan's God was not Cotton Mather's nor the God of most of the people he knew. His God was the God of all the universe, as revealed in what Ethan called "the great book of nature." That was the only God, he would acknowledge.

Judge Robinson, a friend of Ethan's and a peace-loving man besides, did not want to get into a theological argument, and so he said that would do just fine—the natural God was the God he was referring to. Ethan and Fanny had a narrow escape. Had the judge insisted on the God of the church, Ethan would have marched Fanny out of the chambers and into his sleigh, and they would have gone off to Sunderland to live in public sin.

Back in Sunderland, Ethan busied himself with his philosophical treatise, which he now called *Reason the Only Oracle of Man*. The book was finished, but he was having some difficulty about its publication. He had taken it down to Hartford the year before, and several printers had looked and shuddered. What was Ethan trying to do, they asked, run them all out of business and get them as well as himself hanged? The book was a wholesale attack on organized religion.

Not so, thundered Ethan as he moved about Hartford. The book was a philosophical statement to which Americans and others in the world should be exposed, to counteract the cant of the ministers of the Gospel. Dr. Young, Ethan's one-time col-

laborator, had died in 1777 in possession of the manuscript on
which the two had worked, and Ethan had retrieved it. He
began redoing everything, for in the twenty years since he had
begun it, his philosophy had matured. He saw no reason to
quarrel with its original stance, but there was plenty of new
material and many new ideas that he and Dr. Young had never
discussed. So as the book developed, Dr. Young's contribution
faded.

Ethan's book was an attack on both Testaments. Harmony
with nature was Godliness, said Ethan, and that about the size
of his argument, though working out the system took him some
hundred thousand words. The printers objected, for they saw
how the ministers of Hartford, all New England, and probably
all the world were going to hate them and Ethan if the book
should be published.

Previous publishing attempts had failed, but in the summer
of 1784 Ethan persuaded the Bennington press of Haswell &
Russell to take on the job if he would pay as they went. Better
that than nothing, and in a sense better that than Hartford, for
the correction of proofs and all the other work would be sim-
pler to manage closer to home.

Like many another author, Ethan had the feeling that what
he wanted to say was going to be greeted with great interest by
the public. He was, after all, an accomplished pamphleteer, having achieved more than modest success in that field in the war
years. But when *Reason the Only Oracle* was published Ethan
discovered that the guiding principles of his life, his whole
philosophy, were of very little interest to the world at large.
The book became known cynically as Allen's Bible, and gained
a great deal more publicity as an object of attack in the
churches than in any other way. Only two hundred of the fifteen hundred copies printed were sold (most of them probably
to persons who wanted to attack the work) and *The Oracle*
turned out to be the greatest single disaster Ethan ever suffered,
with the possible exception of his first marriage.

Timothy Dwight, later a famous president of Yale, despised
Ethan's treatise. The Calvinist educator predictably attacked

the book as "crude and vulgar . . . coarse . . . flimsy and unmeaningful." In Europe, and particularly in Paris, however, the book was received with a certain cool approval—for it was the very first American attack on organized religion. Continental Europeans, of course, had been wrestling with religious orthodoxy since the days of Giordano Bruno and before, but they were interested to see that someone on the other side of the Atlantic was able to take his mind off material things long enough to worry about philosophy.

It was a disappointment to Ethan that fellow Vermonters and fellow Americans could not all be made to see the light, but he overcame it. He settled down to an admirably happy second marriage. As soon as the book was published he planned to move from Sunderland up to the Onion River country, and in the fall of 1784 he wrote Ira with plans for a 24-by-24 foot house, two stories tall, and asked that the wood be cut for it that year and wintered over. It was all very well to live in the Sunderland place, but there were too many dusty dreams in the closets, too many soggy memories from that unhappy first marriage to Mary, the religious scold. His new love affair with Fanny was not to be blighted.

Ethan suffered seriously from money troubles in these years. This was hardly strange—the whole continent was hurting from what later accountants would call a poor cash flow. The problem was land: Ethan had lots of land, but he found it sold slowly, and by the time a piece was sold, creditors were hounding him for the proceeds. He was in and out of court, sued again and again by creditors.

Ethan got involved in another great land controversy in the summer of 1785. People he had known in Connecticut, who knew what he had done in the Hampshire Grants, called on him to come down to the Wyoming Valley of Pennsylvania, where Wilkes-Barre is now located. The area had been claimed by both Connecticut and Pennsylvania, and in the fighting, which was not so much different from that between New York and New Hampshire over Vermont, the thoughts of the Connecticut men turned to Ethan; they hoped he would do for the

Wyoming Valley what he had done for Vermont. For his interest, he was to have forty-five hundred acres of Wyoming Valley land.

Ethan did go down to Pennsylvania. An independent state like Vermont was just what was needed there, he said. He made plans to bring a bunch of the Green Mountain Boys down and "vindicate the right of soil to those proprietors of that territory." But nothing much came of Ethan's visit; he was never seriously involved in the Wyoming scheme. Still, because he was known as the most successful of all rebels, he got interesting offers. Another one came from Daniel Shays, the leader of Shays's Rebellion in Massachusetts, who promised to make Ethan king of Massachusetts if he would lead the poor farmers in their struggle against the landholders.

But Ethan did not want to be king of Massachusetts. He wanted to go to the Onion River.

Like Ethan, Ira was slowly withdrawing from the political scene to devote his time to business affairs. He was elected Vermont's treasurer again in 1785, but he was not in the governing Council. He did not want to be tied down by offices, but he had to settle up the accounts of the past, for the opposition politicians, led by Isaac Tichenor, were trying to prove that Ira and the others had enriched themselves by misuse of the public purse. This battle was fought during 1785. By fall Ira had withdrawn completely from government except to stand as a member of the Assembly from Colchester. He moved there from Sunderland just as Ethan moved up from the south to the Onion River country. Up north, Ethan and Ira made a new business arrangement. Ethan turned over to Ira a great deal of property around Ira's sawmills, and Ira gave Ethan a thousand-acre farm near Burlington and agreed to furnish goods from the Onion River store for the next seven years to meet Ethan's expenses.

The three brothers were now reunited. Levi stayed in Canada much of the time, handling trade with the north. Ira traveled about Vermont and in the American states, seeking trade and investment commitments. Ethan stayed home and spun tales, considered his philosophy, and maintained the position simply of being Ethan Allen.

By the spring of 1787, his fifty-first year, Ethan's robust health began to fail badly. He knew it, but he would not give up. He went up to Burlington to break ground for his new farm and supervise the building of his house, while Fanny stayed back in Bennington. Ethan was delighted with his farm, which finally totalled fourteen hundred acres, much of it river bottom and upland meadow, with grain fields and pasture land, and all of it well watered. Fanny came up when the house was finished, and they settled down to real happiness. Ethan was writing another philosophical tract, *An Essay on the Universal Plentitude of Being,* and he was carrying on a fairly large correspondence with several French friends and others in England. He had little contact in North America outside Vermont and Canada. Congress still hated all Allens. New York and New Hampshire particularly detested Ethan, and many others considered him a traitor. Whatever they thought of Ethan, his reciprocal dislike of the United States of America was even greater. But these were satisfying and happy times; Ethan, the warrior, had ended his war and was taking his rest.

The End of the Dream

THE winter of 1788 was promising; the snow fell heavily, and that presaged a good crop and a good year for Vermont. But spring brought almost unceasing rains. The seed corn rotted and drowned in the ground when it was planted in May. The hay, cut in June, mildewed before it could be put into the barns, and much of the crop was lost. The summer was cold and the crops that survived did not grow well. So the harvest was poor, and that winter real famine stalked the land. Ethan and Ira survived. The Allens' resources were such that although they might be pinched, they always managed to make out by hanging together.

Congregational ministers from other parts of America offered the hopeful thought that the famine that visited Vermont was heavenly judgment for Vermont's sins in defying New York, New Hampshire, and the Union, playing with the British and the devil, and putting up with that godless sinner, Ethan Allen. So the wolf of famine was laid at Ethan's door by the superstitious. He heard and he laughed.

Ethan minded his farm and worried over his new book. In February, because of the hay shortage, he looked for a supply and discovered that Cousin Ebenezer, who had moved to South Hero Island, had a pretty good stock of hay left. Ebenezer was more than willing to accommodate Ethan, so Ethan and one of his black hired men set out with a hay wagon. They loaded all day long in the heavy weather and then spent the night at Ebenezer's farm before heading south in the stiff wind of winter. Next morning they came home across the ice. Just as they entered the mouth of the Onion River, Ethan suffered what must have been a cerebral hemorrhage and fell back in the sleigh, unconscious. The hired man had to support him and carry him into the house. There Fanny saw her husband, thought he was drunk, and fled to another part of the house in

anger and anguish. And there lay Ethan, her husband, for once
in his life totally innocent of wrongdoing.

He never recovered consciousness, although they brought a
doctor who bled him. He died on the afternoon of February 12,
1789, in a way that would have made him happy enough. No
fuss, no muss, no religious rigamarole.

The death of Ethan Allen marked the end of the dream of the
Republic of Vermont. For several years he had stoutly held that
Vermont would never become one with the United States, and
had used all his influence to prevent such a merger. He had
kept up correspondence with the British, hoping that one day at
least an economic union could be arranged with Britain and
Canada. Ethan had no use for the pusillanimous, lying, snivel-
ing Congress that had played the Yorker game for so long.

On Ethan's death the ministers of the Gospel rejoiced. The
Reverend Uzal Ogden in Newark lambasted the dead Ethan, as
did Ezra Stiles and Timothy Dwight of Yale College, a fine pair
who never failed to bring Ethan to the snorting stage in life.
The Reverend Nathan Perkins, an adventurous divine from
Connecticut, came all the way north to see Ethan's grave and
make sure he was dead. He viewed the site with pious horror
and intoned, "One of the wickedest men that ever walked the
guilty globe."

But Vermonters did not listen to the flatland foreigners, the
Jersey Slickers and the Yorkers. On February 16, 1789, they
gathered by the hundreds in the cold at Burlington to pay their
final respects. Considering the difficulties of travel in Vermont
in the eighteenth century—by sleigh through blizzard and back
through the long night—it was a touching tribute that so many
hundreds came from every part of the Republic. And most of
them, with the exception of Tom Chittenden and a handful of
others, were ordinary people, not politicians.

They saw Ethan off handsomely. He had a soldier's funeral,
with drums and guns and cannon roaring. They carried him
across the ice above the millpond dam on the Onion River and
to the burial ground. The body was lowered into the frozen

earth while six platoons of Vermont militia fired the farewell shots. Ethan had his send-off.

Oddly enough, except for the constant recurrence of tales and legends, there is very little about Ethan left in Vermont. They never named a town or a place for him. They named them for Ira and Tom Chittenden and others, but not for Ethan. But Ethan lived on—God, how he lived on. The reverends could not get enough of hating him. They passed it down from one genera- tion to another to make sure that if the prayers of ministers would have any influence on the Almighty, Ethan would stay safely down in hell. Sometime in the 1850's the stone his friends had erected over his grave disappeared, and various divines in Vermont and elsewhere declared that it had been blasted into oblivion by their unforgiving God.

Well, He wasn't ever Ethan's God anyhow, so Ethan wouldn't have cared what happened to the headstone. He had fought and lived for Vermont, and troubled as the Republic might be in the hour of his death, it was still the Republic, independent and proud.

A Man of Desperate Fortunes

EVEN as Ethan Allen's ghost went to peace—or to perdition, depending on the viewer—changes were being wrought that would bring about the alliance he detested. Down in New York, John Jay and a number of others petitioned the legislature to drop all claims on Vermont lands. They knew Vermont would never join the Union if the claims persisted, and they wanted Vermont in the Union for reasons of their own, both economic and geographic. The tax burden of the Revolution was almost more than the people of America could bear; the southern states threatened to dominate Congress. Vermont's admission to the United States could help with both of these difficulties.

Times were very hard in Vermont. One of the few areas where life was fairly easy was the Onion River community, largely because Ira supplied farmers there with seed and credit that spring. His trade with Canada continued to be brisk in the items he could supply. Levi stayed on in Quebec, and between them they managed to do rather well in spite of the depression that frowned on the land.

One of the principal exports Ira was sending to Quebec was lumber, and he had a number of rafts ready to go this spring. All looked rosy until the buyers in Quebec decided that too many of the boards were frost-cracked, and they arbitrarily cut the price, leaving Ira and Levi in a financial hole.

Levi, always the itinerant one, skipped on to London to seek his fortune, leaving Ira to manage his affairs in Vermont and Canada. Levi's trouble did not end so easily, though. The ship on which he sailed sprang a leak and he had to land at Cork and take a small boat to London. He was seeking the British navy's contracts for masts and spars; he soon learned bidding on the contracts had been closed down the week before. But Levi was not dismayed. He set about learning the political ropes of British naval acquisition. He and Ira began pushing more for a trade agreement between Britain and Vermont.

As for Ira, he was in his early thirties now, and he had been thinking about marriage. Until this time he had been caring for one or another of the widows of the family, but Heber's widow had died and her children were grown, so there was no woman in his house. Ira had been taken by Jerusha Enos, Jr., named for her mother, and in September he went to her in Hartland and they were married. As a wedding present he gave her the town of Irasburg, which consisted of twenty-three thousand acres of land.

That autumn of 1789 brought an end to the era of the Allens in Vermont. In the state elections, for the first time, Tom Chittenden failed to get a majority, although he led all the other candidates, and as a compromise the electors chose Moses Robinson as the new governor. The Allen power had always been wielded through Tom Chittenden and through close ties with the governing Council, and now it had ended. Ethan in his grave was beginning to be but a memory. Time was passing the Allens by.

But there was more than a holler left in Ira and Levi. Early in 1790 Levi got involved in a coffee-house dispute with a Major Jessup in London, and very nearly got into a duel. Levi challenged the major, as he had once challenged Ethan, but the major slunk off without fighting. This quite made Levi's reputation in London, and helped his business arrangements no end. The whole affair was a matter of honor concerning Americans, and Levi never stopped to consider that with his record he was an odd one to be upholding the honor of a country to which he did not even claim adherence.

In Congress matters had changed much since Ethan's death. Northerners were constantly upset about the predominance of the southern states, and particularly Virginia, in the government. The solution, from the northern point of view, was to secure admission of a new northern state, and there was then only one real candidate—the Republic of Vermont. Also, James Duane and the other landholders had lost much of their influence in New York in the changing times. Ira, schemer that he was, persuaded John Jay and some other Vermont landholders

to give up New York's quitclaim to all Vermont holdings for a
mere $30,000. Thus, at about the time Kentucky was agitating
for admission to the Union as a southern state, Vermont was
ready to come in as a northern state.

But Ira was no longer really concerned about politics. Family
and business matters took up all his time. He was doing his best
to stabilize what would either be a vast fortune or a failure,
depending on how he managed it in the next few years. He still
had tremendous responsibility as guardian of Remember
Baker's children, Heman's family, and Heber's family. Now he
also looked after Fanny and Ethan's children—young Fanny, son
Hannibal, and a posthumous son, Ethan Alphonso.

Young Joseph Allen, Heber's son and Ira's nephew, was sent
up to St. John's to manage the absent Levi's affairs, but the
young man so mismanaged them that Levi's Canadian enterprise was completely ruined in two years, and in 1790 Levi was
forced to hide out in London for several months from a sheriff
armed with writs that would have put Levi in debtor's prison.

Since Jra was one of the richest men in the state, he did what
he could to help Levi, but his obligations were too great. Levi
had his own talents: he managed to secure a cargo of goods for
Vermont entirely on credit in England and headed home with
them. But problems at sea caused them to land the cargo at
Charleston, South Carolina, instead of in Canada, which created
more difficulty.

Levi finally disposed of his shipload of goods and then set
forth again for London, leaving a string of debts behind for Ira
to pay off. Levi had the makings of a scoundrel, all right. Perhaps all the Allens did, but Ira, Ethan, Heman, and Heber in
their own ways had always been possessed of a dream; that ideal-
ism had been left out of Levi's character. He played Crown
politics, trading on the abysmal ignorance of the British about
American affairs. He played with various Tories and others who
wanted to come to Vermont. He once indicated to a Reverend
Samuel Peters that he could get him appointed Bishop of
Vermont.

Thus commercial and family affairs occupied Ira's and Levi's
lives in these years. In 1791, however, Ira went down to Ben-

nington with Tom Chittenden to be on hand for an historic occasion. He and Chittenden were two of the 109 members of a convention that would decide whether or not to accept the Constitution of the United States and join that Union. Chittenden and Ira were among only five in the group whose service and memory went back to the original founding of Vermont as a republic.

There was some spark of independence left, but the convention was overwhelmingly in favor of ratification. Whatever Ira might have felt personally, he contented himself politically with making sure New York would recognize Vermont's land status and not try to wrest away the Onion River country.

Ira might have been a United States senator. He certainly must have had support. But in 1791 business affairs came first. He still had parts of his complex affairs as treasurer and surveyor general to settle with the state, and changing politics always made this a dreary and even dangerous problem. He also had land quarrels up north to settle, and he busied himself with a plan for a university in Vermont.

Like Ethan before him, Ira was always in hot water over money. He had a fortune in land, but in order to capitalize on it he had to keep it in trade, and this demanded cash. So he was always behind in his bills, scurrying for credit to pay up.

Meanwhile his old political enemy, Isaac Tichenor, the Jersey Slick, kept after Ira in the legislature, doing all he could to obstruct the settlement of Ira's old accounts. Finally, late in October of 1793, Ira challenged Tichenor to a duel. Tichenor made a great show of accepting, and Ira hastened to make arrangements for the place and time. Then Tichenor and his seconds notified the authorities, who showed up to interfere. That was the way of the Jersey Slick.

As creditors pressed harder every year, Ira came to the conclusion that if he was not to go broke, he would have to go to the real money market to find backing. That meant travel to Europe. As trustee for practically the entire family of heirs (Ethan, Heman, Zimri, and Remember Baker's estates) Ira was constantly bailing out the young folks from one difficulty or another, and it all cost money.

So Ira set out for Europe. Tom Chittenden, again governor, gave Ira a letter indicating that Ira's purpose abroad was to purchase arms for the Vermont militia. Ira also had an idea for a canal to connect the St. Lawrence with Lake Champlain, and thus make a major international waterway of Champlain and a major seaport of Burlington. (Ira, then, anticipated in his vision the St. Lawrence Seaway of today.)

On December 11, 1795, Ira and young Heman, his nephew, sailed for London aboard the ship *Minerva*. On January 2 the ship dropped anchor at Falmouth harbor in waters so rough they dared not go ashore til next day. Almost the first sight to greet Ira's eye was Pendennis Castle, where Ethan had been imprisoned. He set out overland for London. En route he was nearly robbed by highwaymen who schemed with a wicked inn-keeper to do him in, but he so raised his voice and threatened death to the coachman that the man was frightened and abandoned the plan.

In London, Ira and Heman lodged at the Adelphia Hotel. In order to do his business, it was necessary that Ira stop looking the homespun farmer from Vermont, so his first act was to send for D. Owen, a tailor of Norfolk Street, who sent him his first suit of clothing within twenty-four hours. Then Ira could go out in society.

Ira lost no time in trying to mend his financial affairs. Soon he met with the Duke of Portland and others of the ruling group to discuss the St. Lawrence canal. Then he set about making the acquaintance of various merchants in London, Leeds, Liverpool, and Birmingham.

These were difficult times in England and on the continent, and Americans were often suspect. England and France were at war. The French Revolution, with its Reign of Terror, had frightened the British ruling class half to death. An American in London might be a businessman—but he might also be a French agent and a bloody revolutionary.

Ira was there in his role as businessman, but there were many who remembered him as a violent rebel who defied the king at every turn. Ira now wore Ethan's mantle as well as his own, and because nothing had ever come of the Allen negotiations with Canada, there were many who felt they had always been no more than a smoke screen.

When he left England, Ira flagrantly broke British law. The law prohibited the shipment of gold to France, and in his trunk Ira had £2,000 in gold with which to buy arms for the militia.

In France Ira joined select company. James Monroe was the American minister, and he asked Ira to dine. At the embassy, Ira met Thomas Paine and Joel Barlow, a prominent American then living in Paris. He talked openly of his desire to buy guns for Vermont and his intention of shopping around.

In this delicate and worrisome period an undeclared war continued between the United States and France. Americans, while not actually jailed in Paris, were greeted with vast suspicion, as the papers were filled with accounts of friction, privateering, and seizures of property. All American ships in French ports were seized by the government. But Ira needed a great cash infusion to save his land empire, and the commission on the purchase of the arms would do it for him. So he pursued the matter in the face of the gravest personal danger.

With an insouciance that had made him known across America in the old days, Ira went directly to the Directory that ruled France in 1796, without a letter of introduction or any credentials other than his face and bearing. He explained that he wanted to buy twenty thousand muskets, bayonets, and cannon. He did not explain that he had only about £3,000 in cash and that he would have to buy on credit.

Nor did Ira admit that he was engaged in the rankest speculation. True, Vermont's militia did need arms, and Tom Chittenden had not lied in the letter he had given Ira. But the need was not desperate. When Ira came home, it was his intention to offer the guns first to Vermont, but then sell any excess to the highest bidders. And he hoped to get at least $200,000 for them, enough to discharge his urgent debts and straighten out his financial problems. It was a desperate venture.

On the first of July, Ira received a signal invitation. He was asked to dine by L. N. M. Carnot, the president of the Directory. Ira rushed out and bought a silk coat and a fancy waistcoat for the affair, and hied himself to the Luxembourg Palace, where Carnot lived in state.

Ten days later he had his muskets—all twenty thousand of them, with bayonets—and twenty-four brass four-pounder pieces. The French shipped them to Ostend, a North Sea port.

Ira had to put down £10,000, but he did not have the money. Yankee inventiveness came to the fore: he encountered a wealthy speculator named Peter Capa, and sold him £6,000 worth of his Vermont lands.

Ira's problem now was to get the arms shipped, since no French vessel would carry goods for America and no American ships were allowed to touch French ports. Certainly it was going to be a risk to get the guns home, for if a French frigate or a privateer captured the cargo vessel all would be lost. Not even Carnot could help Ira there.

There was only one thing to do. Ira went back to London and chartered an American ship, the *Olive Branch*. This vessel had been engaged in some rather shady transactions recently (about which Ira knew nothing), and she was held suspect by the customs agents of half a dozen lands. She managed to carry cargoes from England to France, even though the countries were at war, by declaring for Spain and then landing at Dunkirk in northern France.

On September 11, 1796, the *Olive Branch* sailed from London, again ostensibly for Spain, and again she arrived at Dunkirk. She discharged her cargo and then went to Ostend to pick up Ira's guns.

Ira went back to Ostend, only to discover that the French bureaucracy had broken down and the guns had not been received. It took two weeks to straighten out that mess, and when it was cleared away he discovered that the *Olive Branch* could take only three-quarters of the load, which meant a big loss in potential profit.

Then Captain Bryant of the *Olive Branch* announced he did not like the idea of shipping guns. He complained so loudly that crew members heard him. Several crewmen, scenting the price of a number of hogsheads of rum in the air, stole a barge and took it to England, where they notified the Admiralty that an American was shipping guns out in the *Olive Branch.* Whitehall sent two frigates to patrol off the port of Ostend.

Ira learned the warships were coming, and it did not take him long to figure out why. He went ashore and bought paints and brushes, then went back aboard ship and made friends with Captain Bryant. Both moves were essential to his plan.

What Ira contemplated was a desperate venture: heading out to sea in a ship only ninety feet long, manned by six sailors, directly into the guns of the British frigates.

Captain Bryant started out from Ostend and took the short route, which meant the shallows, in order to reach Dunkirk. Thus they passed well inshore of the British, who could not make such shoal water safely. On the trip out the sailors were busy changing the colors of the hull, adding a pair of streaks on the sides so that she did not match the description given of the *Olive Branch.*

At high tide on the evening of November 12, they went over the great Channel sandbar in their new colors. They were stopped briefly by a French squadron, but when Carnot's papers were produced the Frenchmen waved them on. Before daylight they were off the English coast, the high cliffs clearly in view. They kept along that coast, passing a dozen British men-of-war but being careful not to speak to any of them or in any way to gain their attention.

At last they were out on the broad North Atlantic, and all seemed safe. They sailed before a fair wind, day after day, making excellent time on the westerly crossing. Then, at noon on Sunday, November 20, when they were eight days out, they sighted their first sail. Two hours later they were stopped by the British ship of the line *Audacious,* a seventy-four gun vessel under Captain Gould. The captain was coming home after three years on the western station, and this was only a routine check occasioned by the war with France. But soon Captain Bryant and Ira were sent for and were closeted with the British captain. Ira took along his copy of Jay's Treaty of 1794 between the

United States and England, and his papers showing how and why he had acquired the cargo of weapons.

But the fact remained that they were weapons, and Captain Gould decided he must seize them and carry them to port. He might have let them go but for the damning fact that the ship's log showed she had previously been carrying contraband goods from London to Dunkirk, which made the ship a legal prize.

It was plain bad luck. Captain Gould's instructions ordered him to seize all armament cargoes in neutral bottoms. The *Olive Branch* had obviously broken the British rules of war. There was really nothing to do but to argue. Argue Ira did all the way back to Portsmouth, where they arrived on December 11.

Immediately Ira was on his way to London to be in touch with Minister Rufus King of the United States. There was some value at least in belonging to the United States—it gave the Vermonters foreign representation for the first time. King was in touch with Lord Grenville, the foreign secretary. And the wheels began to grind, very, very slowly.

Time was precisely what Ira did not have. The whole venture had been an attempt to raise cash quickly for the Allen enterprises. From one side and another the demands for money began to come in on Ira. Back in Vermont a businessman named John Kelly got a judgment against him for £1,300. The Jersey Slick, still trying to embarrass the Allens, insisted that Ira owed Vermont another £1,300 from his days as treasurer.

The British were suspicious. They expected some kind of attempt by the French in Quebec to stage an uprising to help the war in Europe, and they wondered if Ira's guns were actually intended to arm the French Canadians or be used by Americans, under Ira's command, in a joint action against the British in Canada. They distrusted the Allens because the Haldimand negotiations had gone on so long without producing anything. They distrusted Vermont as too damned independent. American minister King even indicated his own distrust, for he wrote Secretary of State Timothy Pickering with very serious questions about Ira's good faith. Had Ira been willing enough to reveal the speculation in which he was involved, it still would not have convinced everyone. Ira, without yet knowing it, was in deep trouble.

The battle raged, involving men in the highest places. Representative Matthew Lyon of Vermont wrote asking that the arms be released. He assured the Secretary of State that Ira was only trying to serve Vermont. Pickering asked London to release the arms; that was what the President wanted, he said. British Minister Robert Liston wrote from America that he thought the arms ought to be released. But General Prescott, the new governor of Canada in 1796 and an old Allen foe, was still suspicious. He wrote the Duke of Portland that he had no proof of any wrongdoing—but then he stuck in the dagger: "I may add that Ira Allen is well known here as being a man of desperate fortunes; and that the lands he boasts of being possessed of are so deeply mortgaged as to be of little or no real value to him."

The delay went on and on.

It was May of 1796 when Ira's case finally was heard in the Court of Admiralty. But what kind of justice could Ira expect from a judge who exhibited this attitude: "What, the state of Vermont wants twenty thousand arms?" he demanded of Ira's counsel. "No such thing. Four or five hundred would be enough for them; why, they are a young, sucking state, the people were a banditti, transported for crimes from France and England."

Having voiced that opinion of Vermont, the judge denigrated Ira. The arms might well be for revolution against the United States, he said—the Allens were well-known revolutionaries, and Ira's very name connoted rage, revenge, and madness.

Ira gave up on British justice and settled down. He began working on a book, *The Natural and Political History of the State of Vermont* . . . , a remarkable work that he wrote entirely from memory in order to defend himself against critics who spoke adversely about his role in the Haldimand negotiations and other episodes in Vermont's early history. As for the arms—by the end of summer friends were advising him to go home: if the guns were ever freed it would be after the political situation cooled down. Ira seemed to agree and made some plans for departure.

Meanwhile Tom Chittenden died, and Ira lost his greatest and most important friend in Vermont. Levi, who was back in America, apparently saw some way he could make financial hay out of political troubles in Quebec. He went there, to the consternation of the ruling body, and was called in, questioned, and released. But later the Canadian authorities issued a warrant for his arrest on charges of high treason. There really was a plot of sorts, largely an attempt to mulct money out of the French government—the sort of thing that would appeal to Levi. Somehow, by various processes, all this was hooked back to Ira in London.

If anything worse could happen to Ira that fall, it was the election by the legislature of Isaac Tichenor to the governorship of Vermont. Ira had gone away from America with his best friend in the office; now that friend was dead and Ira's worst enemy was governor. One of Tichenor's first acts was to remove Ira as general of the militia because he was out of the country.

In the spring of 1798, as the arms case dragged on, Ira decided to go to France to secure more proof that he had indeed bought the arms openly and that the purpose was for shipment to Vermont. France had changed immensely since he had left. Carnot had been driven from power by a coup d'etat, the dictator Barras had become the most powerful figure in France, and the Duke of Talleyrand was foreign minister. None of them had much use for Carnot or any of his works.

Ira landed at Gravelines and was immediately detained by the French authorities. A passport had to come from Paris, they said, so Ira was taken to a private house and kept there under guard. He saw that he had made a mistake in coming back to a France in turmoil. He asked for permission to leave and return to England. No one could give him the permission. He was a prisoner.

Finally a pass to go to Paris arrived, and Ira set out for that city. He took up residence at the Hôtel de Boston and began trying to see various authorities. Ira was passed from one ministry to another, but it seemed he was finally getting someplace, for he was treated most sympathetically. But he did not know that he had already been denounced as a British spy, and that Carnot, with whom he had dealt, had apparently pocketed most of the money from the arms sale. In any event the whole transaction, when reviewed, was anathema to Barras and the French Directory. On September 1, 1798, Ira was arrested. Barras's secret police came for him in his room at three o'clock in the morning and hustled him off to prison. They said he was arrested because he had not registered with the Ministry of Police. After half a day he was sent to Temple Prison, where Louis XVI and Marie Antoinette had been held, too, if that was any comfort to him. Ira was caught in the coils of the Revolution.

CHAPTER THIRTY-FIVE

The Long Ordeal

CLAPPED in a bare and filthy jail cell, Ira was left alone to live on water and a few scraps of food. After a few days he was summoned to examination by Citizen Martin, a justice of the peace, but he was told nothing. Then he was sent back to his cell. Ira bribed a guard and managed to get a bed sent in from his hotel. He bribed for food and other necessities, and for mailing privileges. Bribery was part of prison tradition.

Three weeks went by and nothing happened. Ira's barrage of letters disappeared into the maw of the French revolutionary government, and he learned nothing.

The months rolled by—the cooling of September, the brisk of October, the chill of November. Ira knew all the time that his imprisonment was occasioned by his nationality: he was a victim of the undeclared war between France and the United States. But what saved him from possible execution as spy or agent of the British was knowledge of the role of the Allens in Vermont's formation. In the end, that revolutionary zeal of years past saved Ira, and freed him on December 7, 1798.

Ira remained in Paris at the Hôtel de Boston, conscious that he was followed wherever he went, and careful in no way to blame the Directory or to indicate that his arrest and imprisonment had been anything but a mistake.

Ira was very lucky, caught up in the turmoil of history, to have saved his life; he was far less lucky in financial matters.

For years Ira was regarded as the shrewdest and richest of the Allens. Obviously there was some truth in it, and some truth in Levi's contention that Ira was the greatest schemer of them all. But seldom has any man been so plagued by charges and lawsuits as Ira Allen was in the last days of the eighteenth century. Part of the reason for it was his generosity. He educated several of his brothers' children, and the whole family came to believe that his resources were without end. Thus, when he was abroad for so long, Lucinda, daughter of Heman, brought a suit against him for $46,000, charging that she and her husband were due it from her father's estates, which had been managed by Ira after Heman's death. This was just one of many problems; Ira might be in Europe, but he employed half a dozen lawyers in Burlington, Boston, and New York to keep his affairs together.

Ira still hoped to get all the documentation he needed to sell his arms in New York, where he might realize $100,000 for his pains and thus solve his problems. He was lulled by his release from prison, and thus was quite unready on December 30th when the police arrested him again and sent him to Pelagée prison, an even worse place than Temple.

Ira ran out of cash quickly and sold most of his clothes to his jailers to get additional food. The man who had given £4,000 for the establishment of the University of Vermont just a few weeks before sailing for Europe was so poor that he was counting on ten louis owed him by the landlady of a Gravelines inn. Mrs. Joel Barlow sent him little bits of money and handled the pawning of his gold watch for him.

Ira fell ill, and the American minister sent a doctor, but the medicine he prescribed was seized by the prison doctor and another substituted. Ira always claimed that the prison doctor tried to poison him, probably on behalf of enemies in England who were trying to get Ira's guns. The guns were like gold—they had an immense value, and any number of fortune hunters were doing their best to get control of this treasure trove and make their own fortunes. One person after another entered the case, each one trying to get something for nothing.

Meanwhile Ira was sitting in a prison full of French citizens, studying a French grammar Mrs. Barlow had sent him. On May 1, 1799, he celebrated his forty-ninth birthday in prison.

Ira's problems were complicated by the internal struggle for power in Paris. In elections the people showed a distaste for the extreme Jacobinism exhibited at that time by the Directory, and this made the men of the Directory more nervous and stubborn than ever. They paid no attention to Ira's pleas and petitions. In jail he sat, day after day, as the seasons changed and summer came to Paris.

Finally Ira's guns were sent on to New York, where they lay in customs, uncollected, and various schemers there figured how they could deprive Ira Allen of them. Ira did not even know about their dispatch for months; his letters outside were usually seized and held by the commissioner of the prison and the Ministry of Police without ever being sent on.

Any number of people interceded for him: Barlow, a succession of American consuls, Thomas Paine, and General Thaddeus Kosciusko, a hero of the American Revolution. A faint hint of light came in the spring of 1799 when the bureaucracy began to change, but what was needed, Ira was sure, was to get the despotic Barras out of the Directory. He was certain Barras had been bribed by enemies in England to keep him in jail.

In September, Ira made one last bold stroke. His health was deteriorating fast, and he did not think he could survive another winter in prison. He wrote a strong letter in his own behalf and sent it to the legislators. To do this was to go over the heads of the Directory, a dangerous move. But Ira felt he had no other choice. He sent the letter, written in French, to Mrs. Barlow, with instructions that she have a thousand copies printed and distributed. Ira was up to the old Allen trick of publicizing his situation, hoping to better it.

Even the dispatch of the letter caused certain uneasiness among the officials. The Minister of Police sent a man to tell Ira he would let him go, if he would promise to stay in Paris and if others would go his bond. Ira refused. He had been trapped once by staying on in Paris. Not again.

Finally on September 14, Ira was released, with the comment by Citizen Fouché of the Ministry of Police that his arrest had been wrong in the first place.

So a sick, penniless Ira Allen came out of jail and went immediately to the Hôtel de Boston. He had no recourse but to stay on in Paris while he gathered his resources about him and recovered his health. It took five months to accomplish the latter. Meanwhile he began assembling a wardrobe of velvet knee britches and silk stockings. Long gone was the boy in homespun who braved the night in the forest of Connecticut to rescue his starving pigs. Europe had made Ira a gentleman and taught him a fine taste for Bordeaux wines and other French delicacies.

Unfortunately the key to his fortune now lay not in France, but in New York, where his guns were rusting. His suits in London had been settled, but there were half a dozen more pending against him in Vermont, and the fact that he had been jailed in Paris did not help much.

Nearly a year later, with all his European affairs finally put in good order, Ira came home. He sailed on the ship *Neptune* from Bordeaux and arrived in Philadelphia on January 2, 1801. It was too late to go home to Vermont, and he spent the winter in Washington.

While he was there, Ira learned that Levi had died in the Burlington jail, where he had been confined for debt. Levi had some assets, about $33,000 worth, but he had more liabilities, and in modern times would have been bankrupt. In the beginning of the nineteenth century life was more cruel: Levi's body could not be reclaimed by relatives, because anyone who claimed a body had to pay the body's debts. So the Burlington jail yard was extended and Levi Allen was buried in the part of the place reserved for paupers.

One of Ethan's heirs sued Ira; one of Remember Baker's daughters sued him. His affairs in Vermont were in dreadful shape, and he had not heard from his wife Jerusha in months, nor she from him. For some reason that Ira was never able to fathom, most of his letters to Vermont went astray.

When some of the people who had been speculating in Ira's lands and renting his properties learned that Ira was home, they held a meeting to decide how to welcome him. They suggested that they ought to meet him with a company of horsemen, make a public procession through Burlington, and end with a testimonial dinner.

They took that suggestion to Judge John Law, an old friend of Ira's who had watched the leases and the wriggling and the lawsuits all these years. He looked up at them with a level glance.

"Waal," he drawled, "I think maybe General Allen would

consider it a greater compliment if you would give up the lands you stole from him."

Thus ended the subscription dinner plan.

In the spring Ira went to Richmond and tried to sell his guns to Governor James Monroe, whom he had known in Paris, but with no success. He went back to Vermont in May, after an absence of five years. Jerusha hardly recognized him. He had become a man of the world; he had aged and was thin. He in turn hardly recognized the family. Ira H., his oldest son, was eleven; Zimri Enos was eight; Maria Juliette was six.

The family reunion was warm, the regional one less so. There was no testimonial dinner; instead, Ira was greeted by a whole new handful of lawsuits. At least Jefferson was President and the Republican surge was moving across the land; the opposing Federalist party had lost its kick, and the Jersey Slick saw some of his power and influence in Vermont begin to wane.

So desperate were Ira's affairs in 1801 and 1802 that he maintained his personal freedom only because the Vermont legislature granted him special immunity from arrest in the many cases pending against him. Most of these grew either out of manipulation of his property by trusted persons, or outright theft of it. Some suits came from relatives—the new generation of Allens, with the exception of young Heman, his brother's son, seemed to have lost all the old Allen spunk, and were determined to have what was theirs without regard for how they got it. Young Heman would do well. He would later go to Congress and become American minister to Chile. One of Ethan's daughters, Fanny, would become celebrated when she converted to Catholicism, became a nun, and worked very diligently in Montreal. The lives of the others were undistinguished.

Ira's affairs went from bad to worse. When Ethan and Heman were alive, the three had worked through a loose partnership. But their heirs had no concern for anything but money, and now they secured huge judgments against Ira, which meant the sacrifice of much of the land of the old Onion River Company. In 1803 his financial worries became so great that Ira deeded all his property to young Heman and the other heirs, including his personal possessions, and fled Vermont to avoid the claims against him. He left Jerusha and the children behind. The only possible way he could free himself from debt was to take up residence in the new state of Kentucky, which had a bankruptcy law that would protect him. Further, his friend Matthew Lyon was living in Kentucky and was about to run for Congress there.

While Ira was riding his horse south, the vultures clustered around Burlington to tear up the remains—the estate of the man who had first seen the whole area and had almost single-handedly founded the state of Vermont. Ira Allen, the last of the clan, was gone, and he would never again set foot in Vermont.

CHAPTER THIRTY-SIX

Envoi

ALL the rest was anticlimax. If Ethan had gone the way of the hero, then Ira went the way of the schemer he had been called by others. All that he had wrought, save only the state of Vermont itself, went down the drain.

The next few years were a recital of lawsuits and claims, the efforts of a middle-aged man to retain what he could of the fruits of his vision and enterprise. Everything rang hollow. He had gotten free on the arms matter. When Britain and France made peace, he had finally sold his guns. But the firm that handled the deal went bankrupt, and Ira's money disappeared into the pit of their failure.

Ira sued the British for all the trouble it had caused him plus the thousands and thousands of dollars of his out-of-pocket expenses. The suit failed. He tried to recoup by putting some property into the hands of friends in Vermont—but the friends were betrayed by associates and the property was seized to become a part of the great tangle of Ira's affairs.

Jerusha chose to stay on in Vermont, and the children remained with her. After that evening in the spring of 1803 when he left the house and headed south along Lake Champlain, Ira was never to see house or wife again.

He stayed most of the time in Philadelphia. He secured quitclaims from all his creditors in England, but dealing with the government after the fact was a tiresome and seldom useful business. Ira's efforts were fruitless for the most part. With the replacement of the Jersey Slick and his henchmen in Vermont politics by a new Republican crowd, Ira's reputation there at least glowed again. Like Ethan, he was a tireless pamphleteer, and he wrote on all subjects dear to him, from his muskets to the ship canal for the St. Lawrence.

He lived on Sixth Street in Philadelphia, overlooking Independence Hall, but he never gave up hope of returning to Vermont. When he saw an advertisement for the sale of his

Colchester farm, he issued a warning to all concerned that it was fraud and he was in the process of suing for the return of his lands.

The legal processes ground very slowly, but at least Ira had some satisfactions in his last years. One of his enemies, Brigadier General William Hull, who had stolen some of Ira's property, was tried and convicted for surrendering Detroit to the British during the War of 1812. Silas Hathaway, who had stolen much of Ira's land when Ira was away in Europe, was sent to jail for his speculations. John Graham, the London swindler whom Ira always accused of arranging his arrest in Paris, moved on to New York and was last heard of salting gold mines in North Carolina.

Ira died one January day in 1814, still living in Philadelphia, where he was listed in the directory as Ira Allen, gentleman. No one of the family was there, and none went to Philadelphia for the funeral. He was carried in lonely silence to the burial ground of the Free Quakers on Fifth Street.

It was the end of the fighting Allens, for there were none to succeed them in character, strength or opportunity. Ira died penniless—so poor that not even a headstone could be erected above his grave—and neglected by all his relatives.

The Allen dream of the Onion River Company was cut up among dozens of heirs. Ira H. Allen, Ira's son, finally inherited enough to make him a very wealthy man before he died in 1866. But the thieves and the heirs got most of the Company's substance, except for a little bit that was saved for the University of Vermont—and that was almost entirely due to Ira's foresight. For the rest, Vermont fell into the hands of speculators more ravenous than the Allens themselves, and even the Onion River disappeared from the maps, to be renamed the Winooski.

Today Vermont exists as a monument to Ethan Allen and his clan. The state would not be what it is if the Allens had not given it leadership during the difficult years when it was being settled and nurtured as a separate entity with its own name and boundaries and government. Boisterous, opportunistic, self-seeking—these things the Allens were. But they were also imaginative, enterprising, and able. Hard-living they were, but also they were hard-working. They lived in trying times, and they died quietly or tragically, but in the fullness of their days they were adventurous, and seized upon the future with zest for all it could afford. American history, in addition to the history of Vermont, is richer because they were equal to the excitement of their era.

☆ AFTERWORD ☆

The Allens in Historical Literature

THE Allen brothers not only shaped the early history of Vermont but also provided historians with essential accounts of the dramatic events of their lives. Ethan Allen, fortunately, recounted his experiences as a British prisoner of war in a lively account which is much more sprightly than its long-winded title would suggest: *A Narrative of Colonel Ethan Allen's Captivity . . . Containing His Voyages and Travels, With the most remarkable Occurrences respecting him and many other Continental Prisoners of different Ranks and Characters . . . Interspersed with some Political Observations.* This has been a popular book with the American reading public, several editions having been published since it first appeared in 1779. Brother Ira wrote an *Autobiography* and also *The natural and political history of the state of Vermont, one of the United States of America. To which is added, an appendix, containing answers to sundry queries, addressed to the author* (1798). Ira's Autobiography is reprinted in James B. Wilbur's *Ira Allen, Founder of Vermont: 1751–1814* (two volumes, 1928), and his *Natural and Political History* was reprinted in 1969 by the Charles E. Tuttle Company of Rutland, Vermont and Tokyo, Japan. An excellent essay about Ira's *History,* and about Ira himself, is "Ira Allen's Vermont" by H. Nicholas Muller III. This is in *Early Nationalist Historians,* the concluding volume in a four-volume set published in 1974 under the general title *The Colonial Legacy.*

Muller is the most recent of several scholars, of whom Wilbur was the first, who have carefully researched the surviving evidence about the Allens and published their findings. John Pell's *Ethan Allen* (1929) came shortly after Wilbur's *Ira Allen,* and Charles A. Jellison's *Ethan Allen: Frontier Rebel* (1969; paperbound reprint 1974) carries on where Pell left off by drawing upon hitherto unknown sources and recent historical thinking to give us an informed portrait of Ethan and his era. Matt B.

Jones gives the most detailed account of the controversies arising from the Hampshire Grants in *Vermont in the Making—1750–1777* (1939) ; and Jones's book is augmented by Chilton Williamson's *Vermont in Quandary: 1763–1825* (1949) .

Stewart Holbrook's *Ethan Allen* (1940) provides the most colorful depiction of this most colorful personality, and Frederic F. Van de Water's *The Reluctant Republic: Vermont 1724–1791* (1941; paperback reprint 1974) is perhaps the most readable popular narrative of Vermont's formative years. The 1974 paperback edition is enriched by an Introduction, written for it by H. N. Muller III, which places this book in the context of modern historical writing about Vermont.

There is still much to be written about Vermont during those tempestuous years when it was conceived as a separate entity. Vermont's future, so predictable to us in hindsight, could have been cast in any number of different directions. From Benning Wentworth's first grant of land in the disputed territory in 1794, until the British and Americans concluded their second war in 1815, Vermont's history deserves careful scrutiny, both in terms of particular occurrences and overarching interpretations. Among the benefits of this new scrutiny, a worthy addition to the bicentennial era now underway would be biographical sketches of those individuals whose lives intersected with the Allens'. Seth Warner is one of these, and Remember Baker and Robert Cochran are two others. The bicentennial era, for Vermont, should properly continue until March 4, 1991, the two hundredth anniversary of Vermont's admission to the Union as the fourteenth state—ample time for research and writing about Vermont's colorful past.

EDWIN P. HOYT

Index

Albany, N.Y., 17–18, 25–6, 30, 33, 35–6,
39, 41, 43–4, 46–8, 52, 67, 74, 101,
108, 125, 173–4, 186, 197, 205–7
Allen, Abigail Beebe, 90
Allen, Ebenezer, 38, 60, 155, 220, 230
Allen, Ethan
  birth & childhood, 3
  education, 4–5
  farming, 7–8, 229–30
  in French & Indian War, 8
  mining business, 8–9, 11
  marries, 8–9
  philosophy, 10–13, 18–19, 30, 114–15
  religion, 10–11, 14, 31, 43, 223, 225–7
  writings, 13–14, 32, 38, 47, 80, 82–3,
    175–6, 181, 189–90, 201, 215, 226,
    229
  pleads case of Hampshire Grants, 18,
    24, 27
  land speculation, 25–6, 38, 51, 60, 66–
    7
  head of Green Mountain Boys, 29
  journey to New York, 62–3
  at Fort Ticonderoga, 91–8
  at Crown Point, 99
  loses St. John's, 102–3
  attack on Canada, 103–9, 114–18, 121
  loses command, 110–11
  captured, 118–20
  prisoner of British, 121–36, 139, 143–
    5
  asked to join British, 146
  in New York, 146–8, 161
  jailed, 161–4
  commissioned as colonel, 169
  Vermont prosecutor, 171
  commands Vermont militia, 184
  supplies militia, 191
  accused of treason, 191
  parlays with British, 192–4, 195–8
  confronts Yorkers, 210–11
  quells Guilford rebellion, 216–18
  opposes union with U.S., 220–1
  role in Vermont republic, 223–4
  second marriage, 224–5
  goes to Pennsylvania, 227–8
  health declines, 228
  death, 231

Allen, Ethan Alphonso (Ethan's son),
  235
Allen, Fanny (Ethan's daughter), 235,
  249
Allen, Fanny Montresor Buchanan
  (Ethan's second wife), 224–5, 227,
  229–30, 235
Allen, Hannibal (Ethan's son), 235
Allen, Heber
  birth & childhood, 3, 7–8
  moves to Salisbury, 12
  buys Hampshire Grants land, 38
  settles in Poultney, 60
  in Green Mountain Regiment, 110
  in early Vt. government, 137, 172
  at Battle of Hubbardton, 152–3, 156–
    7
  death, 216
Allen, Heman
  birth & childhood, 3
  "bastion of family," 7, 176
  farming, 8, 20, 22
  joins foundry business, 9
  fight with Tousley, 10
  opens store, 12
  in tannery, 34
  land speculation, 38
  health, 38, 68, 160
  as Allen family's banker, 51, 176
  in Onion River Co., 60, 67–71
  journey to N.Y., 62–3
  military career, 110, 124, 159
  in early Vt. government, 137–8, 141,
    153, 171
  missions to U.S. Congress, 139–40,
    149–50
  aids Ethan, 146
  death, 165
Allen, Heman (Heman's son), 237, 250
Allen, Ira
  birth & childhood, 3, 7–8
  early experiences on frontier, 20–4
  physical vigor, 23
  in tanning business, 34
  takes up surveying, 35
  buys up land, 34, 38
  adventures in woods, 40–1, 54–7
  explores Onion River, 50–4, 58, 90

Allen, Ira (*cont.*)
  breaks up Rupert settlement, 57
  speculates in Onion River land, 57,
    58–65, 221
  journey to New York, 62–3
  settles Onion River, 66–72
  escapes Yorker trap, 81–2
  escorts prisoners to Canada, 105–6
  in Green Mountain Regiment, 110,
    114
  under Gen. Montgomery, 125
  plans new government, 138–42, 149
  sends money to Ethan, 146
  at Windsor Convention, 151, 153
  raises Vermont militia, 155–7
  takes in Ethan's family, 166
  punishes Tories, 170–2
  quarrel with Levi, 175–8
  leads Vermont Republic, 182–4, 188–
    90, 202–3, 207–10, 212–14
  Vermont's treasurer, 166, 189, 223, 228
  in Haldimand negotiations, 195, 198,
    206–7
  in Guilford rebellion, 217
  business affairs, 223, 228, 235, 236–7
  marries, 234
  political power wanes, 234
  in Europe, 237–48
  arms trading, 238–50
  imprisoned, 244–7
  death, 252
Allen Ira H. (Ira's son), 249, 252
Allen, Joseph, 1–5, 24, 33
Allen, Joseph (Ethan's son), 147
Allen, Joseph (Heber's son), 235
Allen, Levi
  birth & childhood, 3, 7–8
  disposition, 12, 175, 235
  joins Heman in tannery, 34, 38
  business affairs, 60, 90–1, 175
  estrangement from brothers 90–1
  Tory sympathies, 91, 124, 177, 180,
    216
  helps Ethan, 137, 162
  quarrel with brothers, 176–9
  moves south, 180
  reconciliation with brothers, 223
  joins Onion River business, 223, 228
  moves to England, 233
  troubles in England, 234
  debts, 235
  in Canadian politics, 243
  death, 248

Allen, Loraine (Ethan's daughter), 9,
  165, 222
Allen, Lucinda (Heman's daughter),
  245
Allen, Lucy (Ethan's daughter), 165
Allen, Lucy (Mrs. Lewis Beebe), 3, 12,
  90, 216
Allen, Lydia (Mrs. John Finche), 3, 12,
  24, 90
Allen, Maria Juliette (Ira's daughter),
  249
Allen, Mary Ann (Ethan's daughter),
  165
Allen, Mary Baker (Joseph's wife), 1,
  4, 7
Allen, Mary Brownson (Ethan's first
  wife), 8–9, 18, 38, 47, 165–6, 169,
  221–2, 227
Allen, Zimri, 3, 7, 18, 20, 33, 38, 59–60,
  62, 65, 68, 73, 80, 90, 236
Allen, Zimri Enos (Ira's son), 249
Amenia, N.Y., 13, 81–2
American Revolution
  Battle of Lexington, 89–90
  Concord Bridge, 90
  Fort Ticonderoga, 91–8, 147, 153, 158
  Crown Point, 99
  St. John's, 102–3, 122, 139
  Canada campaigns, 122–6, 139
  Battle of Hubbardton, 154, 157–8
  Battle of Saratoga, 156–7, 165
  Battle of Bennington, 158–61
  Battle of Yorktown, 211
Arlington Junto, 200, 201–3, 215, 222
Arlington, Vt., 30, 45–6, 66, 79, 82, 165–
  6, 169, 175, 182, 186, 190, 193, 200,
  202–4
Arnold, Col. Benedict, 91–7, 100–2, 104–
  5, 107–9, 112–13, 122, 125, 139, 169,
  198
Averill, Samuel, 60–2, 64–5

Baker, Desire, 30, 45–6, 54, 167
Baker, Remember, 29–32, 37, 40–1, 45–9,
  52–5, 60, 62–4, 66–72, 75–6, 82, 90,
  99, 107–8, 115, 126, 152, 167, 197,
  235–6, 248
Bennington Board of Confiscation, 173
"Bennington Mob." *See* Green Moun-
  tain Boys
Bennington, Vt.
  disputed settlements in, 16, 18, 24, 36
  Yorker partisans in, 82
  Battle of, 156–9

Vermont Assembly at, 166, 207
  Ethan moves to, 169
  Tory executed in, 171–2
Bolton, Vt., 48, 60, 64–5
Brattleboro, Vt., 86, 88, 182, 215–16, 218
Breakenridge, James, 16–18, 36–8, 67, 80, 138
Brown, John, 84, 92, 116–17, 121, 124, 126
Burgoyne, Gen. John, 146–7, 151, 153–4, 156, 158, 165, 170
Burlington, Vt., 50, 70, 99, 228, 231, 237, 246, 248, 250

Canada
  incited against England, 84
  British army in, 101
  Ethan's plan to attack, 103, 105, 108–9, 113–14
  See also Haldimand, Gen. Frederick; Quebec (province)
Carleton, Gov. Guy, 103, 115, 117–18, 122, 124–6, 197
Carnot, L.N.M., 239–40, 243–4
Carpenter, Isaiah, 26–7
Castleton, Vt., 33, 38, 40, 50, 66, 68, 71, 92, 94, 152, 154–5, 195–6, 207, 210
Catamount Tavern, 29, 31, 37–8, 43, 47, 82, 109, 138, 167, 169, 171–2, 174, 214, 222
Caughnawaga Indians, 105, 107–8
Charlestown, N.H., 157, 208
Chittenden, Thomas, 67, 138, 141, 149, 155, 167, 171–2, 176–7, 182, 185–6, 188, 190–6, 198, 200–2, 205–11, 213–16, 220–4, 231–2, 234, 236–8, 243
Clarendon, Vt., 44, 75–7
Clinton, Gov. George, 170, 173, 175, 181–6, 188, 190, 200, 203–6, 211, 218–19
Cochran, Robert, 35, 42, 47, 76, 88, 94, 123
Cockburn, William, 35, 48–9, 52
Colchester, Vt., 66, 228, 252
Colden, Gov. Cadwallader, 16, 26, 31, 33
Colonies, American, 101, 108, 123, 126, 137, 139, 170, 185, 192–4, 196, 198–200, 216
Committees of Correspondence
  Boston, 84
  Westminster, 85
  Hartford, 91, 104
  Albany, 101

Concord, N.H., 90, 206–7
Congress, U.S.
  Ethan writes to, 101, 165, 201–2
  war policy, 104–5, 156
  Ethan appears before, 108–9, 189
  independence an issue in, 124, 126
  Hampshire Grants' delegations to, 138–40, 141, 149–50, 186, 213
  distrust of Vt., 157, 206
  Ethan's commission from, 164–5, 169
  divided over Vt., 185, 214
  delegation to Vt., 186
  mediates claims to Vt., 188
  cuts off Vt. troops, 190, 195
  Chittenden's letter to, 192
  Vt.'s dissatisfaction with, 193, 195–6, 198, 231
  debates Vt.'s admission, 204, 208, 211, 214, 233, 234
  censures Vt., 219
Connecticut
  settlement, 1–2
  in French & Indian War, 7
  iron mining in, 8
  frontier life in, 20
  Vermont proprietors in, 58–9, 60–1
  militia, 91–3
  Ethan offered land in, 146
  Committee of War, 147
  state legislature, 204
  claims Wyoming Valley, 227
Connecticut Courant, 32, 66, 80, 177–9
Connecticut militia, 91–4, 100, 105, 108
Connecticut River, 14, 79, 85, 141, 149, 157, 171, 174, 186, 202, 205, 212, 214
Connecticut Valley, 85–6, 138, 158, 183–4
Continental Army, 194–5, 202
Cornwall, Conn., 1–5, 7–9, 12, 33
Crown Point, N.Y., 52, 55, 73, 86, 94, 99, 106, 108, 139–40, 151, 203

Delaplace, Capt. William, 96–7, 100, 102
Dorset, Vt., 110–11, 137, 140
Duane, James, 26–7, 30, 35, 48, 53, 63, 204, 219, 234
Durham, N.Y. See Clarendon, Vt.
Dwight, Timothy, 226, 231

Enos, Brig. Gen. Roger, 220
Exeter, N.H., 174, 212

Fay, Dr. Jonas, 47–8, 138–40, 141, 149, 155, 168–9, 186, 189, 213, 221
Fay, Stephen, 29, 31, 37, 43, 47–8, 109

Fort Ticonderoga
  early assault on, 30
  military importance, 84
  Col. Skene governor of, 86
  condition of, 91
  British reaction to capture, 101–2
  Ethan's command at, 104, 108
  Gen. Burgoyne recaptures, 151–3
  British reinforce, 196
Fort William Henry, 7–8, 14
French & Indian wars, 7–8, 14, 30
French Revolution, 237, 239–41, 243–7,
  251

Gaspée, H.M.S., 117, 121–2, 125
Gates, Gen. Horatio, 20, 165, 173–4
George III (King of England), 15, 32,
  84, 86, 91, 97, 104, 107, 115, 124,
  126, 145, 147, 193, 197–200, 209–10,
  237
Germain, George Sackville, Lord, 146,
  192, 199
Green Mountain Boys, 31, 33, 35, 37–
  53, 55, 57, 63–8, 73, 75–82, 84–6,
  88–110, 112–15, 123–5, 135, 139,
  151–3, 157, 158–61, 164, 167, 171,
  173–4, 182, 184, 197, 202, 216, 228
Green Mountain Regiment, 110–13, 114,
  147
Green Mountains, 1, 32, 49, 56, 79, 85–
  6, 137, 149, 154–5, 198, 205
Guilford, Vt., 215–18

Haldimand, Gen. Frederick, 195–200,
  203, 207–10, 212, 221–2, 241–2
Halifax, Nova Scotia, 134–6, 143, 179
Hampshire Grants
  origin of, 14–16
  litigation with N.Y., 24–7
  Yorkers move into, 29–30, 35
  Ethan's defense of, 38–9, 42, 49, 68,
  73, 75–9
  Allens purchase land in, 38, 41, 47,
  60, 66
  Yorker strongholds in, 44, 75, 138,
  141, 149
  conventions of, 109–10, 140, 142, 149
  British threat to, 137, 147
  relations with N.H., 137–8
  independence of, 138–9, 149–50, 170
Hartford, Conn., 1, 32, 80, 91–2, 94, 149,
  170, 215, 225–6
Hero Islands, 189, 230
Herrick, Sam, 94, 99–100, 155–8, 167

Hessians, 145, 152, 158–9
Houghton, Daniel, 88
Housatonic River, 1–2, 4, 34
Howe, Gen. Sir William, 146–7, 162
Hoyt, Winthrop, 84, 94
Hubbardton, Vt., 33–5, 40–1, 52, 66, 68,
  111, 152, 154, 157–8
Hudson River, 7, 32, 69, 73, 79, 98, 137,
  151, 158, 164–5, 203–4, 211, 214
Hull, Gen. William, 252

Île-aux-Noix, 107, 114, 207
Indians, 4, 10, 14, 85, 103, 106–7, 114–19,
  135, 140, 167, 175, 221
Ingersoll, Jared, 25, 27

Jay, John, 185, 188–9, 200, 233–4
Jay's Treaty, 240

Kempe, John Tabor, 27–8, 40, 135
Kentucky, 214, 235, 250
Knowlton, Luke, 222

Lake Champlain, 14, 38, 50, 52, 55, 57,
  63, 68–9, 73, 75, 84–5, 91, 96, 98–9,
  101–4, 113–14, 140, 147, 151–2, 158,
  189, 196, 207, 209, 237, 251
Lake George, 7, 8, 104, 158
LaPrairie, Quebec, 116, 124
Lee, Rev. Jonathan, 4–5
Lexington, Mass., 89–90
Litchfield, Conn., 1, 3–5
Livingston, Judge Robert R., 26–7, 36
London, 15–16, 25, 75, 80, 84–6, 105,
  113, 121–4, 126–9, 137, 146, 178,
  188, 192–3, 233–5, 237, 239, 241, 243,
  248, 252
Long Island, 145–7, 161, 176 179
Longueuil, Quebec, 115–16
Lovell, James, 143–5
Lyon, Matthew, 242, 250

McCormick, Robert, 80–2
Manchester, Vt., 60, 79, 83, 153–5, 158–
  60
Marsh, William, 141
Massachusetts, 8, 11–12, 15, 18, 73, 92–4,
  143, 152–3, 156–7, 188–91, 203, 222,
  228
Middlesex, Vt., 60–1, 64–5
Mining, 8–9, 11, 13, 15
Mohawk River, 58, 85
Monroe, James, 238, 249

Montgomery, Gen. Richard, 113–16, 119, 122, 124–6, 139
Montreal, 84, 94, 103, 105, 114–17, 121–4, 126, 143, 151, 249
Mott, Edward, 92–5, 100, 104
Munro, Judge John, 17, 44–8, 197

"New Connecticut," 149–50
New Hampshire, 14–15, 19, 24–5, 32, 79, 137–9, 152–3, 156–9, 174, 177, 186–90, 194, 202–8, 211–16, 227, 229–30
New Haven, Conn., 4, 25, 39, 57, 67
New Lots, N.Y., 146–8, 161
New York
    settlements in Conn., 1
    claim to Hampshire Grants, 14–15, 30
    authority defied, 16–18, 35–7, 67, 75–7
    surveyors from, 15–16, 35, 39, 48, 52
    colonial Supreme Court, 18, 25–7
    land patents issued, 32–3, 75, 181
    settlers harassed, 41–2, 44–5, 57–8, 67–8, 75–6
    delegation to, 47–8
    Allens' journey through, 62–3
    land disputes, 73
    colonial Assembly, 78–9, 109–10
    influence in Connecticut Valley, 79, 86, 137, 141, 149, 181–3
    accommodation with Hampshire Grants, 83, 110, 137–8
    sympathizers in Vt., 172–3
    influence in U.S. Congress, 149, 181, 185–6, 213
    relations with Vt., 181–5, 188
    towns annexed by Vt., 202–4, 211–14
    sympathy for Vt. in, 205
    ships ban Vt. goods, 221
    recognizes Vt. jurisdiction, 236
New York (city), 62–3, 65, 77, 109, 135, 143–6, 161, 174
Northampton, Mass., 11–12, 89

Onion River Company, 66, 68, 72, 83, 90, 108, 112, 175–6, 221, 228, 249, 252
Onion River Territory, Vt., 50–4, 58, 60–4, 66–9, 71–2, 83, 90, 99, 108, 126, 140, 167, 221, 227–8, 230–1, 233, 236
Otter Creek, Vt., 66, 151

Paris, 226, 238, 243–9, 252
Parliament (British), 126–8, 131, 145

Paterson, Sheriff William, 86–8
Patterson, Eleazer, 181–2, 184
Pendennis Castle, 124, 127, 130, 237
Pennsylvania, 101, 185–6, 189, 227–8
Phelps, Noah, 92, 94
Philadelphia, 86, 102–3, 108, 126, 138–40, 147, 149–50, 174, 186–7, 189, 203, 213–14, 219, 248, 251–2
Pittsfield, Mass., 84, 116, 165
Pittsford, Vt., 35, 55–7
Portland, William Bentinck, Duke of, 237, 242
Portsmouth, N.H., 19, 24–5, 27, 138, 241
Poultney, Vt., 33, 35–6, 38, 48, 50, 60, 66, 68, 90, 172, 207
Prescott, Gen. Richard, 119–22, 126–7, 133, 163, 242
Prisoners
    American, 123–36, 143–7, 161–3, 165
    British, 144–5, 173, 203, 206–7
Putney, Vt., 181–2

Quebec (city)
    Arnold's expedition to, 122, 125, 139, 161
Quebec (province)
    Ira's expedition to, 105–6
    Ethan's campaign and capture in, 116–22, 124–5
    Vermont trade with, 223
    Allens' business interests in, 223, 228, 233

Redding, David, 169, 171–2
Reid, Col. John, 39, 42–3, 57, 67–8
Religion, 3, 11–12, 14, 31, 43, 115, 128, 223, 225–7, 231–2, 249
Richelieu River. See Sorel River
Robinson, Col. Moses, 152, 183–4, 234
Rupert, Vt., 42, 57
Rutland, Vt., 44, 138, 154, 190

St. Clair, Gen. Arthur, 20, 151–2
St. John's, Quebec, 99, 102–3, 106–8, 110, 113–15, 121–2, 139, 203, 207, 225
St. Lawrence River, 116, 122, 125, 139, 237
Salisbury, Conn.
    Ethan's schooling in, 4–5
    Allens' foundry in, 8–9
    Allens' life in, 9–10
    Heman's business in, 9, 12, 67
    Hampshire grantees in, 18, 26
    Allens' tannery in, 33–4, 38

Saratoga, N.Y., 113, 151, 156–7, 165, 207
Schuyler, Gen. Philip, 108–13, 116, 125, 154, 156–7, 164–5, 191, 203, 206–7
Scottish settlers, 42, 57–8, 67–8
Shaftsbury, Vt., 26, 45, 48
Sheffield, Mass., 18, 24–5, 38, 41, 47, 72, 83, 147, 165
Sherwood, Justus, 46, 197–8, 207, 209, 222
Shoreham, Vt., 73, 94
Skene, Col. Philip, 85–6, 94, 100, 102, 113, 145, 159–60
Skenesboro, N.Y., 52, 68–9, 86, 94, 152, 196, 208
Small, Maj. John, 16–18, 26–7
Solebay, H.M.S., 128, 130, 132, 134, 139, 172
Sorel River, 99, 103, 115
South Carolina, 180, 185, 235
Spencer, Benjamin, 44–5, 75–7
Stark, Gen. John, 157–9, 173, 201, 211
Sullivan, Gen. John, 139–40
Sunderland, Capt. Peleg, 55, 84, 228
Sunderland, Vt., 22, 77, 165–6, 203–4, 211, 224–5, 227

Tannery business, 34–5, 38
Tichenor, Isaac, 191, 214, 220, 223, 228, 236, 241, 249 251
Ticonderoga. *See* Fort Ticonderoga
Tories, 123, 145–7, 154–5, 159–60, 162, 169–73, 177–9, 193, 197, 206, 216, 222–3, 235
Tryon, Gov. William, 33, 38–42, 43–5, 47–9, 53, 73, 75, 77–9, 83, 122, 135

United States, 221, 229–31, 233, 235–6, 241–2

Vanornam, Isaac, 53–6, 66
Vermont
    as independent republic, 150–7, 166–8, 170–6, 178, 181–92, 195, 197–204, 206, 209–19, 222–32, 234–7
    Committee of Safety, 151, 154–5, 158–9
    Council of State, 155–7, 167–8, 170–2, 182–3, 189–91, 195, 208, 211, 213, 220, 228, 234

Commission of Sequestration, 155
army regiment, 154–5
Assembly, 166–8, 172, 184–5, 188–91, 195, 200–2, 207–9, 215, 220, 228
constitution & laws, 170–1, 183–5, 188, 191, 216–19
Banishment Law, 172–3
new lands, 174, 181–4, 186–90, 202–4, 207, 209, 211–15, 233
militia, 184–5, 190–1, 195–8, 201, 206–7, 211–12, 216–17, 231, 237–44
admission to U.S., 186–7, 189, 192–4, 204, 208–15, 219–21, 231, 233, 235–6
negotiations with British, 191–206, 208, 210, 212–13, 219–21, 230–1, 233, 242
deserters in, 195, 206
prisoners of war, 195–6, 203, 206–7
truce with British, 201, 203, 205, 207–8
new settlers in 221–3
negotiations for arms, 238–50
university, 246, 252
grants immunity to Ira, 249
Virginia, 40, 162, 185, 209, 214, 234
Von Riedesel, Gen. Friedrich, 152, 154–5

Walloomsac River, 159, 160, 211
Warner, Seth, 29–32, 37, 40, 47–9, 77–8, 93, 96, 99, 108, 110–13, 121, 124–5, 151–4, 157–60, 206
War of 1812, 252
Washington, George, 111, 137, 154, 157, 164–5, 174, 176, 178 185, 191, 195–6, 203, 206, 208, 211, 213–14, 222
Watson, Brook, 105–6, 123–4
Wentworth, Gov. Benning, 14–16, 18–19, 24–6, 67, 79, 137
Westminster, Vt., 85–9, 141, 182, 184, 191, 218, 224
Windsor, Vt., 150–3, 184
Wyoming Valley (Pa.), 227–8

Yale College, 4–5, 226, 231
Yorkers. *See* New York
Yorktown, Va., 208, 211
Young, Dr. Thomas, 13–14, 150, 225–6